CONVERSATIONS WITH CATALOGERS IN THE 21ST CENTURY

CONVERSATIONS WITH CATALOGERS IN THE 21ST CENTURY

Elaine R. Sanchez, Editor

Foreword by Michael Gorman

LIBRARIES UNLIMITED LIBRARY MANAGEMENT COLLECTION

Gerard B. McCabe, Series Editor

LIBRARIES UNLIMITED

AN IMPRINT OF ABC-CLIO, LLC
Santa Barbara, California • Denver, Colorado • Oxford, England

Library of Congress Cataloging-in-Publication Data

Conversations with catalogers in the 21st century / Elaine R. Sanchez, editor ; foreword by Michael Gorman.

p. cm. — (Libraries Unlimited library management collection)

Summary: "Authored by cataloging librarians, educators, and information system experts, this book of essays addresses ideas and methods for tackling the modern challenges of cataloging and metadata practices"—Provided by publisher.

Includes bibliographical references and index.

ISBN 978–1–59884–702–4 (pbk. : acid-free paper)

1. Cataloging. I. Sanchez, Elaine R. II. Title: Conversations with catalogers in the twenty-first century.

Z693.C65   2011

025.3—dc22   2010048782

ISBN: 978–1–59884–702–4
EISBN: 978–1–59884–703–1

15 14 13 12 11   1 2 3 4 5

This book is also available on the World Wide Web as an eBook.
Visit www.abc-clio.com for details.

Libraries Unlimited
An Imprint of ABC-CLIO, LLC

ABC-CLIO, LLC
130 Cremona Drive, P.O. Box 1911
Santa Barbara, California 93116-1911

This book is printed on acid-free paper ∞

Manufactured in the United States of America

CONTENTS

CONTENTS

FOREWORD

Michael Gorman

Civilization and learning depend, to a very great extent, on the textual and graphic part of our cultural heritage—the human record—created by human beings since the invention of writing many millennia ago. Librarianship is about many things, but none more important than the stewardship of that human record—a stewardship that consists of acquiring and giving access to subsets of the human record, of working to coordinate the millions of subsets to widen access, of organizing the records of those subsets to facilitate access, and of ensuring that the carriers of texts and images in all formats are preserved for future generations. It is, of course, the texts and images themselves, not the formats in which they are presented and preserved, that is of paramount importance; but some formats are more durable than others, and some formats are more conducive to the preservation and onward transmission of the human record that are the ultimate goals of librarianship and the prime motivation for what we do.

Library school (to use the old-fashioned term) was for me a life-changing experience, as it should be if library education is to be more than a ticket-punching exercise. I went to library school with a vague idea of a career as a reference librarian in public libraries, I emerged, two years later, committed to and fascinated by cataloguing—the enterprise that gives us the bibliographic architecture without which the tasks of facilitating access to the human record and mapping that human record for posterity are impossible. I was, as are all true cataloguers, enthralled by the details of codes, the arcana of corporate headings, uniform titles, Cutter-Sanborn numbers, descriptive abbreviations, faceted classification, the order of names in the headings for Spanish married women, and the like; but, I hope, never lost sight of the fact that catalogues are information retrieval systems to be judged by the eternal verities of precision and recall, or they are nothing. The pantheon of Panizzi, Cutter, Dewey, Ranganathan, and Lubetzky hovered over us as we learned and practised cataloguing in accordance with their teachings, but this was no Casaubon-like amassing of lore for its own sake. To adapt one of Ranganathan's laws, *catalogues are for use*, and the work that goes into them is justified only when they are used to provide speedy and efficient retrieval of relevant carriers of recorded knowledge and information.

These are dark times for cataloguers and cataloguing in many ways. The ubiquity of search engines has made many library users far less demanding than they were. After all, scholarly rigour is absent in someone whose idea of "research" is bunging words and phrases into a search engine and being rewarded, all but instantaneously, with a glittering pile of random texts in random order (or, worse, an order determined by advertisers and other hucksters), from which he or she extracts a few things of vague relevance found on the first screen. Search engines do not make you stupid, but they can, too often, leave you in ignorance. They are cheap and quick, unlike cataloguing, which is labour intensive and time consuming. Small wonder that library administrators (who may belong to the first generation of librarians who have little or no knowledge of cataloguing) believe, or affect to believe, that some search engine–like process can replace real cataloguing and professional cataloguers and trim their personnel budgets accordingly. Small wonder that senior administrators in the Library of Congress have openly talked of abandoning their century-old mission of providing cataloguing data to the nation's libraries. Small wonder that the cataloguers who remain are worried about their futures and the future of libraries. Some feel that current controversies in cataloguing, such as that over the wretched RDA and the fatuities of "metadata," are irrelevant in a time when we can watch libraries twittering, gaming, and grabbing at any technological straws they can as they spiral down into irrelevance.

High levels of precision and recall, the two ways in which we judge any information retrieval system, are dependent on controlled vocabularies and national and international standards—they cannot be obtained by other systems not involving human intervention, no matter what technophiles and billion-dollar advertising companies may tell you. Scholars, researchers, and students depend on systems that give them knowledge of that part of the human record with which they are concerned and will do so for the foreseeable future. For that reason, I think the dark days for cataloguing will come to an end as more and more people realize what we are losing in letting our catalogues decay, and turn to those who have devoted their careers to making the human record accessible.

I am, therefore, very glad to welcome the publication of *Conversations with Catalogers in the 21st Century* and applaud the courage of its editor and contributors as they make a persuasive case for the relevance of cataloguing. There may be disagreements in the field of cataloguing over policies and practices but, as this book shows, there is no disagreement over the fundamental purpose and importance of cataloguing. Civilization and learning require the human record to be organized, accessible, and preserved. Cataloguers play an important role in that great enterprise—an enterprise that is dedicated to no less a purpose than ensuring the people of the future know what we know, thus enabling them to add to that ever-expanding record.

Chicago, January 2010

Michael Gorman worked, for fifty years, in public libraries in London, for the British National Bibliography, the British Library, the University of Illinois library and that of the California State University, Fresno. He was the first editor of AACR2 and AACR2R and the drafter of the first ISBD (the ISBD-M) and of the ISBD-G. He is the author and editor of a number of books and too many articles. He is the recipient of the Margaret Mann Citation and the Melvil Dewey Medal, an Honorary Fellow of the Chartered Institute of Library & Information Professionals, and a past president of the American Library Association.

INTRODUCTION

Elaine R. Sanchez

This book came into being because of the vortex of change in which cataloging is now swirling. These are some of the currents we are in:

- Ever-increasing digital resources, in changing formats, to catalog.
- A proposed "new" structure for the bibliographic universe we are in: FRBR, Functional Requirements for Bibliographic Records, the work of IFLA (International Federation of Library Associations).
- Patrons searching for information and resources now go to for-profit, non-library information entities and use keyword searching instead of our precise and reliable library catalogs with pre-coordinated subject thesaurus terms.
- A new cataloging code based on FRBR is now being tested, RDA (Resource Description and Access), to perhaps replace AACR2.
- New international cataloging principles by IFLA were published in 2009, *Statement of International Cataloguing Principles*, which replace and broaden the 1961 "Paris Principles" and guide the new development and use of cataloging codes.
- The Library of Congress, its Program for Cooperative Cataloging, and OCLC have been decreasing full cataloging description and also providing for more core or floor record standards, now called the Bibco Standard Record (BSR) that can be built upon, rather than starting off at full cataloging level.

- LC formed the Library of Congress Working Group on the Future of Bibliographic Control in 2007 to determine the future of cataloging, suggesting recommendations including using upstream vendor supplied bibliographic data as a cataloging source, considering the use of FRBR, and beginning to research cataloging on the Semantic Web.
- LC commissioned an independent consultant to study MARC record sources in North America, in order to help LC determine its role as a major supplier of these records, and to determine if other sources could be available in order to reduce LC cataloging.
- And, probably much more.

It's enough to make one very seasick. However, catalogers love challenges and problems, so there is good reason to believe we won't sink, and will continue on our journey. We'll just need to keep on course, or the current will turn us around again.

This book was created as an opportunity for the contributors to speak their minds on what is going on in our cataloging world. Each author is unique in his or her cataloging experience, passionate about cataloging and metadata, knowledgeable, creative, genuine, and wise. The book is titled *Conversations with Catalogers in the 21st Century* because I asked them to write on a topic that they wanted to share with other catalogers—what is on their minds at this present time of such difficult and confusing change —just as if they were sitting and talking by the glow of the ancient shelflist. The works that they came up with are just that.

Maybe knowing how this work came about, and how it turned into this book, will provide a little more understanding of the meaning of each author's contribution, and how all the essays together form a whole picture of the worries and visions of a group of varying kinds of catalogers and librarians, with various levels of experience and responsibilities. In a way, the book expresses more than ideas on grouped topics in chapters—it is a snapshot of the richness, purpose, mission, vision, and intelligence of our cataloging and metadata profession and professionals at this time of change. As such, this work is dedicated to all of us, in our current and other times, and to our honorable and important work: preserving the human record, past, present, and future.

I
AACR2 AND RDA

Moving Cataloguing Rules Out of the Library: Goodbye, AACR2?
J. McRee (Mac) Elrod

AACR and RDA: One Cataloguer's Reaction
Helen Buhler

RDA, AACR2, and You: What Catalogers Are Thinking
Elaine R. Sanchez

1 MOVING CATALOGUING RULES OUT OF THE LIBRARY: GOODBYE, AACR2?

J. McRee (Mac) Elrod

Resource Description and Access (RDA)[1] is an effort to develop more general cataloguing rules, so that they may be used beyond the library community to organize information resources. It is intended to replace Anglo American Cataloguing Rules Second Edition (AACR2).[2] The date of implementation keeps being pushed back, but is currently said to be 2011, with release in 2010.

Even though RDA is intended to be general enough for use outside the library community, and more international than AACR2, it is in fact so complex that it is unlikely to find usage outside the library community, and perhaps not even in smaller libraries within the library community. It is far more Anglocentric than AACR2, substituting "language of the catalogue" (examples are English) for the Latin abbreviations used in International Standard Bibliographic Description (ISBD).[3]

Special Libraries Cataloguing (SLC) has found AACR2 quite "general" in that it adequately addresses the cataloguing of all library materials, particularly now that AACR2 allows collation for remote electronic resources, as does the Provider Neutral (PN)[4] E-Book Record. Some SLC clients find PN use of "1 online resource" to be too general, since that specific material designation (SMD) could apply to a Web site, an electronic document, or a streaming video.

The description of electronic resources is very important to SLC since, at present, 75 percent of SLC's original cataloguing is of remote electronic resources. This essay presents many RDA changes and options that will affect SLC and all cataloguing agencies, including: description; AACR2 and RDA; Machine Readable Cataloging (MARC21)[5] record structure; language of the catalogue; consistency, completeness, and reliability of RDA cataloguing records; online catalog display; access points; and more. SLC's own implementation[6] of

RDA (its issues and options), and the company's plan to continue using much of AACR2, are discussed in the last section for other libraries to consider.

TESTING AND IMPLEMENTATION

Since RDA's purpose is to provide cataloguing rules that all kinds of information entities can use, it has less restrictive standards and many more options for this larger group. Many options are included (initially, even transcribing place of publication was optional), so what libraries may be using, rather than RDA itself, is the implementation plan drawn up by the U.S. Library of Congress. The joint implementation plan by U.S. "national libraries" (Library of Congress, National Library of Medicine, National Agricultural Library), and the earlier planned Anglo national libraries' joint implementation plan (the AACR2 authors), seem to have been replaced by a selection of more than a score of "test sites," chosen by the Library of Congress to use both RDA and AACR2 rules to create sample records. Fortunately, those test sites include a variety of libraries, and a cataloguing vendor. It will be interesting to see the variety of records for the same items produced by RDA test sites, due to the many options available. For example, a collection without a collective title may have a cataloguer-supplied title and, according to a sample RDA record[7] created by the Library of Congress, MARC21 246s (Varying Form of Title) for individual titles as well as individual MARC21 700at (Added Entry-Personal Name author and title subfield) access points.

The use of UKMARC's 248 field (Title and Statement of Responsibility for Multipart Items field, which allows multiple-level records) would have been a much more consistent solution to works within works. British librarians did not insist on field 248 when joining MARC21. German cataloguing, using the MAB (Maschinelle Austauschformat für Bibliotheken) format (rather than MARC21), still also has the tradition of multiple-level cataloguing, although many German libraries are considering moving to MARC21.

There are some welcome ideas in RDA, which will probably be included in any implementation plan. Some are: square brackets only when the information is nowhere in the item (and brackets do not carry across MARC21 subfields); simplification of entry for treaties (always use first nation mentioned regardless of number); cataloguer-supplied titles may be given to collections without a collective title already mentioned; O.T. (Old Testament) and N.T. (New Testament) spelled out for those collections, but omitted between "Bible" and the name of the book; and separation of carrier and content into separate elements, replacing the General Material Designation (GMD). In AACR2, there is a mix of content and carrier in GMDs, and particularly in the sample SMDs for remote electronic resources. It is helpful to patrons to know both carrier and content. It is unfortunate that some RDA terms for both of these are too long for convenient display, and that the numbering of the MARC21 336–338 fields are no longer from general to specific (media type, carrier, and content) as originally proposed (336 Content Type, 337 Media Type, 338 Carrier Type).

Also unfortunately, several helpful ideas have been dropped from implementation. These include: removal of alternate title from title proper; change from B.C. and A.D. to the faith-neutral B.C.E. (Before Common Era), and C.E. (Common Era); and entering compilations of the work of several authors under compiler, in keeping with scholarly bibliographic practice.

MARC21, ISBD, AND RDA

Some suggest that the lifetime of MARC21 is limited. So far, no viable alternative has gained acceptance to the language- and largely script-neutral numbered MARC21 field tags. RDA does not specify either ISBD, with its choice and order of elements and punctuation, or MARC21 coding, although both are addressed in appendices. It is unfortunate that many consider ISBD to be a set of punctuation marks. More important even than the order of elements is the choice of elements, and both are far more important than punctuation. The choice and order of elements is based on over a century of experience with what patrons require. It is premature to consider the abandonment of the two most successful library international standards ever created, which for over thirty years have increased standardization and international exchange of bibliographic records. MARC21 will almost certainly continue to be used for RDA cataloguing records, at least until another more versatile and reliable standard takes the stage.

The announcement (without prior consultation or reference to rule justification) of the joint plan of the Program for Cooperative Cataloging (PCC) and the Library of Congress (LC) to implement repeating MARC21 field 260 (Imprint) for integrating resources, serials, and sets-in-progress points to the growing role of MARC21 as a de facto set of rules.

New MARC fields have been proposed to accommodate new data elements introduced by RDA. Three new fields are 336, content type; 337, media type; and 338, carrier type. The 336 content type field describes the form of communication through which the work is expressed. For example, a recording of a musical group's performance would have content recorded as 336 $a performed music, and carrier recorded as 338 $a audio disc. Field 337, media type (in this case "audio"), is optional. Fields 338 and 336 could be used to create a compound GMD of [audio disc: performed music]. An e-book via the Web would be [online resource: text].

Using the same musical performance by our musical group as an example, this would be coded in an RDA/MARC21 record as 336 $a performed music, 337 $a audio, and 338 $a audio disc. When and if integrated library systems (ILS) implement the MARC21 336–338 fields for content, media type, and carrier, these will replace 245$h GMD. It is not yet clear how they will be displayed. If they are displayed in field order after collation, they would be out of logical general to specific sequence. ISBD Area 0 (content form and media type area) suggests that they be displayed at the beginning of the record.

Another major change that RDA will require, which also employs MARC coding, is the universal application of relators that relate creators to their works.

MARC21 has $e relator terms, and $4 relator codes, but they have been seldom used. They *will* be used with RDA.

The relationship between RDA as a cataloguing code and MARC21 as the communication format can be expected to continue for some time. There is much legacy bibliographic data in thousands of databases across the world as well, which cannot be ignored or easily converted to a new format. SLC has had no difficulty creating cross walks from MARC21 to other formats used by some library systems. But efforts to reverse the process do not work, because of MARC21's greater granularity. If a new cataloguing code were adopted, and a new communication format were developed and used, this would mean that the library's database must be replaced when system migration time came.

RDA AND LANGUAGE OF THE CATALOGUE

Problematic for bilingual or multilingual catalogues is RDA's substitution of spelled-out phrases in the "language of the catalogue" for ISBD Latin abbreviations, e.g., [S.l.] and [s.n.], when place of publication, or publisher, is lacking from the item and is not known. In a bilingual English-French catalogue, for example, English could be used for English texts and French for French texts, but what about for German and Spanish texts? This will be difficult for officially bilingual provinces and countries. This abandonment of ISBD Latin inclusions also hampers the International Federation of Library Association's (IFLA) Universal Bibliographic Control (UBC) program, in which the bibliographic record produced in the country of publication is to be used internationally.

OTHER RDA CHANGES AND IMPACT ON CATALOGUES

There are other descriptive changes from AACR2 in RDA. The following paragraphs highlight a few of those changes that will have some impact on catalogues and record displays.

Although optional in RDA, it will be possible to continue to use ISBD punctuation. There is an appendix with examples applying ISBD punctuation to RDA records. This is important for those libraries that wish to continue this practice in their online catalogs. Other changes from AACR2 practice will make brief displays less informative: the omission of "[sic]" after a typographical error in the title will make it difficult to know if there is a mistake in transcription; omission of a missing jurisdiction after city of publication will mean the patron won't know whether the item was published in London, England, or London, Ontario, based on the brief display. Many patrons do not go beyond the brief display, and few read notes, in our experience. In RDA, AACR2 abbreviations are abandoned. Words are transcribed as found, with abbreviations used only if found in the item. This also includes spelling out abbreviations such as "ed." in edition statement; "p.," "v.," and "ill." in collation; years in imprint if given as words; and terms and numbers for series. Fortunately, "cm" has been accepted as a symbol and need not be spelled out. While most measurements will be given in cm, "in." is also allowed. This will result in a variety of descriptive practices in bibliographic descriptions, which will be possibly confusing and certainly longer.

Another RDA change, which will be welcome to many, is a more meaningful description of media format as SMDs in the physical description of the carriers, such as CD, CD-ROM, DVD, DVD-ROM, and VHS, rather than digital disk, digital disc, and optical disc, for example.

Finally, another major change, addressed in the prior section on MARC21, is the universal application of relator terms to creators in access points, describing the relationship between the person and the work. This could be useful, or helpful, if the user wants to immediately know if the name they find is an author, editor, translator, composer, illustrator, and so on. It may, however, create split files in some ILS.

ACCESS POINTS

One of the major changes in RDA from AACR2 is the abandonment of the rule of three, in which AACR2 states that works by four of more authors must be entered under title, with an added entry for the first author mentioned only. The impact of RDA entry of monographs, written by four or more people, under first author is yet to be seen; it does produce inconsistencies with earlier records. With the adoption of AACR2, many of us changed older records on an encounter basis. It will not be possible to add additional authors to statements of responsibility without having the item in hand, even if the first author mentioned is made main (prime) entry (i.e., changing from MARC21 700 added author, to 100 main entry author). For treaties, dropping the rule of three will greatly simplify practice. With RDA, treaties will always be entered under the first country mentioned as opposed to first country alphabetically as in AACR2, if three or fewer are mentioned. With AACR2 rules, for example, NAFTA is lost under Canada in a single entry bibliography. Some of us would have preferred entry under title for all treaties, but at least more uniformity will result from this change.

SPECIAL LIBRARIES CATALOGUING (SLC): RDA IMPLEMENTATION

The percentage of national catalogue agency records SLC's clients use varies from 10 percent for the very specialized collection, to 90 percent for a small public library. For many libraries, editing RDA records to preferred AACR2 forms would be prohibitively expensive and time consuming. Thus, SLC will selectively implement RDA practices, but will continue to utilize some AACR2 practices, in order to be practical, provide consistent quality, and remain cost effective for our clients.

One major change is the universal application of relators to authors, i.e., MARC21 $e relator terms, or $4 relator codes. SLC has so far not implemented them. One of SLC's early products was printed book catalogues. The relationship of the author to the first title under the name might differ from the relationship of that author to subsequent title(s). The same would apply to titles under an author's name in an Online Public Access Catalogue (OPAC). Currently, SLC is considering retaining $e and $4 relator terms and codes in derived records, but all clients who have responded wish them excluded from exported records. I assume libraries could deal with the problem by excluding $e and $4 codes from display mapping, unless and until Integrated Library System (ILS) vendors address how to display the relationships in a non-confusing way. Their presence in new records, and absence from older ones, would be a major inconsistency in OPAC display, as well as possibly causing split files.

Because of SLC's multilingual and multinational client base, we will edit spelled out English phrases to ISBD Latin abbreviations. If the phrases are standard enough, this could be done by macros. We certainly can't expect a Québécois, European, or Asian client to accept a record for a French, Spanish, or German text with English inclusions. While inclusions in the language of the text is a possibility, that would be more work intensive than continuing ISBD Latin abbreviations. Since "[et al.]" is no more, due to the end of the rule of three, and lacking imprint (MARC21 subfield 260$b) subfields is relatively rare, this will not be labour intensive. We will continue the AACR2 practice of guessing place and date of publication with brackets and question mark, so would rarely have "[S.l.]" and never "[n.d.]."

Although optional in RDA, SLC will also continue ISBD punctuation. The use of "/" in MARC21 245 title, for example, frees us from having to supply the equivalent of "[by]" in the language of the text.

RDA provisions that SLC will adopt include: square brackets only when information is not in the resource (no retrospective change need be made); treaties under first signatory (leaving older treaties under first country alphabetically, and changing on an encounter basis those entered under title to the first named country, i.e., MARC21 710 added corporate author, to 110 main entry corporate author); not entering "O.T." and "N.T." between "Bible" and the name of a book, and spelling "Old Testament," and "New Testament" for those collections of works (this biblical entry change can be done retrospectively by automation).

The RDA/MARC21 fields 338 and 336 will be used to create a compound 245$h[gmd], e.g., [online resource : text], carrier and content fields, as mentioned earlier.

If we adopt the optional RDA/MARC21 media type, we would certainly use IFLA's ISBD Area 0 "electronic" rather than RDA's "computer." To our patrons, "computer" would indicate an item of equipment. If media type were to be displayed, we would advise our clients not to display MARC21 337 media type "unmediated," just as AACR2's GMD "text" is not used.

SLC will not adopt the RDA rule omitting jurisdiction from imprint if it is absent from the work. To make brief displays more informative, jurisdiction will be transcribed or supplied (continuing to use AACR2 abbreviations in brackets when supplied), and substituting AACR2 abbreviations for postal codes to achieve uniqueness. For example, "CA" can be California or Canada, "WA" can be Washington State or Western Australia, so differentiation is necessary. Supplying missing information in a note is not as helpful to patrons as having it in the ISBD position.

AACR2's rule for transcription and supplying of jurisdiction is one of the most misunderstood and poorly applied rules of AACR2, and always supplying jurisdiction has been popular with SLC clients; a city known in Washington D.C.'s Beltway may not be so well known in Canada, Europe, or Asia.

The RDA change to patron familiar SMDs such as CD, CD-ROM, DVD, DVD-ROM, and VHS is a welcome one. For other carriers, SLC would use terms from the RDA's carrier type (MARC21 338). SLC will adopt the RDA change of tracing all authors as opposed to limiting it to only the second and third authors, after the first, or the first if more than three. We already trace more than three actors for video recordings of motion pictures.

Finally, based on RDA's complexity, multiple options, and cost of access, I suspect SLC cataloguers will not be alone in continuing to consult AACR2 and MARC21 print binders for original cataloguing guidance. Some annotated changes can be added to those tools to create greater consistency with derived records.

A list of RDA changes from AACR2 may be found at http://www.rda-jsc.org/docs/5sec7rev.pdf. It might be worth printing this out and placing it in the front of the AACR2 and MARC21 binders, later annotating both with practices that are accepted, and making notes in the appropriate places in the AACR2 and MARC21 text.

CONCLUSION

Most RDA records will interfile with AACR2 ones. Choice of entry for works by more than three authors and treaties does not create a problem for interfiling. The change of the form of biblical headings will require retrospective change to avoid split files. Whether creator access point relator $e terms, and $4 codes, will create split files will need to be investigated in each ILS.

To be cost effective, editing of incoming RDA records should be held to a minimum. Until the library's ILS can cope with new RDA/MARC21 content, media type, and carrier fields 336–338, some means may need to be found to translate 338 and 336 into a compound 245$h GMD. Some MARC21 336 content terms may need to be truncated, since they are too long to display in MARC21 245$h position. If optional MARC21 337 media type is used, RDA's "computer" should be changed to ISBD Area 0's "electronic" to avoid confusion. See suggestions regarding treatment of the new 336–338 fields below.[8]

Serious consideration should be given, particularly in multilingual situations, to continuing ISBD abbreviation inclusions as opposed to phrases "in the language of the catalogue." Spelling out well-known abbreviations such as "ed.," "p.," "v.," and "ill." can probably not be avoided.

NOTES

1. Joint Steering Committee for Development of RDA, "RDA: Resource Description and Access," http://www.rda-jsc.org/rda.html (accessed May 4, 2010).

2. AACR2 Products, http://www.aacr2.org/canada/products_aacr2.html (accessed May 4, 2010).

3. IFLA Cataloguing Section and ISBD Review Group, *International Standard Bibliographic Description*, http://www.ifla.org/publications/international-standard-bibliographic-description (accessed May 4, 2010).

4. Becky Culbertson, Yael Mandelstam, and George Prager, "Provider-Neutral E-Monograph MARC Record Guide" (Washington, DC: Program for Cooperative Cataloging, 2009), http://www.loc.gov/catdir/pcc/bibco/PN-Guide.pdf (accessed May 4, 2010).

5. Library of Congress, Network Development and MARC Standards Office, MARC Standards, http://www.loc.gov/marc/ (accessed May 4, 2010).

6. J. McRee (Mac) Elrod, "SLC Practices Incorporating RDA," http://slc.bc.ca/cheats/practices.htm (accessed May 4, 2010).

7. "Examples for RDA—Compared to AACR2 (work in progress) For Texas Library Association Conference Workshop on Nuts & Bolts of RDA," March 31, 2009, Revised April 14, 2009, http://www.txla2.org/conference/handouts/Nuts and Bolts Handout.pdf (accessed September 19, 2010).

8. MARC21 Fields for RDA Content, Media Type, and Carrier Terms (SLC Modifications).

336 Content type

For systems requiring 245$h, field 336 is exported as second half of a compound GMD, e.g., 245$h[online resource : text] where "text" is the 336 field data.

Follow each term below with $2rdacontent.

- For cartographic materials, SLC exports "cartographic"; the SMD is a specific term.
  o cartographic dataset
  o cartographic image
  o cartographic moving image
  o cartographic tactile image
  o cartographic tactile three-dimensional form
  o cartographic three-dimensional form
- computer dataset
- computer program
- notated movement
- notated music
- performed music
- sounds
- spoken word
- still image [For still image the SMD is a more specific term, e.g., "engraving," "painting."]
- For tactile works, SLC exports "tactile"; the SMD is a specific term.
  o tactile image
  o tactile music
  o tactile notated movement
  o tactile text
  o tactile three-dimensional form
- text [Do not create 245$h if 338 is "volume" and 336 is "text."]

- three-dimensional form [SLC exports "form."]
- three-dimensional moving image [SLC exports "3-D moving image."]
- two-dimensional moving image [SLC exports "moving image."]

MARC codes for RDA Content:
http://www.loc.gov/standards/valuelist/rdacontent.html (accessed September 19, 2010).

337 Media type
The 337 field is not exported as part of 245$h.
Change "computer" to "electronic$2isbdarea0" if present.

Follow each term below, except "electronic," with $2rdamedia.

- audio
- [electronic] [SLC uses ISBD Area 0 term, rather than RDA's "computer."]
- microform
- microscopic
- projected
- stereographic
- unmediated [SLC suppresses if 338 displayed.]
- video

MARC codes for RDA Media:
http://www.loc.gov/standards/valuelist/rdamedia.html (accessed September 19, 2010).

338 Carrier type
For systems requiring 245$h, field 338 is exported as first half of a compound GMD, e.g., 245$h [online resource : text] where "online resource" is the 338 field data.

Follow each term with $2rdacarrier.
Notice two additions at Unmediated.

1. Audio carriers
   - audio cartridge
   - audio cylinder
   - audio discsound-track reel
   - audio roll
   - audiocassette
   - audiotape reel
2. Electronic carriers
   - computer card
   - computer chip cartridge
   - computer disc
   - computer disc cartridge
   - computer tape cartridge

  o computer tape cassette
  o computer tape reel
  o online resource
3. Microform carriers
  o aperture card
  o microfiche
  o microfiche cassette
  o microfilm cartridge
  o microfilm cassette
  o microfilm reel
  o microfilm roll
  o microfilm slip
  o microopaque
4. Microscopic carriers
  o microscope slide
5. Projected image carriers
  o film cartridge
  o film cassette
  o film reel
  o film roll
  o filmslip
  o filmstrip
  o filmstrip cartridge
  o overhead transparency
  o slide [Use for photographic slides only]
6. Stereographic carriers
  o stereograph card
  o stereograph disc
7. Unmediated carriers
  o card
  o [equipment]
  o flipchart
  o [object]
  o rollsheet
  o volume [Do not export; do not create 245$h if 338 is "volume" and 336 is "text."]
8. Video carriers
  o video cartridge
  o videocassette
  o videodisc
  o videotape reel

MARC codes for RDA Carriers:
http://www.loc.gov/standards/valuelist/rdacarrier.html (accessed September 19, 2010).

2 AACR AND RDA: ONE CATALOGUER'S REACTION

Helen Buhler

A NEW CODE WAS NEEDED

AACR 1967[1] was replaced by AACR2[2] in 1988, and that has undergone a series of revisions and updates since. New media have created new cataloguing situations, and the days when what crossed our desks was a book, a serial, or perhaps a microform, are long gone. Cataloguing is now mainly shared. The days are far behind us when the main outside sources of cataloguing were the Library of Congress printed cards or BNB (British National Biography) cards for the British, and perhaps membership in OCLC or BLCMP (Birmingham Libraries Mechanisation Project) for British libraries. Cataloguing is now international. Libraries take records from the source that has good-quality records, often from abroad if the book comes from another country. Our world has changed, and a new cataloguing code that is supposed to handle this change better than AACR2 is being tested as I write—RDA (Resource Description and Access).[3] Cataloguers outside the Anglophone area expect RDA to be more responsive to their needs, and less Anglocentric in a multi-language and multi-script environment.

Since 2004, working cataloguers have been reading and commenting on successive drafts of each chapter of RDA. Online discussion lists have enabled us to be notified of the arrival of new chapters, and have encouraged us to comment on, criticise, and discuss this internationally. We know (more or less, barring major last-minute changes) what we're going to get, although there is still a list of matters to be considered.

This is in complete contrast to earlier codes. I started cataloguing in October 1966 as Student Assistant (a pre-library school post) at Queen Mary College, University of London. The first version of AACR was almost due when my post ended, and I can remember much head-scratching about how we would file author cards, since entry would in future be under one name only, instead of up to three as we were used to with the Anglo-American rules of 1908.[4] What eventually happened I don't know, but we certainly didn't hear very much about the provisions of what was to be a very different code, or have the opportunity to discuss them—there were no online discussion lists. I found out at library school. Interestingly, AA1908 was to be the last completely international text for eighty years until AACR2 in 1978.

When AACR2 arrived, there was little fuss then, either. There were many changes, but we took them (more or less anyway) in our stride. Some changes were quietly ignored for the sake of large libraries which would have massive changes to make, such as "Department" for "Dept." in government headings, and cataloguing microform reprints as such. Again, there was no e-mail to inform us or bring us into a discussion of AACR2, and we couldn't get our hands on the forthcoming code to analyse and criticise it. Those involved in AACR2's development got on with the job without our input. We couldn't discuss then as we do now.

RDA, however, has been developed in the electronic age. Since its inception, there has been a Web site, http://www.collectionscanada.gc.ca/jsc, that subsequently became http://www.rda-jsc.org, as well as an official discussion list, RDA-L@LISTSERV.LAC-BAC.GC.CA. Needless to say, RDA has also been discussed at length on many other lists, AUTOCAT and OCLC-CAT among them. Working cataloguers have examined every new draft of every new chapter as it appeared, and commented at length for four years. RDA must be one of the most discussed documents ever, and as of this writing, it is undergoing six months' testing in working libraries. It is hoped that all this discussion and testing by working cataloguers should help to produce an outstanding cataloguing code. We have had the chapters to examine as they were drafted, we have had lists on which to discuss them—and we have made full use of them.

RDA WORRIES

But RDA really worries me. This has nothing to do with the shock of the new, or with, "What on earth is going to be in this new code?" No forthcoming cataloguing code has ever had so much advance attention from those who will use it. So why am I worried? It is not because there are to be big changes from the current code; this has happened before. Neither is it because the format will also change—from paper to Web-based. We can cope with that (if we or our libraries can afford the subscription). My worries take several forms: (1) lack of writing clarity and RDA's basis on theoretical FRBR; (2) record-sharing problems and inefficient cataloguing; and (3) language of the cataloguing agency.

RDA WRITING STYLE AND THEORETICAL FRBR

Basically, RDA will be far more difficult to use because it isn't written clearly. In *Howard's End Is on the Landing*, Susan Hill says: "But linguistic or stylistic obscurity is a hindrance to understanding."[5] This is quite different from the

FRBR (Functional Requirements for Bibliographic Records) vocabulary, which still confuses many as the concepts behind FRBR require a different way of thinking and have not yet come into general use, but at least it is adequately written. This is not the case with RDA. It is the difference between content and carrier. Even experienced cataloguers have found difficulty in understanding newly released RDA chapters; if they find it difficult to comprehend, how will library school students fare? Library school educators will also have a difficult time trying to explain cataloguing concepts that are written in tortuous prose. The convoluted English and prolixity of RDA, which is based on the still largely theoretical FRBR, was so daunting a prospect that the Working Group on Bibliographic Control at the Library of Congress[6] recommended that work on RDA should be suspended until FRBR had been fully tested. These factors make RDA difficult both to follow and to apply. A good editor with a sense of style could improve RDA immensely. If we could work out what the code says, we would stand a better chance of being able to apply it effectively. Understanding FRBR (has it yet been fully tested?) is a different problem entirely, without going into the question of whether our ILS can handle FRBR.

RDA lacks clear and concise structure. For a code that was billed as "principle-based," there seems to be a shortage of clearly stated principles. The IFLA (International Federation of Library Associations) Frankfurt Principles[7] were formulated at the same time as RDA, and are a model of rigor and clarity. These are intended to formulate the basic principles on which cataloguing and authority control should be based, not to be prescriptive. (I have wondered why, if new IFLA principles were to be produced, work on RDA could not have waited until these were available to use as a basis.)

Here are two examples (many others could have been chosen) that demonstrate just some of RDA's unnecessarily wordy and unclear content.

- Selection of which part of the work to use as the authorized "source" (title page, container, cover, etc.) for description of the work has a basic rule in AACR2, which is 1.0.A.1. It is contained in seven lines in the print version of AACR2. RDA's rule for source of description is 2.2.2.1. It needs half a page in the PDF version to state its concept, with references to specific rules.
- When it comes to place of publication, AACR 2.4.C.1 states unequivocally: "Give the place of publication, distribution, etc. as instructed in 1.4.C."[8] This, in turn, states: "Transcribe the place of publication, etc. in the form, and the grammatical case, in which it appears. If the name of a place appears in more than one language or script, give the form in the language or script of the title proper. If this criterion does not apply, give the form that appears first."[9] The same concept in RDA 2.8 states: "Core element: Publisher's name and date of publication are core elements for published resources. Place of publication is optional."[10] However, 2.8.2, "Place of Publication," is followed by five and a half pages of instructions on how to record the place(s) of publication. (As an aside,

the place of publication has now been added to the list of core elements in 0.6.2 of RDA, which is to be welcomed, as making mention of the place of publication mandatory.)

RDA RULES FOR DESCRIPTION AND RECORD-SHARING IMPLICATIONS

RDA's step back from clear and standard cataloguing rules seems to have implications for record sharing and easily usable cataloguing records. The days are long gone when a library acquired cataloguing from LC (Library of Congress) or the BNB (British National Bibliography). Now, when a good record is needed for an item to be catalogued, not only does OCLC provide cataloguing records in WorldCat from libraries in many countries, but individual libraries download records from library catalogues all over the world. In order to be able to do this and obtain or share good quality records, it is necessary to adhere to and understand agreed-upon standards, or it will take as much work to change or upgrade the records to standard format as it would to catalogue the item from scratch. It will also take more work to determine if the catalogue record found actually represents the work in hand.

There are many long and confusing rule changes in RDA, but here is an example of one that could confuse an unsuspecting cataloguer. The optional addition to RDA rule 2.8.2.3 for place of publication—"Include the full address as part of the local place name if it is considered to be important for identification or access,"[11]—is likely to cause confusion when a cataloguer finds a full address in what appears to be a standard record. Surely this is a rare-books situation, for perhaps the local history collection, rather than normal cataloguing? Someone not aware that this is just a new RDA option, unrelated to the description of rare books, might have doubts as to whether the book in hand was actually the one described in the record. Why would this rule be necessary, and is it worth the confusion it might cause? Optional additions to general rules simply create confusion. Some libraries may feel that this option is worth adopting for all records; some only where they know of a place name that exists in several places, and others may use it only for exceptional items. How do those who want a record for that book know? Rochester is a cathedral city in Kent to me. A friend in Michigan tells me that there is not only a Rochester there, but one in every contiguous state. How many elsewhere? A library deliberately deciding to use an option or to depart from a rule in its own catalogue, but upload a standard version to the shared database, is one thing. A situation where more than one possibility is equally valid and official is very much another.

Some of the language rules in RDA have other, more widespread implications for record sharing. These changes in the language of description rules may affect both efficient cataloguing and record sharing. AACR follows the ISBD (International Standard Bibliographic Description) in using Latin abbreviations. RDA has dropped the requirement for ISBD Latin abbreviations, and allows spelled-out words in the language of the cataloguing agency. Granted, Latin is no longer the lingua franca of scholarship that it used to be, but [sic] and fl. are known internationally, and record sharing is international because library collections are international. These international abbreviations, such as et al. and those already described, are language-neutral, and once learned, they are applicable in records from any source. The location of the cataloguing agency, and its associated language, may be half a world away from the library acquiring the item. If each library cataloguing agency is free to use its particular language, will this increase the time it takes to catalogue the work for another cataloguing agency using a different language? Cataloguers will have to learn and translate the text to understand what the actual description is. Will this increase the difficulty of determining whether the record with the foreign-language description is actually the same as the item they are cataloguing? The same applies to such English abbreviations as b. or d. in name headings. Libraries routinely acquire items in many languages (and scripts, but that's another problem altogether).

International migration in the late twentieth century has seen large populations of immigrants from Asia and Africa in what used to be English-speaking areas. Spanish is widely spoken in many parts of the United States. Notes and subject headings can be translated locally, but abbreviations may not be easily guessed, and in an international situation will cause problems. At least Latin is international. Both [sic] and [et al.] appear in the ISBD. Surely if we have an International Standard Bibliographic Description, which states what should be in a record and is far more than just prescribed punctuation, we should use it. This and the previously mentioned Frankfurt Principles (Statement of International Cataloguing Principles), which are a short statement of basic principles, have been hammered out internationally and multilingually. RDA is intended to be used beyond the Anglo community, and allowing multiple possible language abbreviations and descriptions does not support records that can be easily understood and used by all libraries, no matter what the language of their particular cataloguing agency. Latin does have the merit of being standard, and familiar to many.

Another option with the same potential for linguistic problems is that of the statement of responsibility. AACR2 states in 1.1F5 that "If a single statement of responsibility names more than three persons or corporate bodies performing the same function, or with the same degree of responsibility, omit all but the first of such persons or bodies. Indicate the omission by the mark of omission . . . and add [et al.] (or its equivalent in a non-roman script) in square brackets."[12]

This same situation in RDA is handled quite differently, allowing the addition of descriptive text in the language of the cataloguing agency: 2.4.1.5: "Record a statement of responsibility naming more than one person, etc., as a single statement, regardless of whether the persons, families or corporate bodies named in it perform the same function or different functions."[13] It then gives the optional exception: "If a single statement of responsibility names more than three persons, families, or corporate bodies performing the same function, or with the same degree of responsibility, omit all but the first of each of such persons, families, or corporate bodies. Indicate the omission by summarizing the omission in the language and script of the agency preparing the description. Enclose the summary of the omission in square brackets."[14]

So, if a library encounters a record produced by a library in a country that uses another language and/or script, it has to be able to translate and understand the text to be sure that the record represents their particular item, or if they should instead seek another record; decide whether to accept the "foreign language" record as is; or decide whether or not to translate the text into the "home" language. This seems likely to lead to some interesting discussions on international record sharing and efficient cataloguing.

RDA AND AACR2: WHAT IS OLD IS NEW AGAIN

Some apparently "new" changes are in fact holdovers from AACR2. The recent announcement by the Library of Congress that Dept. will change to Department has caused consternation because of the huge amount of records to be changed. Global change capabilities in online catalogues will help here. In fact, Department dates back to the advent of AACR2, but was not implemented because of the enormous problems then of making the change. Or, as with AACR2, will we all decide collectively to ignore the decision?

The provision that square brackets be used only (in the 2XX title fields) for material not found in the item harks back to a similar instruction for music cataloguing in 1966.[15] I welcome this—it made catalogue records much cleaner and easier to read!

CONCLUSION

So what will RDA be like? How much of it will actually be implemented by the national libraries? How will we cope with it when we actually get it and find ourselves using it? We'll have to wait and see.

NOTES

1. *Anglo-American Cataloging Rules*, prepared by the American Library Association, the Library of Congress, the Library Association, and the Canadian Library Association, North American text (Chicago: American Library Association, 1967).

2. Michael Gorman and Paul W. Winkler, ed., *Anglo-American Cataloguing Rules*, prepared under the direction of the Joint Steering Committee for Revision of AACR, a committee of the American Library Association, the Australian Committee on Cataloguing, the British Library, the Canadian Committee on Cataloguing, the Library Association, and the Library of Congress, 2nd ed. (Ottawa: Canadian Library Association; and Chicago: American Library Association, 1988).

3. "RDA: Full Draft, 11/24/08," RDA: Resource Description & Access Toolkit, RDA Constituency Review, http://www.rdatoolkit.org/constituencyreview (accessed May 5, 2010).

4. *Cataloguing Rules: Author and Title Entries*, compiled by committees of the Library Association and of the American Library Association, English ed. (London: Library Association, 1908).

5. Susan Hill, *Howard's End Is on the Landing* (London: Profile Books, 2009), 189.

6. "On the Record: Report of the Library of Congress Working Group on the Future of Bibliographic Control," January 9, 2008, http://www.loc.gov/bibliographic-future/news/lcwg-ontherecord-jan08-final.pdf (accessed May 5, 2010).

7. IFLA Cataloguing Section and IFLA Meetings of Experts on an International Cataloguing Code, "Statement of International Cataloguing Principles," 2009, http://www.ifla.org/files/cataloguing/icp/icp_2009-en.pdf (accessed May 5, 2010).

8. *AACR2: Anglo-American Cataloging Rules*, "Part I Description. Chapter 2. Books, Pamphlets, and Printed Sheets. 2.4. Publication, Distribution, Etc., Area. 2.4C. Place of Publication, distribution, etc.," in Cataloger's Desktop, http://desktop.loc.gov/php/login.php?referrer=http%3A%2F%2Fdesktop.loc.gov%2Ftemplate.htm%3Fview%3Dmain%26h_action%3Dclear (accessed May 5, 2010).

9. Ibid., "Chapter 1. General Rules for Description. 1.4. Publication, Distribution, Etc., Area. 1.4C. Place of Publication, distribution, etc.," in Cataloger's Desktop, http://desktop.loc.gov/php/login.php?referrer=http%3A%2F%2Fdesktop.loc.gov%2Ftemplate.htm%3Fview%3Dmain%26h_action%3Dclear (accessed May 5, 2010).

10. "RDA: Full Draft, 11/24/08," "2. Identifying Manifestations and Items. 2.8. Publication Statement," 119, http://www.rdatoolkit.org/constituencyreview (accessed May 5, 2010).

11. Ibid., "2.8.2. Place of Publication. 2.8.2.3. Recording Place of Publication," 122, http://www.rdatoolkit.org/constituencyreview (accessed May 5, 2010).

12. *AACR2: Anglo-American Cataloging Rules*, "Part I Description. Chapter 1. General Rules for Description. 1.1. Title and Statement of Responsibility. 1.1F. Statement of Responsibility. 1.1F5," in Cataloger's Desktop, http://desktop.loc.gov/php/login.php?referrer=http%3A%2F%2Fdesktop.loc.gov%2Ftemplate.htm%3Fview%3Dmain%26h_action%3Dclear (accessed May 5, 2010).

13. "RDA: Full Draft, 11/24/08," "2. Identifying Manifestations and Items. 2.4. Statement of Responsibility. 2.4.1. Basic Instructions on Recording Statements of Responsibility. 2.4.1.5. Statement Naming More than One Person, etc.," 62, http://www.rdatoolkit.org/constituencyreview (accessed May 5, 2010).

14. Ibid., 63.

15. Brian L. Redfern, *Organizing Music in Libraries* (London: Bingley, 1966).

3 RDA, AACR2, AND YOU: WHAT CATALOGERS ARE THINKING

Elaine R. Sanchez

A new cataloging code, based on the bibliographic framework of IFLA's (International Federation of Library Associations) FRBR (Functional Requirements for Bibliographic Records) construction for relating works, entities, and subjects, was finally made available for review in the cataloging world in late 2008 through February 2009. RDA (Resource Description and Access) "provides a set of guidelines and instructions on formulating descriptive data and access point control data to support resource discovery."[1] The objectives and principles for development of RDA, as stated by the committee tasked for its creation, the Joint Steering Committee for Development of RDA,[2] sound right to catalogers: comprehensive, consistent, clear, and rational cataloging guidelines and instructions that are responsive to new types of resources, compatible with established cataloging standards and models, easily adaptable for libraries and others, and easy and efficient to use. This does *sound* good. The problem, even after listening to so many of its ardent and vocal supporters, was actually seeing its monolithic online presence, and trying to imagine how to use this new code to achieve all the nobly stated objectives and principles in real life. It hasn't been achieved. Neither FRBR nor RDA has been tested in production and outcomes reviewed (even though the Library of Congress and its testing associates are in the midst of this process), and FRBR remains a theoretical notion of the bibliographic universe that is still neither concrete nor available in the only platform most libraries use to provide access to their collections: online catalogs. Plus, the cost of RDA itself is prohibitive for many libraries, training will be difficult and costly, and the learning curve will negatively and significantly affect all cataloging agencies. My question is, and all this is for *what*?

That prompted me to wonder if we could retain AACR2 and its updating device, LCRIs (Library of Congress Rule Interpretations), for those libraries that cannot afford to move to RDA, as well as having RDA (if implemented by the Library of Congress) available for those who want to utilize this code. This survey was written and administered to gather answers from practitioners and all interested parties on this question, and many other temperature-taking questions, to see what we are all thinking and doing regarding RDA and AACR2, and other issues.

There were 685 respondents to the survey, with a final count of 459 completed and usable responses. Ninety-one percent of the respondents to this survey were from the United States. Canada was the second-highest respondent at 3 percent, followed by the UK at 2 percent, and Mexico and Australia at 1 percent each. The remaining ten countries completed the last 2 percent of the respondents: China, England, Italy, Lebanon, Malaysia, New Zealand, Singapore, South Africa, Spain, and Sweden.

Most of the respondents, as just noted, are from the United States. The positions of survey respondents, in Figure 3.1,[3] following, also have a predominance of a certain type of position—cataloging librarians.

Figure 3.1 shows that basic catalogers and their administrators responded in the highest percentage (71%). Systems librarians (3%), library administrators (2%),

Figure 3.1 Question 3 on survey
Your position. (All title and copyrights in and to the Software are owned by SurveyMonkey. Material is copyright and trademark protected.)

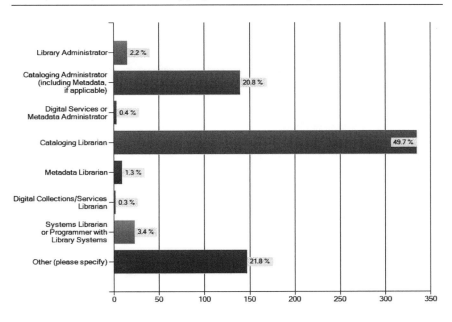

and metadata librarians (1%) followed in response percentages. In addition to the positions listed in Figure 3.1, many other types of respondents fell into the "Other" category, including the following main position types: technical services librarian/coordinator/head, cataloging technician, library educator/instructor, collection manager, research and instruction librarian, special collections librarian, database manager/specialist, library associate, graduate assistant, library director, archives manager, technical assistant, knowledge management, paraprofessional cataloger, electronic resources librarian, acquisition clerk/librarian, reader development and stock librarian, consultant, and many kinds of format catalogers.

Just as catalogers dominated the number of responses, academic libraries were the predominant respondents, as shown in Figure 3.2.

It should come as no surprise that most respondents to the survey (53%) work in academic libraries; however, public libraries also participated in high numbers (23% of the total), as did special libraries (16%). In all the types of library categories shown in Figure 3.2, the survey had at least one respondent. In addition to the categories of libraries above, and their percentage of responses, the 106 special libraries that responded to the survey included the following basic types: Law libraries of all kinds (20%); art/photography/film museum

Figure 3.2 Question 4 on survey
Your organization. (All title and copyrights in and to the Software are owned by SurveyMonkey. Material is copyright and trademark protected.)

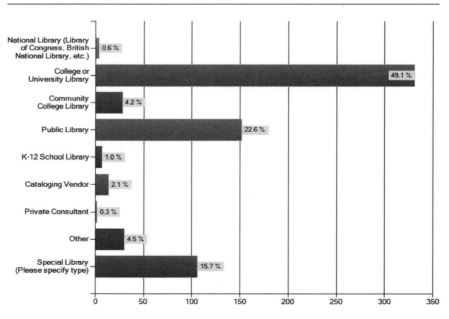

22

libraries (15%); state and state agency libraries (12%); consortiums of all kinds (8%); government research libraries (6%); historical research, society, and genealogy libraries (5%); seminary and theological libraries (4%). The remainder of the libraries, comprising 30 percent, were fairly all equal in low actual numbers of one or two per category: archives and media archives, botanical, corporate, federal, federal and state court, health sciences, humanities research, legal depository, legislative, medical, membership, nonprofit organization, private contractor for government agency, private research, rare books and special collections, and science.

The survey was designed to capture feelings toward RDA and AACR2 and its implementation, as well as facts and knowledge levels of respondents. Figure 3.3 reflects the specific feelings of respondents.

Uncertainty (62%) and curiosity (43%) are the two feelings expressed most commonly by the respondents as shown in Figure 3.3, with resignation (34%) and interest (34%) not far behind. Hower, 43 percent in total have negative feelings (fear, distrust, anxiety) compared to 28 percent with positive feelings (acceptance, positive anticipation, glad it's coming). Seventeen percent of the respondents also described their feelings in the "Other" category.

Figure 3.3 Question 6 on survey
Words that most closely match your feelings toward RDA. (All title and copyrights in and to the Software are owned by SurveyMonkey. Material is copyright and trademark protected.)

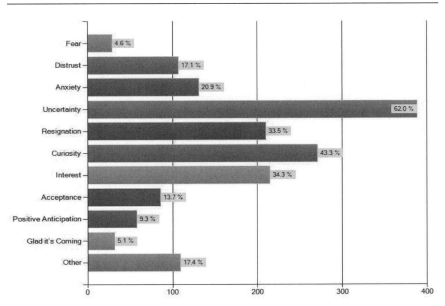

The percentages in the following ambivalent, negative, and positive categories are percentages of the overall 17 percent in the "Other" category.

- Ambivalent feelings: Apathy, ambivalence (4%); ignorance about RDA (4%); confusion (3%); doesn't change the fundamentals of cataloging (1%); and some other categories with only one respondent: sounds good in theory, but cataloging is already strained by bare-bones operations; make it easier to understand; will learn when we need to, right now it's waiting and watching; want improvements to AACR2
- Negative feelings: Disappointment/despair/disillusion (11%); annoyance/frustration/irritation (9%); it is complicated, vague, and full of jargon (6%); disgust/dislike (4%); worry about cost and usefulness (4%); farce, hyped, skeptical, cynical (4%); not necessary, it's reinventing the wheel (3%); antipathy, loathing, anger, resentment, resistence (3%); don't see a cost-benefit (3%); waste of time and money (3%); nervous, hesitant (3%); exhausted by all the talk (3%); wish to retire before it comes (2%); fear of losing job and losing the value of cataloging (1%); and others at one response—unimplementable or will take much work; won't be good enough; boondoggle; already obselete; draconian solution to unclear problem; cataloger won't have access to the Toolkit; not serve users as well as AACR2; RDA won't be used by other agencies outside the library
- Positive feelings: It's our responsibility and professional duty as well as curiousity to see what RDA is and can do (3%); cautious optimism and a hope that it will be a better standard for library services (3%); library will follow other major libraries (2%); and with one category that had only one respondent: some aspects of it may be okay.

In the next section of the survey, represented by Figures 3.4 and 3.5, catalogers are asked to respond to questions that attempt to identify the level of their understanding of RDA concepts.

Connecting the categories with the highest percentages, in Figure 3.4, may show us how the majority of catalogers (and others) rank their knowledge of the listed RDA issues or components. Most respondents (39%) rank themselves in the middle category, average, in regard to knowing why RDA was created and AACR2 was left behind. Most (32%) are not as knowledgeable or comfortable with understanding the use of RDA as a cataloging metadata application profile for non-library entities, but still have some knowledge. Similarly, most respondents (40%) are not as knowledgeable or comfortable with understanding the use of RDA element sets, but have some knowledge of them. Finally, in the same fashion, most respondents (41%) are not as knowledgeable or comfortable with the use of RDA vocabularies. It is also enlightening to review the lowest knowledge rankings and percentages in column 1, "No knowledge," and compare them to the higher 4 and 5 category rankings and percentages. Somehow, in order for RDA to be effectively used in order to maintain consistent good quality records in our shared databases, the gap between these two extremes in knowledge will have to be lessened.

Figure 3.4 Question 7 on survey
Knowledge or understanding of RDA components. (All title and copyrights in
and to the Software are owned by SurveyMonkey. Material is copyright and
trademark protected.)

7. Please explain your knowledge or understanding of the following 🕑 Create Chart ⬇ Download
RDA issues or components, using the scale of 1-5, with 1 as the lowest: "No knowledge" and 5 as the highest: "Expert knowledge." Select only one scale value per topic.

	1 No Knowledge	2	3	4	5 Expert Knowledge	Rating Average	Response Count
1. The reasons why RDA was created, and modification of AACR2 was abandoned	8.6% (47)	22.7% (124)	38.6% (211)	27.4% (150)	2.7% (15)	1.00	547
2. The use of RDA as a cataloging metadata application profile for non-library entities	30.0% (164)	32.2% (176)	28.3% (155)	8.8% (48)	0.7% (4)	1.00	547
3. Use of RDA Element sets	26.4% (143)	39.9% (216)	26.6% (144)	6.7% (36)	0.4% (2)	1.00	541
4. Use of RDA Vocabularies	24.8% (136)	41.0% (225)	27.0% (148)	6.9% (38)	0.4% (2)	1.00	549

Figure 3.5 continues the rating of knowledge and understanding of RDA
concepts, as well as introducing the opportunity to comment on whether the
respondent believes the statements are true, or agrees with them.

Using the same approach to analysis as in Figure 3.4, let's look at the categories with the highest percentages in Figure 3.5, as these may show us how the
majority of catalogers (and others) rank their understanding of and agreement
with the statements regarding RDA. Most respondents (41%) understand and
agree that RDA's defined element set allows bibliographic data to be more easily
shared in other formats than MARC. An even larger percentage (59%) also
understands the FRBR model and linking relationships between entities. But,
when it gets to specific components of RDA, such as the RDA vocabulary and
element set, this same percent of respondents (59%) either don't understand or
don't know about these documents. The next part of RDA in this question concerns its basis of FRBR as the underlying model of bibliographic organization.
Thirty percent of catalogers (and others) agree with the statement that FRBR
is a necessary requirement for future online catalogs. It is fairly close in number
to those who have no opinion or don't understand, as well as the 25 percent
who disagree, so this may indicate some ambivalence about this statement.
RDA's next feature, the "take-what-you-see" transcription approach, seems

Figure 3.5 Question 8 on survey
Level of understanding and agreement with statements regarding RDA. (All title and copyrights in and to the Software are owned by SurveyMonkey. Material is copyright and trademark protected.)

8. Indicate your level of understanding and agreement with the following statements regarding RDA, choosing only one level per topic.   🔵 Create Chart   ⬇ Download

	1 Strongly Agree and Understand	2 Agree and Understand	3 No opinion and/or Don't Understand	4 Disagree and Understand	5 Strongly Disagree and Understand	Rating Average	Response Count
1. RDA's defined element set allows our bibliographic data to be more easily shared in many different formats other than only MARC	3.9% (21)	41.4% (225)	36.1% (196)	16.4% (89)	2.2% (12)	2.72	543
2. The underlying FRBR model supports linking between entities, such as works and persons, allowing the description of relationships between them	10.5% (57)	59.1% (321)	21.2% (115)	7.2% (39)	2.0% (11)	2.31	543
3. RDA's Vocabularies and Element set have consistent and complete terminology to describe the relationships between FRBR and RDA elements, etc.	1.3% (7)	16.1% (87)	59.0% (318)	18.9% (102)	4.6% (25)	3.09	539
4. FRBRized catalogs, using RDA rules linking all types of works, expressions, manifestations and items, is a necessary requirement for future online catalogs	7.2% (39)	29.9% (162)	28.4% (154)	25.1% (136)	9.4% (51)	3.00	542
5. RDA's take-what-you-see in transcription approach facilitates re-use of metadata from non-library entities and enables automated machine matching	3.5% (19)	29.4% (159)	44.2% (239)	16.5% (89)	6.5% (35)	2.93	541
6. AACR2's transcription rules and exceptions for corrections and abbreviations impedes automated data re-use and causes difficulties for non-library entities	7.2% (39)	30.9% (167)	28.1% (152)	25.4% (137)	8.3% (45)	2.97	540
7. AACR2 is too bound to the limitations of the card environment	16.1% (87)	31.2% (169)	12.4% (67)	29.8% (161)	10.5% (57)	2.87	541
8. RDA's elimination of tracing only 3 added authors increases user access, improves machine-processing, provides better representation of the resource	25.3% (137)	48.3% (262)	10.5% (57)	12.2% (66)	3.7% (20)	2.21	542
9. Machine-generated, automatically applied publisher and vendor data is sufficient for a basic record, providing the necessary quality data for subsequent building on that record	2.6% (14)	21.1% (114)	18.3% (99)	31.8% (172)	26.2% (142)	3.58	541
10. Latin abbreviations no longer transcend linguistic boundaries	10.3% (55)	27.8% (149)	28.5% (153)	24.4% (131)	9.0% (48)	2.94	536
11. It is important to encourage publisher or distributor RDA use, and to begin to use their upstream bibliographic data so that some data doesn't have to be re-entered when cataloging, and it is less important to be overly concerned about the quality of the publisher or distributor-supplied data	6.5% (35)	24.1% (130)	19.4% (105)	29.1% (157)	20.9% (113)	3.34	540

unfamiliar with most respondents, as 44 percent don't understand this, or don't have an opinion. Thirty-one percent of catalogers think that AACR2's transcription rules, which are heavily standardized and abbreviated, impede automated data reuse and usage by non-library entities, close to the same percentage rate (31%) of those who believe AACR2 is bound by these limitations, which were set by the card environment. Related to this is the statement that Latin abbreviations, as used in AACR2 and the card environment, no longer are useful across all countries. Twenty-nine of the respondents are uncertain about that notion. RDA's change to allow more than three author added entries is approved by 48 percent. Most catalogers and others (32%) disagree on the statement, which proposes that machine-generated vendor records are sufficient for a starting bibliographic record. This idea is related to the last item in Figure 3.5, which says upstream bibliographic data use, such as vendor records, is efficient for the distribution of cataloging. Again, the largest number of respondents feel negatively about this, as 29 percent disagreed.

Figures 3.6 through 3.8, following, concern catalogers' (and others') thoughts on RDA and training issues, such as numbers of staff to train, the amount of time training will involve, and from what source funding for this training will come.

Percentages in Figure 3.6 indicate that most respondents (56%) had five or fewer staff to train. As the number of staff increased, generally the number of libraries represented decreased until the last category of thirty or more staff, which garnered more library respondents than three of the prior categories. Five to ten staff to train: 19 percent; ten to fifteen staff to train: 11 percent; fifteen to twenty staff to train: 4 percent; twenty to twenty-five staff to train: 3 percent; twenty-five to thirty staff to train: 3 percent; thirty staff and up: 5 percent.

The next section on training, shown in Figure 3.7, reviews staff training time. Although this was hard for respondents to gauge, not having any experience with RDA or the training needs it will require, many gave it their best estimates.

The majority of respondents, as reflected in Figure 3.7, sensibly noted that they don't know and can't determine the estimated training time for librarians

Figure 3.6 Question 9 on survey
Number of staff to train on RDA. (All title and copyrights in and to the Software are owned by SurveyMonkey. Material is copyright and trademark protected.)

9. Please guesstimate the number of staff to train for RDA, selecting the range of staff that matches your agency. ⬇ Download							
Number of staff to train							
	1-5	5-10	10-15	15-20	20-25	25-30	30 or more	Response Count
Ranges of staff numbers	55.5% (288)	19.1% (99)	10.6% (55)	4.2% (22)	2.9% (15)	2.5% (13)	5.2% (27)	519

Figure 3.7 Question 10 on survey
Estimated staff training time for RDA, FRBR, and ILS functionality for
FRBRized displays. (All title and copyrights in and to the Software are owned
by SurveyMonkey. Material is copyright and trademark protected.)

10. Estimated training time per staff: please estimate training time   Create Chart Download
per type of staff member as categorized in the following table. All training hours are guesstimates
only. Training would include RDA, FRBR, and new ILS functionality for FRBRized displays. If a
guesstimate cannot be provided, go to question 13.

	5-10 hrs.	10-20 hrs.	20-30 hrs.	30+ hrs.	Don't know/Can't say	Response Count
Librarian	9.6% (49)	16.6% (85)	13.5% (69)	23.2% (119)	37.1% (190)	512
Paraprofessional	10.2% (49)	12.9% (62)	10.2% (49)	22.4% (108)	44.4% (214)	482

and paraprofessionals. For those who train librarians, 37 percent could not estimate training time. This is compared to the 44 percent who train paraprofessionals, and who are unable to estimate training time. The comparison of training
time percentages between librarians and paraprofessionals may not serve any
purpose for this essay, but it is worth pointing out that for both types of library
workers, respondents estimated training time of 30 or more hours at the highest
percentages, 23 percent for librarians, and 22 percent for paraprofessionals. This
is a significant recognition of the training commitment that will be required for
everyone to learn RDA, FRBR, and ILS functionality for the new cataloging
code, the new bibliographic universe structure, and the changes they will evoke
in integrated library systems.

Figure 3.8 shows the last responses regarding training in this survey, which is
funding and training preferences.

Most libraries do not currently know where funding for RDA training is coming from (33%), but would prefer regional training by ALCTS and other library
entities (33%). Figure 3.8 percentages show that fully 30 percent of the respondents do not have money for training at all, but 44 percent have identified training funding possibilities such as travel and professional development funds.
The 11 percent of "Other" comments by respondents include categories as follows: Wherever training is from, it should be free, Web-based training, an online
interactive webinar (13%); many libraries will have some in-house training, for
main and branch libraries, generally sending someone for outside training which
is then brought in house (13%); can't send library staff out for training, nor can it
be afforded to bring in trainers from the outside, due to budget cuts now and in
the future (13%); several libraries prefer local or regional OCLC training,
Minitex, Lyrisis, NYlink, state consortia (11%); libraries in Alaska are remote,
and may need much training funding (perhaps grants) for small libraries to be
trained, hopefully in the major cities, or perhaps via distance education as
on-site training would be cost prohibitive (7%); some libraries will send staff to

Figure 3.8 Question 11 on survey
Funding and regional training preference for RDA training. (All title and copyrights in and to the Software are owned by SurveyMonkey. Material is copyright and trademark protected.)

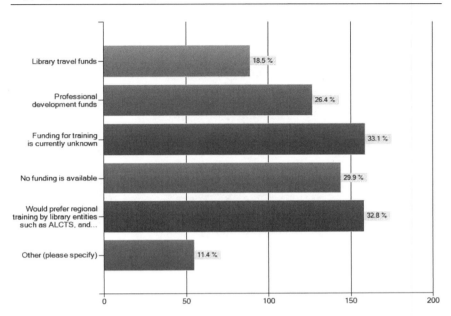

ALA to receive training, which they will bring back for on-site local training, but travel to ALA is also in question (7%); statewide budget cut crisis puts training funds at risk, and RDA training needs couldn't have come at a worse time (7%); several have funds available only for in-state travel, and would prefer training in one of the three largest cities (4%); a couple of libraries indicated that RDA developers should do this training, and have them foot the bill (4%); a few said that they were official RDA test sites, and would do their own in-house training (4%); and the remainder of comments were generated by only single libraries: prefer same day, within driving distance, no overnight stay training; OCLC and/or ALCTS should offer a free or low-cost training schedule, either online or in person; the survey assumes that libraries will train staff in the use of RDA, but this library won't as it is irrelevant (however, they will monitor the situation); in-person training is essential, as webinars are all but useless for this kind of training; this will cost a lot of money; one person sincerely hopes she won't have to train the 150 people who work with her!

Figure 3.8 reflected catalogers' views on funding for training. Figure 3.9 expands this funding question beyond training to the actual training document itself, RDA, in order to determine respondents' views on how this cataloging code will be paid for, so that library staff can train, learn, and work with it in

Figure 3.9 Question 12 on survey
How would your library fund the subscription to RDA? (All title and copyrights in and to the Software are owned by SurveyMonkey. Material is copyright and trademark protected.)

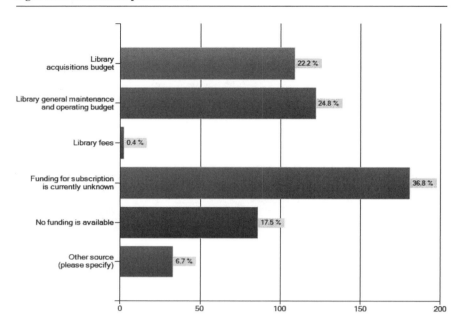

cataloging. Having RDA available for training is essential, and the cost of the
RDA subscription is considerable, growing with additional concurrent users.

Figure 3.9 clearly indicates that most libraries do not know where funding for
the RDA subscription will come from (37%), or there will be no funding available at all (18%). For those libraries that know the funding source, it seems that
the library general maintenance and operating budget is the most likely candi-
date for RDA (25%), followed closely by the acquisitions budget (22%).

Comments in the "Other source" category in this question indicate that 25 percent of respondents just don't know where the money will come from to pay for an
annual subscription to RDA. Another 25 percent suggest funding from areas such
as cataloging funds, technical services operating budget, library technology budget
(although it has been cut in half), from the university library, staff development
fund, and from cooperation with the university's library school program. Nineteen
percent of the comments indicate that these libraries are part of a consortium and
will use this arrangement to share costs, although their budgets are also stretched.
Thirteen percent indicate that they are not going to implement RDA, one because
it fears their library cannot afford RDA (its budget already cut in half), and one
doesn't see a cost-benefit when subscription prices are so high and benefits so
slight. The remaining comments include a few different ideas, such as: decreasing

OCLC services to pay for RDA; definitely paying for RDA if LC (the Library of Congress) adopts it; a vendor will use general overhead budgets which customers pay for; and a library educator worries how to provide access to multiple LIS (Library and Information Science) students.

This last comment from the library educator, who worries how to provide multiple user access to RDA, is further explored in the next question on the survey: Given the cost of RDA, what would this mean at your cataloging agency regarding the availability of this code for the staff that need it? In order to understand this issue better, the current cost of RDA, in May 2010, is as follows. RDA cost is based on concurrent users. $325 for the first user; 2 to 9 concurrent users will be charged an additional $55 for each designated user; 10 to 19 concurrent users will be charged an additional $50 for each designated user; 20 or more concurrent users will be charged an additional $45 for each designated user. Comments and percentages regarding this question are categorized into Table 3.1 and represent a large swing of opinions.

Respondents in Table 3.1 who either will not purchase RDA, will purchase it but with economic difficulty, are uncertain of obtaining RDA because of the cost, or will limit access to concurrent users because of the cost, totaled 53 percent.

Table 3.1
Comments: Considering RDA's cost, what would this mean at your cataloging agency regarding the availability of this code for the staff that need it?

Category of Comment	Percent of Respondents
BUDGET ISSUES: WE WON'T SUBSCRIBE TO RDA, OR ARE NOT SURE	
Unknown if we'll buy or not.	8
Tight budget, expensive title; would have to subscribe, but might need to cut something else to be able to afford.	7
We had to reduce budget; not sure we can afford or justify cost.	1
No budget for it this year, especially in these economic conditions.	5
Unlikely to subscribe, can't afford.	8
Can't afford it in the future unless library funding increases.	1
Total Percentage	30%

(continued)

Table 3.1. (*continued*)

Category of Comment	Percent of Respondents
ACCESS ISSUES	
We would have to limit access as we can't afford one for everyone.	11
We will only get one user, even though we need one for staff.	12
Total Percentage	23%
WE'LL SUBSCRIBE TO RDA	
We can afford it, it's not a problem, or it is at least doable; staff that need it will get it.	20
Cost is low, or nominal; it will be available to all that need it.	1
We'll subscribe.	1
Total Percentage	22%
OTHER COMMENTS	
It's very expensive.	5
We are in a consortium, and hope our group can get special group pricing; but, we're not sure how our group will handle this.	4
We want to pay for it once; the pricing model for annual subscription is not good, and we can't do this method.	3
After initial training, libraries will probably reduce users, because as much access won't be needed.	2
If the entity responsible for RDA wants catalogers to adopt it, it should be open access or free; needs to be available in an affordable, indexed print version, or as basic online text for a much lower price; we plan to print out relevant rules or whole chapters as a convenience and cost-savings method.	2

OTHER COMMENTS	Percent of Respondents
Small and school libraries find it prohibitive, puts them at a disadvantage.	2
The changes in RDA are not enough to justify the cost of its manual.	2
RDA means we may or will have go to vendor cataloging and eliminate local cataloging.	1
It is hard to justify, along with cost of Cataloger's Desktop and RDA. Could we get a discount if we utilize both?	1
For Library and Information Science students: how will this be paid for, as they need access. Could it be free? We need information on the cost to library schools.	1
Productivity and cataloging quality and efficiency will go down as we can't afford the needed consecutive users.	1
Library administration will resist purchasing RDA as they don't see the need for it, or this change for cataloging.	1
Percentage	25%

Those who indicated that they will purchase RDA and make it available to all staff that need it totaled 22 percent. If these numbers remain steady, this will represent a large inequity in access to and availability of the new RDA cataloging rules, which will perhaps have one of the consequences that was mentioned in a comment in the above table: Productivity and cataloging quality and efficiency will go down as we can't afford the needed consecutive users (1% envisioned this).

Considering this question of cataloging productivity and efficiency, Figure 3.10 and Table 3.2 portray catalogers' (and others') views on whether RDA will be cost effective in relation to the quality of the cataloging records produced by its use, and the ability of catalogers to immediately, and effectively, begin using it as a working cataloging code.

Almost half of the respondents in Figure 3.10 fall into the "No, it won't" category (46%) on the question: Will RDA be cost effective in relation to its cataloging results and its immediate ability to serve as a useful and useable cataloging code for your cataloging agency? Six percent are optimistic, and think it will be cost effective and able to serve as a useful cataloging code nearly immediately. The highest combined number of respondents (48%), though, either replied

Figure 3.10 Question 14 on survey
Will RDA be cost effective in relation to its cataloging results and its immediate ability to serve as a useful and useable cataloging code for your cataloging agency? (All title and copyrights in and to the Software are owned by SurveyMonkey. Material is copyright and trademark protected.)

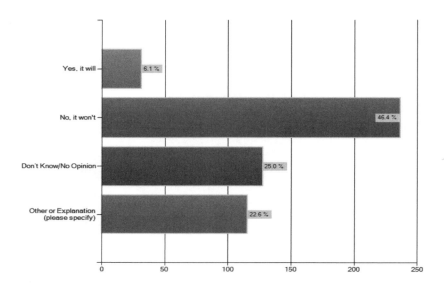

"Don't Know/No Opinion" (25 %), or cannot so easily judge yet whether RDA will be immediately useful, thus they prefer to explain their thoughts in the "Other or Explanation" (23%) category. The comments are analyzed in Table 3.2 and are in order by the categories with the highest, to lowest, percentages.

It seems that many catalogers (and others) are looking forward to RDA and FRBR as better and more modern, flexible, user-friendly cataloging and bibliographic organization standards (21%). Of course, there are the caveats as with anything new, such as testing, and waiting to see how RDA and its implementation work out, and 17 percent of the respondents indicated that this was a sensible thing to do. Thirty-three percent of those who responded leaned toward questioning the cost-effectiveness and ready implementation and use of RDA as a cataloging code: 13 percent noted that ILS systems are not yet ready for FRBR, along with other problems; 11 percent declared RDA to be too expensive to be cost effective; and 9 percent wrote about their uncertainties regarding the use, benefits, and implementation of RDA. The remaining 29 percent were unique comments, but interesting enough to put into Table 3.2.

Table 3.2
Comments: Will RDA be cost effective in relation to its cataloging results and its immediate ability to serve as a useful and useable cataloging code for your cataloging agency?

Category of Comment	Percent of Respondents
AACR2 OUTDATED, RDA AND FRBR ARE THE HOPE OF THE FUTURE	
We need to move on, AACR2 is outdated and can't be easily linked to other web data; FRBR will help with user displays; it will cost more in the future to do nothing; there is also a cost to continuing with AACR2. There are many technological features to consider and we may look back and say it was a failure, but we will not know until we try.	7
It depends—if it does what is hoped, it will be quite cost effective, although this may not be immediate; however, if RDA becomes the standard of the cataloging community, the results will be immediate and useful; the implementation will be long and unknown, so let's hope for the best.	11
It will be wonderful, and the sooner we start, the better; we will just have to backtrack later if we don't do it now.	3
Total Percentage	21%
WAIT TO SEE TESTING RESULTS AND HOW RDA WORKS	
Wait and see testing results and how it works.	10
As the national libraries go, so will we, so that we can serve our customers. We will follow their standards, but the benefit is not clear.	5
We hope the RDA testing process will provide data for evaluation of its effectiveness and use.	2
Total Percentage	17%
ILS DETAILS HAMPER COST-EFFECTIVENESS	
It's not just the cataloging costs, but also reindexing of existing records and retooling of the mapping/indexing for the public catalog; working with our vendor and IT department.	3

(*continued*)

Table 3.2. (*continued*)

ILS DETAILS HAMPER COST-EFFECTIVENESS	Percent of Respondents
It won't be cost effective because our systems are not set up to work with RDA effectively yet.	3
If our ILS doesn't adjust to the new FRBR and RDA fields and displays, this is all moot anyway. How will RDA work in ILS?	7
Total Percentage	13%

TOO EXPENSIVE	
I can't see how it is a good use of funds, especially with the economy as it currently is. We are lucky at this point to have money to purchase books! We cannot afford it, budget is tight, hiring freezes are possible.	8
I was on board with RDA until the pricing structure came out. If not all libraries can afford to purchase the new structure then it will never work as an international standard. The training costs are high but to access the documents is prohibitive.	2
Have RDA already included in the subscription pricing for Cataloger's Desktop and it will be more cost effective.	1
Total Percentage	11%

UNCERTAINTY OF COST-EFFECTIVENESS AND QUALITY OF RESULTS	
Initially it won't be cost effective, as time and money for training and the Toolkit is required; it is unclear what the learning curve will be, and it will take time for catalogers to achieve the same level of quality currently experienced.	6
Not sure how widely it will be used, nor what savings this brings to libraries.	3
Total Percentage	9%

OTHER COMMENTS	
We already have enough bib maintenance and cataloging to do, and we know AACR2. Who will do my work when I'm learning RDA?	4

OTHER COMMENTS	Percent of Respondents
The real cost is in "old dogs" trying to learn a lot of new tricks, so backlogs may grow, making public services and patrons unhappy; quality might decline.	4
RDA's success depends on LC, OCLC, staff training, and individual ILS systems, so few immediate results might be possible; however, the worry is that once all these changes are made, we will have to change again as it will take considerable time.	3
RDA is mired in confusion and indecisiveness, and FRBR and RDA are explained in vague ways, so it is hard to form an opinion.	2
No, it won't be immediately useable, as it is too large and will take too much time to learn to use it online, and we'll need funding for larger or multiple monitors.	2
If vendors and major libraries adopt RDA, it will eventually cost less for smaller libraries; or, shared cataloging between larger and smaller systems will disappear; but cost, now, for small libraries is significant.	2
Implementation will be gradual, perhaps a multiyear implementation period in which all interested libraries receive extensive free training at their own pace prior to enforced implementation.	2
This survey seems to be written to push people to fear RDA, think it isn't cost effective, and give an overall negative view of it. RDA is necessary, may be cost effective.	2
Having a print product would make it easier to share on with the team, and more cost-effective. Please!	2
Cost-effectiveness is not an applicable concept in regards to catalog codes; at least, after a certain common-sense point. That view is one of the problems that has gotten us where we are. Cataloging is always changing, and we don't usually ask if it's cost-effective or not. When a subject heading changes, we just change it. It's something we have to do in order to fully participate in the universe of shared cataloging. I wonder if people asked this question when AACR was published.	2

(*continued*)

Table 3.2. (*continued*)

OTHER COMMENTS	Percent of Respondents
RDA looks nearly identical to AACR2, so there isn't much change.	2
We have a consortial catalog and our choice of cataloging code is determined at the consortial level.	1
FRBR is pretty much useless without proper catalog display and relationships, especially for Rare Books and Special Collections. We could achieve much of the desired interoperability with MARC XML and concentrate on implementation of FRAD.	1
Total Percentage	29%

Respondents shared their thoughts on RDA's cost-effectiveness and usability in Figure 3.10 and Table 3.2. This question is expanded in Figure 3.11, as the survey asks whether RDA is better suited to the future, when linked bibliographic and authority data on the Semantic Web will be available for data mashup and reuse.

Although those who support the effort to implement RDA as a cataloging code for the Semantic Web, as shown in Figure 3.11, represent a large number, 15 percent, the majority of respondents (33%) feel that it will not be worth the cost and effort to implement RDA. Close to this number, 29 percent are refraining from offering their opinion, most likely because they either don't know, or because it is still very hard to realize what implementation of such a new idea as a FRBRized cataloging code will mean. The "Other or Explanation" category of 24 percent is where most of the thoughts on this topic will be found.

There were 108 comments analyzed, and they are categorized, with percentages of respondents, in Table 3.3, by order of percentage of responses.

Table 3.3 comments resemble the percentages in Figure 3.11: a good number want RDA to be successful and think or hope it will be; others are sure it will not meet its goals and wonder about its necessity and cost; and a large number are still uncertain of its usefulness, but are unable to judge whether it will be worth the cost to implement it, and move away from AACR2.

The concern that cataloger productivity will decline if RDA is implemented has been mentioned in prior figures and discussions of respondents' comments. It is yet another worry among several, linked to RDA training and learning curve, quality of cataloging, and the necessity to keep up with current materials, so as to avoid stockpiling uncataloged materials. Figure 3.12 includes respondents views on how RDA implementation will affect productivity and cataloging backlogs.

There are many statements in Figure 3.12 concerning various predictions of RDA's effect on cataloger productivity. The survey posed these questions to determine catalogers' (and others') reactions. To determine the mainstream of

Figure 3.11 Question 15 on survey
Will it be worth the cost and effort to implement RDA, as it will be a useful and more forward-looking cataloging code than AACR2, better suited to the future of automated reuse of publisher and other linked bibliographic and authority metadata available on the Semantic Web? (All title and copyrights in and to the Software are owned by SurveyMonkey. Material is copyright and trademark protected.)

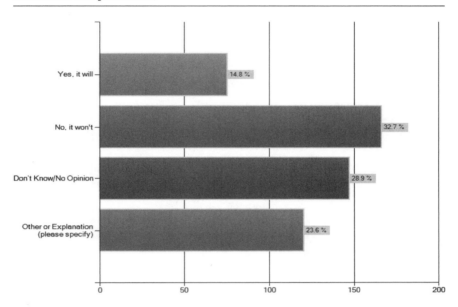

cataloger reactions from those responding to the survey, the entries with the largest percentages in each category will be discussed. Thirty-two percent agree that RDA implementation will slow down cataloging production for a significant amount of time, but the larger number of respondents (51%) think it will only be for a limited time when catalogers are learning to apply RDA. It's close, but 36 percent of the respondents agree that RDA will require significant restructuring of cataloging workflows, compared to 35 percent who think it will have minimal or no affect. From the percentages on Figure 3.12, no matter how it is viewed, respondents definitely agree that increasing cataloging turnaround is something to be avoided. Similarly, a backlog *is* expected to develop due to the RDA learning curve; 39 percent agree with this. Thirty-nine percent think that having to type in phrases, as RDA requires, instead of abbreviations, as AACR2 requires, will increase cataloging time. Finally, 60 percent expect some negative impact on cataloging productivity or turnaround time due to RDA.

Since cataloger productivity is an issue, the idea was presented to continue AACR2 and LCRIs, as well as RDA. Libraries could choose their cataloging code, and both would be acceptable. Figure 3.13 shows catalogers (and others) response to this idea.

Table 3.3

Comments: Will RDA be worth the cost and effort to implement, because it will be a useful and more forward-looking cataloging code than AACR2?

Category of Comment	Percent of Respondents
Not enough evidence yet that RDA will meet all its goals and objectives.	12
Implementation will be long and hard, but RDA will eventually be worth the effort. Let's hope there is money to train and implement it.	10
Depends on ILS vendor and OCLC to implement RDA and FRBR functionality.	8
Time and usage of RDA will tell.	8
Sources of cataloging other than catalogers will increase, and the outlook for quality data is not optimal, unless we work with providers; need to consider ramifications of lower quality cataloging, dumbing down cataloging.	8
FRBR and RDA are very theoretical and hard to envision; I'll have to use it to see.	6
AACR2 works fine and does what it is supposed to do.	4
Hope so.	4
AACR2, as RDA, is librarian-centered, so they are really very similar, and there won't be much change; however, it is good to change.	4
Not at this time of budget cuts and fiscal uncertainty; cost is a big factor.	4
Would like to see how it works for a user in the PAC, to see if it delivers better search results; PACs don't use much of our data now, would RDA make it better?	4
RDA doesn't go far enough, and perhaps FRBR is outdated.	4

Category of Comment	Percent of Respondents
The national test will give a better idea of cost and usage.	3
If publishers start using RDA, it has the potential to be useful and improve reuse of metadata, but reality is far from theory.	3
Superiority of RDA over AACR2 has not yet been proven.	3
Libraries get mostly copy, and some original, so either way they will have a mix of RDA and AACR2 to work on.	2
Several 1 percent respondent-rated comments included: RDA would be better for nonbooks; wouldn't be better for nonbooks (especially DVDs); would be better for books than nonbooks; would be better for digital formats; seems a cosmetic solution to adapting catalogs to the Semantic Web; its language hinders its usefulness; school and small libraries will not be able to afford RDA; and so on.	13

Fifty-five percent of those surveyed agreed that a fully maintained AACR2 should be available as well as AACR2—33 percent agreed with this strongly. Nineteen percent stated their disagreement with this idea—6 percent of them strongly. The difference between the two sets of percentages (55% supporting the idea, 33% against it) seems to indicate acceptance of the idea is fairly strong. However, 13 percent of the respondents selected "Other," and the statistical analysis of their responses shows that this group believes that maintaining two cataloging codes is not an optimal action, among other things.

- Thirty-five percent disagreed, and are against the idea of maintaining AACR2 and RDA.
- Twenty-two percent agreed that a fully maintained AACR2 should be available.
- Fifteen percent believe that LC's decision will be one that they will follow, and they think LC (and RDA's Joint Steering Committee) cannot support both AACR2 and RDA—it is unrealistic.
- Seven percent believe maintaining two cataloging codes would be expensive, redundant, and/or confusing.
- Seven percent think that RDA should be scrapped or revamped, with more modern theoretical grounding.

Figure 3.12 Question 16 on survey
RDA implementation and cataloger productivity. (All title and copyrights in
and to the Software are owned by SurveyMonkey. Material is copyright and
trademark protected.)

16. RDA Implementation and Cataloger Productivity: please indicate 🌀 Create Chart ⬇ Download
your level of agreement with the statements below, choosing only one per statement.

	1 Strongly Agree	2 Agree	3 No Opinion/Don't Know	4 Disagree	5 Strongly Disagree	Rating Average	Response Count
1. RDA implementation will slow down cataloging production for the foreseeable future	22.6% (109)	32.2% (155)	27.0% (130)	17.0% (82)	1.2% (6)	1.00	482
2. RDA will slow down cataloging production only for a limited time as catalogers learn the rules	14.9% (72)	51.0% (246)	15.1% (73)	15.6% (75)	3.3% (16)	1.00	482
3. Cataloging workflows WILL require significant restructuring to implement RDA	17.6% (85)	27.7% (134)	36.4% (176)	16.7% (81)	1.7% (8)	1.00	484
4. Cataloging workflows will require MINIMAL OR NO restructuring to implement RDA	1.9% (9)	16.4% (79)	34.6% (167)	33.8% (163)	13.3% (64)	1.00	482
5. Increasing cataloging turnaround time (from receipt to patron) is NOT a service problem at my agency	10.0% (48)	27.7% (133)	8.5% (41)	34.7% (167)	19.1% (92)	1.00	481
6. Increasing cataloging turnaround time (from receipt to patron) IS a service problem at my agency	21.2% (102)	33.1% (159)	8.9% (43)	27.4% (132)	9.4% (45)	1.00	481
7. NO INCREASE in backlogs is expected due to RDA implementation (RDA learning curve WON'T increase backlog growth)	1.9% (9)	13.3% (64)	30.0% (144)	34.2% (164)	20.6% (99)	1.00	480
8. An increase in backlogs IS EXPECTED due to RDA (RDA learning curve WILL increase backlog growth)	20.3% (98)	39.4% (190)	25.9% (125)	11.8% (57)	2.5% (12)	1.00	482
9. As required by RDA, typing "Place of publication not identified" for S.l., and providing spelled out abbreviations in the transcription rather than using shortened forms, will NOT increase cataloging time	5.2% (25)	23.5% (113)	15.4% (74)	40.2% (193)	15.6% (75)	1.00	480
10. As required by RDA, typing "Place of publication not identified" for S.l., and providing spelled out abbreviations in the transcription rather than using shortened forms, WILL increase cataloging time	18.2% (88)	38.8% (188)	16.1% (78)	22.3% (108)	4.5% (22)	1.00	484
11. I anticipate NO negative impact on cataloging productivity or turnaround time due to RDA	1.9% (9)	4.6% (22)	17.6% (85)	49.8% (240)	26.1% (126)	1.00	482
12. I anticipate SOME negative impact on cataloging productivity or turnaround time due to RDA	23.9% (116)	59.3% (288)	11.3% (55)	4.3% (21)	1.2% (6)	1.00	486

Figure 3.13 Question 17 on survey
Select the choice that most closely matches your opinion on this statement: A fully updated and maintained AACR2, with continuing LC and Joint Steering Committee for Development of RDA support, and LCRI service, should be maintained in addition to RDA for those libraries that choose not to utilize RDA cataloging rules. (All title and copyrights in and to the Software are owned by SurveyMonkey. Material is copyright and trademark protected.)

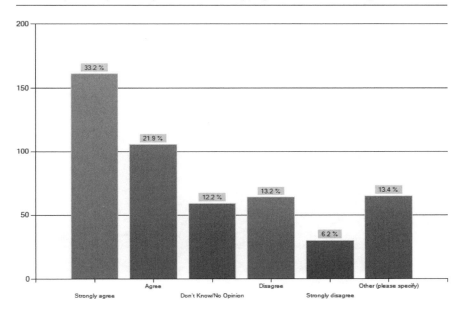

- Five percent of the respondents in the "Other" category think AACR2 should be available, but not fully maintained and/or updated—it could die a slow death and allow libraries to start working with RDA when they were ready.
- The remainder of the "Other" responses, which make up the remaining 9 percent, includes these ideas: better to use ISBDs for descriptive rules; if RDA, as it is supposed to do, simplifies the process of cataloging, can't it be made easier? AACR2 is outdated; some RDA principles are valid, but it is complicated and there is not an inexpensive print version; incorporate some RDA ideas into AACR2.

AACR2 as a continuing, viable cataloging code has support, although many disagree and feel it would be impractical to have two cataloging codes. Figure 3.14 questions catalogers on their opinions regarding for which formats AACR2 could still function as an effective cataloging code. Figure 3.15 asks a similar question, but addresses use of the RDA cataloging code.

Figure 3.14 Question 18 on survey
If AACR2 were to continue as a fully maintained cataloging code, in addition to RDA, what formats could continue to be effectively cataloged *using* AACR2? Choose all that apply. (All title and copyrights in and to the Software are owned by SurveyMonkey. Material is copyright and trademark protected.)

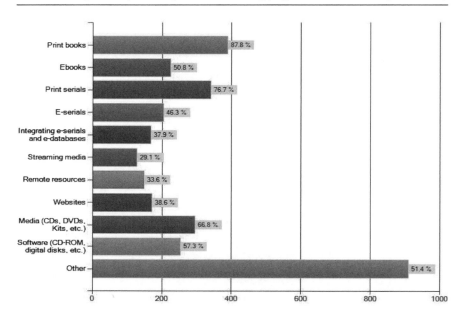

From Figure 3.14, it is clear that catalogers are confident in AACR2's ability to handle print materials, as they rate AACR2 at an average of 83 percent in being an effective cataloging code for print books and serials, together. AACR2 for cataloging media and software is rated by an average of 63 percent of the catalogers as effective for these resources. Digital resources have a lower statistical rating, although catalogers deem that e-books and e-serials can be handled moderately well, with 51 percent and 46 percent ratings, respectively. It is the other digital resources that catalogers feel less confident about AACR2's ability to be an effective cataloging code. Catalogers (and others) have rated AACR2's effectiveness in handling integrating resources, streaming media, remote resources, and Web sites together at an average of 35 percent.

"Other" responses in this figure (51%) represent catalogers' thoughts on either other formats not covered in the list of material types, or general comments. Comments are listed in percentage order, from highest to lowest, in the following categories.

- We already use AACR2 for all the things on this list, and it can be developed as new formats develop: 39 percent.

- Opposed to continuing to use AACR2; let's be done with it: 19 percent.
- In addition, the following resources can be cataloged using AACR2: Unpublished materials, realia, manuscripts, microforms, 2-D collections, archival collections, manuscripts, music, oral history, kits, puppets: 14 percent.
- Using both AACR2 and RDA at the same time would be confusing, and cause national level standard problems: 12 percent.
- Don't know enough about RDA versus AACR2 to say: 4 percent.
- All formats can benefit from RDA: 4 percent.
- Remaining three categories, all with 2 percent each: AACR2 needs to be updated for nonprint resources; we already have conflicting rules from AACR2, CONSER, BSR, e-book neutral; takes more time to catalog e-books with AACR2; and, not necessarily any of the above can be cataloged better by AACR2.

Figure 3.14 has given a very good overview on catalogers' thoughts regarding AACR2's ability to handle different types of resources. Let's compare all these percentages to RDA's handling of the same, as shown in Figure 3.15.

Figure 3.15 Question 19 on survey
If AACR2 were to continue as a fully maintained cataloging code, in addition to RDA, what formats would be cataloged most effectively *using RDA*? Please choose all that apply. (All title and copyrights in and to the Software are owned by SurveyMonkey. Material is copyright and trademark protected.)

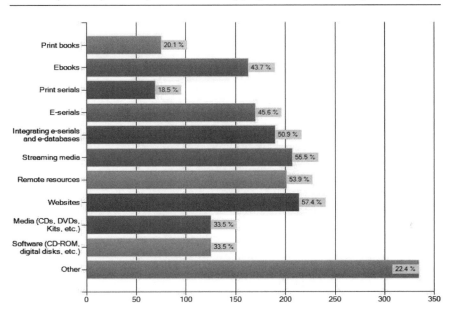

Catalogers are considerably less confident about RDA's ability to be an effective cataloging code for both print books and serials, averaging 20 percent who believe RDA can handle both formats effectively. This is much lower than AACR2's average percentage of 83 percent for print. The average percentage for the effectiveness of RDA to catalog media and software is 34 percent. AACR2 has an average of 63 percent. This clearly demonstrates that for "traditional" formats, catalogers rate AACR2 significantly higher than RDA as an effective cataloging code. Perhaps e-books and e-serials might be considered a little more traditional, as they have been in existence for some time. The percentages reflect this, as catalogers rated RDA's efficacy as a cataloging code for e-books at 44 percent (compared to 51% for AACR2) and 46 percent for e-serials (the same as AACR2's 46%). The difference in confidence is in RDA's functionality with newer digital media. Catalogers (and others) have rated RDA's effectiveness in handling integrating resources, streaming media, remote resources, and Web sites together at an average of 55 percent, which is markedly higher than AACR2's 35 percent for these same digital formats.

There were a large number of comments (22%), which are contained in the "Other" category. They can be categorized into the several types of responses in the list below. Comments are listed in percentage order, from highest to lowest, in the following categories.

- Don't know enough about RDA versus AACR2 to say: 53 percent.
- RDA will perhaps prove itself more suitable for online and e-materials, new formats, blogs, podcasts, with the new content, carrier fields, and works with accompanying material, while AACR2 still can excellently serve traditional resources, music: 8 percent.
- RDA is designed to effectively catalog all the above: 8 percent.
- Not necessarily any of the above can be cataloged better by RDA: 8 percent.
- Using both AACR2 and RDA at the same time would be confusing, cause national level standard problems: 3 percent.
- AACR2 should not continue: 3 percent.
- AACR2 can work for any of these: 3 percent.
- In theory, RDA should be more effective for cataloging nonprint resources, streaming media, Web sites: 3 percent.
- Can't answer until I start using it and see how it interacts with my ILS and other things: 3 percent.
- Either RDA or AACR2 would work fine: 3 percent.
- RDA is not effective cataloging, will create sloppy database construction and maintenance, disservice to scholars: 1 percent.
- None will be more effectively cataloged using RDA than AACR2; problems will be in transitioning between one system and another: 1 percent.
- RDA description looks good, as do entry changes. Will change accordingly and ignore FRBRization: 1 percent.

Figure 3.16 Question 20 on survey
Indicate your level of agreement with these statements regarding AACR2 and RDA. (All title and copyrights in and to the Software are owned by Survey-Monkey. Material is copyright and trademark protected.)

20. Please indicate your level of agreement with the following statements, choosing only one per topic.						🗘 Create Chart ⬇ Download	
	1 Strongly Agree	2 Agree	3 No Opinion/Don't Know	4 Disagree	5 Strongly Disagree	Rating Average	Response Count
1. RDA is going to replace AACR2	9.1% (44)	38.1% (184)	38.3% (185)	11.4% (55)	3.1% (15)	2.61	483
2. Changing to RDA from AACR2 is something all catalogers need to be ready to implement	6.2% (30)	50.8% (246)	22.3% (108)	16.1% (78)	4.5% (22)	2.62	484
3. AACR2 is still an excellent, easy to use, inexpensive set of rules with a viable updating LCRI mechanism, and remains a useful cataloging code	30.1% (145)	45.4% (219)	7.1% (34)	15.4% (74)	2.1% (10)	2.14	482
4. AACR2 can handle the cataloging of digital resources as effectively as RDA	15.5% (75)	21.7% (105)	39.5% (191)	19.2% (93)	4.1% (20)	2.75	484

- RDA must be tested first: 1 percent.
- A good cataloger can catalog anything with any set of rules: 1 percent.

In Figures 3.14 and 3.15, catalogers gave their observations on how they believe AACR2 and RDA would effectively handle the cataloging of the varying specific material types or formats, and comparisons are analyzed and described. Figure 3.16 demonstrates catalogers' views on several statements comparing the two cataloging codes and their relationship.

In order to see the most prevalent view, let's compile the rankings of these statements with the highest percentage of respondents. The highest number of catalogers (38%) do not know, or have no opinion, on whether RDA is going to replace AACR2. This is sensible—the rules aren't even tested yet. Over half of respondents (51%) think that catalogers do need to be ready to move to RDA from AACR2, if this becomes necessary. Catalogers, in the majority (45%), believe that AACR2 is still an excellent, easy-to-use, inexpensive, and viable cataloging code. The last statement concerns AACR2's ability to handle the cataloging of digital resources as well as RDA, and most catalogers are still uncertain about this: 40 percent have no opinion or don't know—again, a sensible response, since RDA is as yet untested and unused in daily cataloging.

Since the comparison of AACR2 and RDA is such a strong indicator of catalogers' views on the usefulness of the respective cataloging codes, a short analysis of the overall positive ("I agree") and negative ("I disagree") responses is enlightening. Combining ranking categories 1 and 2 gives the overall "agree" responses, and combining categories 3 and 4 does the same for the "disagree" responses. Forty-seven percent of catalogers (and others) in this survey believe that RDA will replace AACR2. Fifty-seven percent think that catalogers need at least to be ready to move to RDA and leave AACR2 behind. In the minds of catalogers, 75 percent believe that AACR2 is still an excellent, easy-to-use, inexpensive, and viable cataloging code. Finally, 37 percent have the opinion that AACR2 can handle digital resource cataloging as well as RDA.

In contrast, the combined negative responses show that 14 percent of the catalogers who responded to the survey think that AACR2 will not be replaced by RDA. Twenty-one percent hold the view that catalogers do not need to be ready (at least for now) to implement RDA and leave AACR2. Seventeen percent disagree with the statement that AACR2 is still an excellent, easy-to-use, inexpensive, and viable cataloging code. Twenty-three percent of respondents feel that AACR2 cannot handle digital resources cataloging as effectively as RDA will be able to.

Comparisons of AACR2 to RDA in Figure 3.16, and the prior comparisons regarding how respondents think both cataloging codes would handle different formats, in Figures 3.14 and 3.15, have created a fairly thorough impression for the views of the respondents on these topics. The survey next asks for catalogers' (and others') viewpoints on the problems and limitations of AACR2 and how or if AACR2 could be improved to maintain its viability for present and future cataloging needs. Respondents answered the AACR2 improvement and viability question frequently in relation to RDA, but always in a variety of thoughtful ways. Their comments are categorized below in Table 3.4, and are in percentage order from highest to lowest.

Catalogers have a lot invested in AACR2, and many still believe it to be as useful as ever, with a few updates and modifications. Many others believe, though, that AACR2 has outlived its usefulness, and new digital formats and new online catalog structures, as well as FRBR, require a new cataloging code. Table 3.4 covers many of their suggestions for this, as well as many comparisons to RDA, and is a possible source of information for those who would change both codes to more closely adhere to perceived cataloging needs for better access, description, and display.

Catalogers (and others) have a wide range of opinions on the viability and future of AACR2, as the survey has shown. Some feel AACR2 should be continued and maintained, and of course, others don't. This is a common thread that shows through many of the survey respondents' answers to various survey questions. Figure 3.17 contains the responses to the next logical question for catalogers, given their feelings about AACR2's viability: Would you support an AACR2 maintained by a cataloging community, if its official supporting agency did not?

Table 3.4
Please explain your thoughts, if any, on problems or limitations of AACR2, and how or if AACR2 can be improved to maintain its viability for present and future cataloging needs.

Category	Percentage of Respondents
AACR2 is adequate for cataloging, should be adapted to accommodate new and digital media as they evolve; keep using it; keep it updated to match RDA if this is what will work.	29
AACR2 is too based on card environment, for example: rule of three example, punctuation.	11
Dynamic, digital forms of communication cause problems for cataloging descriptions in AACR2, such as digital resources, new formats, and more future forms.	7
In AACR2 there are too many options and exceptions, esoteric abbreviations, card-bound rules, too much repetition.	7
Eliminate Festschriften in AACR2; get rid of GMDs and only use SMDs; add new fields for material designators; get more explicit instructions on including data support FRBR linkages; update the carrier-versus-content fields; adopt RDA's expansion of rule of three, update chapters 21–25 and FRBRize them.	7
AACR2 is conceptually outmoded and needs to be abandoned.	6
AACR2 is mostly print oriented, and books oriented.	3
The problems with AACR2 are more to do with MARC; MARC needs enhancement.	3
FRBR is very worthwhile and AACR2 can't make very good use of it, can't describe relationships of resources	3
AACR2's rules provide a philosophical and methodological framework, which is without question an excellent one.	2

(continued)

Table 3.4. (*continued*)

Category	Percentage of Respondents
AACR2 and RDA are both all right, similar, and need streamlining and changes.	2
Need a code that reflects the Web environment, computer-to-computer communication, language, and structure, which AACR2 is not strong in.	2
AACR2 is too tied to the physical manifestation of the work being described and not to the actual intellectual content of the work.	2
AACR2 is not as easy to work with for nonprint media.	1
RDA is not true change, nor in the right direction, and we need something that will have a true understanding of data presentation.	1
Need a code that reflects the new types of ILS coming, handles the new and different way that information is shared and used, and AACR2 doesn't do this.	1
Cataloging interfaces need improvement, not the cataloging codes.	1
RDA doesn't seem to go far enough.	1
Several other comments, equaling 11 percent: AACR2 needs support from the highest levels of the cataloging profession; use of outside rule interpretations to keep AACR2 up to date is inflexible; AACR2 is just as adaptable to FRBR as RDA; RDA will most likely handle digital media better; RDA will enable more data mining from upstream sources of all kinds; special materials can be cataloged with AACR2, with no problem; make AACR2 easier so that people other than catalogers can use it; AACR2 can be maintained and updated more cheaply than implementing RDA—use a wiki if JSC won't cooperate; release AACR2 as an open source alternative to RDA.	11

Forty percent of the respondents indicated they would support an AACR2 maintained by a cataloging community, with voluntary discussion and adoption of standards and changes, but almost half that, 19 percent, would not. A significant amount of respondents indicated that they had no opinions at present, so

Figure 3.17 Question 22 on survey
if AACR2 were not maintained by its official agency, Joint Steering Committee on Development of RDA, would you support an AACR2 maintained by a
cataloging community, with voluntary discussion and adoption of standards
and changes? (All title and copyrights in and to the Software are owned by
SurveyMonkey. Material is copyright and trademark protected.)

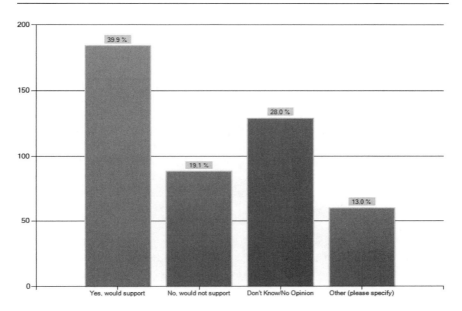

many of them are most likely waiting to see how the testing of RDA ends, and
what national libraries will do regarding RDA implementation. Comments on
this question varied as much as the percentages of responses. Here is just a sample of some repeated themes, and some interesting remarks:

- Huge task, and if it's not authoritative, what would its value be?
- Yes, I would support, but assume it would be a transition, and eventually
  shut down.
- Wouldn't like to see a listserv handle rule changes.
- This depends on which institutions populated this "cataloging community."
- Yes, I would support, because I don't believe LC will commit to support-
  ing two codes, and I believe it is completely "on board" with the gang of
  infidels who are pushing RDA as a panacea!
- No, I would not support it as it would be even slower and more chaotic
  than now.
- This suggestion is not even possible and reflects a lack of understanding
  of the JSC's last few years of work. WE are the JSC (ALA, LC, LAC,
  BL, etc.).

- Although I do not want to abandon AACR2 for RDA, I do not believe that it is in the best interests of the cataloging community to maintain two separate cataloging codes, diminishing the benefits of shared cataloging.
- AACR2 should not be a Wikipedia; some body in authority should maintain it.
- Yes, but that is inefficient; the JSC needs to be chastised and replaced within the existing structure; we already paid for their work and should have a result that we can work with without having to try to reinvent the wheel.
- AACR2 is a published resource covered by copyright so you could only do this to a certain extent without the rights.

The responses in Figure 3.17 indicate a general consensus for some kind of interim support of AACR2 as a community standard, if it were not continued by its responsible agencies, although this is not viewed as a very workable way to maintain cataloging standards. Figure 3.18 follows this topic and asks if libraries would be willing to subsidize or pay a small subscription fee to continue AACR2 and LCRI updates.

Figure 3.18 Question 23 on survey
Would your agency be willing to subsidize or pay a small subscription fee to continue AARC2 and LCRI updates? (All title and copyrights in and to the Software are owned by SurveyMonkey. Material is copyright and trademark protected.)

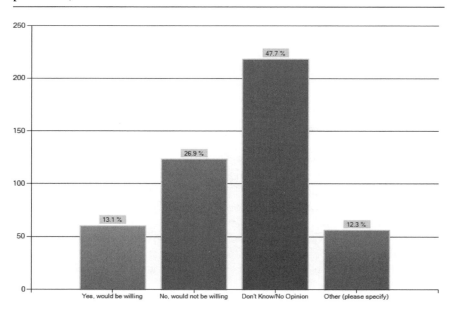

Money is tight, especially during a time of economic hardship. Not unexpectedly, when having to select a yes or no answer to provide monetary support, most (27%) indicated they would not subsidize or pay a small subscription fee to continue AACR2 and LCRI updates. Half that number (13%) would be willing. The majority, though (48%) are not sure, which is reasonable, because the future of RDA and AACR2 is not written, and anything could be possible. The main types of comments for this question, and some other interesting ideas from respondents, are covered in the following list:

- I would personally be willing to subsidize the continuing development of AACR2 and LCRIs. Because of my library's special circumstances, I'm not sure it would be willing or able to make such a commitment.
- Only if RDA is not used on a national level; I disagree with having two standards.
- The open-source software community offers an excellent model for what needs to be done here; the success of Firefox and Linux proves that it really CAN be done.
- I don't see any reason to do anything but maintain the status quo of AACR2 until all libraries can adapt to RDA; therefore, subscriptions will not be necessary.
- In this economy, it would have to be a small subscription fee.
- Cataloging as a practice should move forward with everyone involved. It seems like most of the practicing catalogers are not sold on RDA so are not ready to incorporate it. Or they may know it is just a solution in search of a problem. To be part of the global cataloging community, we should not split into RDA and AACR2 camps. Would we not use the sharing and the value of our records?
- The cost of buying access to the new RDA was a shock. I would be willing to pay a fee to have AACR2 continue, but only as a stop gap to a better code, more affordable code than RDA. I would prefer for RDA to be affordable and functional, but right now I fear it is neither.
- Define "small."
- We will adopt RDA if NLM and our peer institutions do. So we would not be willing to pay to maintain AACR2 even if we felt it was the better alternative.
- Only if we didn't buy into RDA.
- We would be willing to continue to pay what we are paying now for AACR2, LC:SCM, and LCSH updates.

While the question that Figure 3.18 covers demonstrates respondents' views on whether libraries would help pay to continue AACR2 and LCRI updates, Figure 3.19 asks catalogers (and others) to actually comment on particular AACR2 and RDA rule changes and workarounds.

As has been done in prior analyses, let's take the middle-of-the-road approach and use percentages that reflect the majority of responses in Figure 3.19.

Figure 3.19 Question 24 on survey
Please categorize your level acceptance of the following RDA rules that differ from AACR2, and your acceptance of selected workarounds. (All title and copyrights in and to the Software are owned by SurveyMonkey. Material is copyright and trademark protected.)

	1 Would accept	2 Consider accepting	3 No Opinion/Don't Know	4 Won't accept	Response Count
1. Accept RDA O.T./N.T. changes. Globally fix the O.T./N.T. differences to be implemented by RDA in your online catalog	31.4% (143)	26.5% (121)	39.0% (178)	3.1% (14)	456
2. Map the new MARC fields 336 (content type) 337 (media type) 338 (carrier type) to a modified 245 $h [GMD]	17.8% (81)	35.5% (161)	38.3% (174)	8.4% (38)	454
3. Don't use or map the 336-338 fields and instead insert usual 245 $h[GMD]	13.5% (61)	19.0% (86)	50.3% (228)	17.2% (78)	453
4. Use the new MARC 336-338 fields as is, once online catalog displays allow this	27.2% (123)	32.2% (146)	37.3% (169)	3.3% (15)	453
5. Adjust to spelled out Department as per RDA (instead of Dept. as per AACR2)	40.9% (186)	33.0% (150)	15.4% (70)	10.8% (49)	455
6. Use or add in spelled out words, instead of AACR2 abbreviations	41.0% (188)	35.4% (162)	14.2% (65)	9.4% (43)	458
7. Use RDA rule of main entry for treaties under the first country to appear on source	28.7% (131)	28.9% (132)	39.3% (179)	3.1% (14)	456
8. Follow the dissolution of the rule of 3 added entries and add as many as found	47.9% (219)	33.5% (153)	11.8% (54)	6.8% (31)	457

Further analysis of the extremes can be left for another time. In the five following RDA rules, most catalogers don't know whether they would use the workarounds! There are current system limitations, and we aren't cataloging with RDA yet, so that makes perfect sense.

1. Accept RDA O.T./N.T. changes. Globally fix the O.T./N.T. differences to be implemented by RDA in your online catalog: 39 percent don't know if they would do this; however, 58 percent might consider it, or would accept it.
2. Map the new MARC fields 336 (content type) 337 (media type) 338 (carrier type) to a modified 245 $h[GMD]: 38 percent don't know if this is what they want to do with these fields, but 54 percent might consider it, or would accept it.
3. Don't use or map the 336–338 fields and instead insert usual 245 $h [GMD]: 50 percent aren't sure if they would do this; 33 percent might consider it, though.
4. Use the new MARC 336–338 fields as is, once online catalog displays allow this: 37 percent haven't yet made up their mind to use these fields (most likely due to system limitations); but, 59 percent would do it or consider it (once it becomes available in OCLC and our online systems).

5. Use RDA rule of main entry for treaties under the first country to appear on source: 39 percent are not certain about this rule; but 58 percent would use it, or consider using it.

The remaining two categories are both viewed favorably by respondents, who indicate they would accept the rules:

1. Adjust to spelled-out Department as per RDA (instead of Dept. as per AACR2): 40 percent of catalogers said they would accept this. Add to that the percentage of those who would consider it, and that's a large percentage of respondents who might actually use this RDA rule: 74 percent.
2. Follow the dissolution of the rule of three added entries and add as many as found: When you combine percentages of those who would (48%) and those would consider it (34%), the result is 82 percent who would use this rule, the largest percentage of all, so far. It is a popular rule!

The survey now changes its focus from cataloging rules to the adoption and implementation of RDA. Figure 3.20 is an important question for libraries, as most libraries depend on cataloging done by the Library of Congress to provide records for their online catalogs.

Figure 3.20 Question 25 on survey
If LC adopts RDA either in total or in part, what will your cataloging agency do?
(All title and copyrights in and to the Software are owned by SurveyMonkey.
Material is copyright and trademark protected.)

25. If LC adopts RDA either in total or in part, what will your cataloging agency do? Please select one response.		Create Chart Download	
		Response Percent	Response Count
Utilize LC's RDA implementation plan, follow LC completely		21.3%	98
Adopt parts or the whole of LC's RDA implementation plan in principle, but establish local practices that vary from LC's		26.2%	121
Do not follow LC's RDA implementation plan, but do establish your agency's own RDA implementation plan and practices		4.6%	21
Do not follow LC's RDA implementation plan, and continue using AACR2		3.5%	16
Don't know/No opinion		24.9%	115
Show replies Other (please specify)		19.5%	90

Following the lead of LC is a popular choice of survey respondents. Most libraries, 26 percent, will utilize LC's RDA implementation plan, but adapt it to local needs. Close behind that, 21 percent will follow LC completely. In the cataloging world, this acceptance of LC's lead is pragmatic (most cataloging copy for many libraries comes from LC), and clings to the hope and dwindling tradition that LC will choose the method that offers excellent quality cataloging. Five percent will make their own way, without LC's example, and 4 percent have already determined that they will not utilize RDA, but will remain with AACR2. Those 25 percent with no opinion are just waiting to see the results of the national RDA cataloging experiment before they commit to a course of action. The comments are very telling: catalogers are trying to use logic, keep costs down, follow standards, and come up with an implementation plan that will work for them. Here are a few representative comments that are repeated in the entire group of comments, as well as a few interesting ones:

- I am in a consortium. The group would decide, not just I, so I would follow the group's decision.
- I would hope that we would establish local practices that vary from LC/RDA, but again, this would depend on whether there is a large enough number of fellow institutions doing their own thing. We would not wish to become isolated.
- Again, I don't know enough—plus we can't imagine being able to afford the RDA yearly subscription cost, so that may drive how much we are able to do and when. We may just end up following Mac Elrod's cheat sheets.
- We will probably follow LC, and accept their cataloging as is, but may also allow varied practice locally. We have to accept large tape loads from other sources, and their practices may vary from LC. We can't recatalog things we already own, so we will have a hybrid no matter what we implement.
- [We] hope there is an alternative that allows libraries to continue using AACR.
- Why does LC have to be the ones to which we look? I am interested in learning about other institutions implementation as well. I will not propagate the continual reverence of LC when they will not step up and take any responsibility. They are an entity too big to make effective changes in this profession.
- In terms of teaching, until we know the outcome of the LC and British Library trials, it is impossible to know what to do!
- For us it will probably depend on what our customers' request. We will probably have customers on both sides and will have to walk a path between the two.
- We tend to wait and see what everyone does. I believe we will wait at least six months from the conclusion of LC's testing phase, take a look at how it went for LC and also what other libraries are doing, look at

what accommodations OCLC and our ILS have made for RDA display, look at the number of RDA compliant records in OCLC, and train, and when all those factors reach a critical mass, then we will implement.

- We have not talked about it, at all.
- If LC adopts RDA, I will need to teach both RDA and AACR2 for a while so students can understand all of the records that currently exist and the new ones being created.
- We would still wait for Library and Archives Canada to lead the way for us, but LC's full adoption would certainly affect our view of how and when that would happen, and how we should prepare.
- Keep AACR2 and implement RDA only when we must.
- Will not adopt RDA due to lack of funding for rules and training.
- I think we are going to try implementing it, but to what extent, I haven't a clue. I'm kind of being forced to learn about all this, and don't really want to. I have only 3.5 years until retirement and I don't want to have to learn a new system this late in the game.
- We will teach RDA, and probably not teach AACR2.

Everyone is looking for the right answer for their institution, and all the information to find the answer is not yet available!

In Figure 3.20, and elsewhere in this essay, mention has been made regarding the RDA testing by national libraries, because the results of the testing will drive many libraries toward a decision whether to go with RDA, stay with AACR2, or take a hybrid approach. There has been much discussion on cataloging listservs that even though libraries are testing RDA, there may be a certain "done deal" effect in place, meaning that the decision to implement RDA has already been made by LC and other national libraries, regardless of the results of the test. Figure 3.21 responses show catalogers' views on this possible situation.

Forty-five percent of the respondents believe that there will be discussion among the testing libraries, and that the RDA implementation decision will be made based on the testing results. It is encouraging that most libraries still believe in the integrity of the process. Thirty-five percent, however, think that the decision has already been made to go with RDA. The 15 percent who indicated that they don't know are being safe in their response, because no one really knows! Selected comments, reflecting the majority of opinions, and some unique ones that are of interest, are as follows.

- RDA acceptance is a done deal; testing may result in some modifications.
- Too much time and money has been invested to abandon it.
- About one year ago, it seemed RDA had been shelved; too unclear to most; now going forward and to be released in June. But nowhere has clear information on what it will mean to our daily work been distributed. Very late notification and awareness of what this actually means to people doing daily cataloging of thousands of materials, especially

Figure 3.21 Question 26 on survey
Do you believe that RDA acceptance is already a done deal, or do you believe
that it is still possible the U.S. National Libraries and RDA test partner libraries
will confer to recommend the best possible choice? (All title and copyrights in
and to the Software are owned by SurveyMonkey. Material is copyright and
trademark protected.)

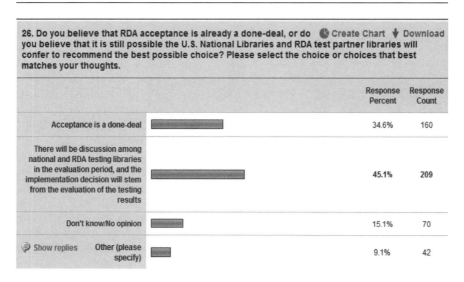

with budget issues. At conferences, RDA talk is heated and jargon
based, and nothing that is practical or daily use is discussed.
• While partisans of RDA (many of whom do not at all understand the
implications) want us to believe that the change is inevitable, I hope
at least that it may be stopped and re-evaluated realistically, which has
not yet happened.
• National libraries and test partners will have to confer to justify their
work to their constituencies. Unconceivable that LC would renege on
RDA. LC has already done quite a bit of RDA/MARC revision. Part
of the consideration will be the opportunity to discontinue the LCRI
apparatus. LC's reduction in staff, and history of scaling back on legacy
operations, and given philosophy that LC cannot be "the" national
library, LC will approve the move to RDA.
• I think it's a done deal but that the cataloging community will be the
Party of No and do everything to slow it down. It will happen, though.
• Can't be a done deal, if I'm not dealing with it yet.
• I think there will be a pretty even split, not at all based on the merits of
either standard. Some stubborn librarians will refuse to toss out RDA
simply because they put so much time and effort into it, and some

stubborn librarians will refuse to accept RDA on principle, even if they eventually get it right.

- I hope it isn't a done deal!
- Hope there is a discussion after some release of this project can be tested on a wide scale.
- I would hope the test libraries comments will be taken into consideration.
- As one of the testing institutions, we certainly plan to offer criticisms and comments.
- The testing libraries, who probably didn't have to pay for it, will give it an impartial test. But because the financial considerations aren't being included, a HUGE part of the impact on other libraries isn't being assessed. This is a mistake.
- I would like to think that discussion resulting from evaluation would rule, but I do not believe that. There is only one K–12 testing site, and those least affected are the ones making the decisions. I am very disappointed in the lack of democracy in this entire project.
- I think for LC it's pretty much a done deal, but if the rest of the country doesn't obediently follow they might have to reconsider.
- It's probably a done deal, since there seem to be no better options on the table. But there is still the hope that the hand-picked on-board libraries will realize that it is no better for emerging standards and no more adaptable than AACR2.
- I am on a testing committee so I believe that the testing is sincere.

So, those are the moods of the catalogers in the country regarding the national testing of RDA.

The survey turns to FRBR and RDA in the next few questions, Figures 3.22 and 3.23.

Forty-three percent of the respondents state that FRBR is currently not able to be implemented in current ILS. The next highest response rate is 35 percent, who don't know whether it can be or not. Only 8 percent think it can be implemented. A lot of catalogers (and others) need more information on FRBR before they can imagine its use in their online catalogs. Of the 14 percent in the "Other" category, representative, and unique, comments from this group are:

- Yes, it could work. We have Primo, and Ex Libris is trying to make it work there.
- Pieces of it are implemented in principle, but I don't think any implement it fully.
- No, because of holds issues—even now cannot place holds on all vol. 1 copies. Once you have series like graphic novels, it resorts to item level holds. Think what that would mean if you tried to place hold on best seller available in audiobook, hardback, LP, paperback, three different publishers, different editions, etc., and they were all on one record. With consortia, a user would be faced with dozens or over a hundred

Figure 3.22 Question 27 on survey
Is FRBR able to currently be implemented in our current ILS (integrated library systems)? (All title and copyrights in and to the Software are owned by SurveyMonkey. Material is copyright and trademark protected.)

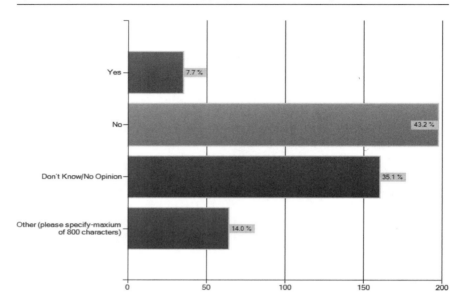

choices very frequently. There is no way now within one bibliographic record to place separate queues within groups of items. Either bibliographic hold or actual copy/item level holds are required.

- Yes, but the interface is often clunky and getting specific editions may not happen.
- To a very limited extent, since our current data and standards contain inadequate information to identify relationships, which is the most important improvement FRBR brings to cataloging.
- Yes, in part, as a III user I know that they tried one way that failed and have yet to come up with an acceptable way to implement FRBRization of search results.
- No, as evidenced by the lack of ability to display and work with hierarchical subject concepts, which have been in place since practically the beginning of time (except for WorldCat, of course, that can almost get it right!).
- There will probably need to be software changes from the ILS vendors.
- Our Systems Librarian has developed our OPAC and has incorporated some FRBR elements.
- Most examples of FRBR are a disaster in current ILS systems. We are a rare book library and manifestation, and especially item level descriptions

are vital to our mission. FRBR as it stands requires not only a complete retraining of professional staff, redesign of ILS systems, but also a reeducation of the public user. Is this practical?

- When I was in library school, eight years ago, FRBR was the "next big thing." We're still waiting.
- We have Polaris ILS. Not sure if it is ready for this.
- It is impossible to say with certainty that an ILS will be able to "do" FRBR; however, I have confidence that it will work and am excited about the increased access and easy of availability of varied resources.
- No. Even AACR2 uniform titles are a mishmash of Work, Expression, and Manifestation (e.g. "Aida. Vocal score"). Until we have relational databases that can pull work information from a single work record and house only expression/manifestation/item information in the bibliographic record, our current ILSs cannot fully accommodate all the principles behind FRBR and FRAD.
- Yes, with next-gen OPAC overlays.
- It's probably able to be implemented, but should we? For starters, it points out all the problems when you don't keep up with authority work (and we don't have the time or money or support from higher up to keep up that well).
- I'm sure FRBR could be implemented anywhere when higher quality standards are not sought. In my opinion, FRBR is extremely unstructured and will continue the "dumbing down" of cataloging records that has become so pervasive with vendor records and the acceptance of abbreviated records on OCLC. It doesn't seem to me that consistent quality is something associated with FRBR.
- Too many catalogers still don't fully understand it. Has it really been properly tested on different media and relationships?
- FRBR is not well defined and far too nebulous in its concepts. At the training that I went to there was no agreement in the room about the examples posited—supposedly chosen by the presenter because they displayed the various levels so clearly. Everyone was sort of bewildered that he seemed to think that it was so clear, and he was unable to counter the various perceptions in the room in any sort of logical way to explain why it was supposed to be the way that he perceived it.
- Since I use open source, the community will probably implement it as quickly as any commercial agency.
- It is possible, but it would require: (1) changes in OPAC display by ILS vendors, and (2) changes in MARC cataloging practice, e.g., rigorously apply 77X-78X linking fields to ALL materials to indicate relationships.

The ability to implement FRBR is linked to its usefulness as a user tool to bring together works, entities, manifestations, and items in meaningful relationships and displays. Figure 3.23 gathers respondents views on whether FRBR does this well, and if it is still a workable model of the bibliographic universe.

Figure 3.23 Question 28 on survey
Indicate your opinions on this statement: FRBR is a useful and up-to-date model of the bibliographic universe and relationships between its entities (authors, works, etc.), and is well suited to meet user information needs in the Web and digital environment. (All title and copyrights in and to the Software are owned by SurveyMonkey. Material is copyright and trademark protected.)

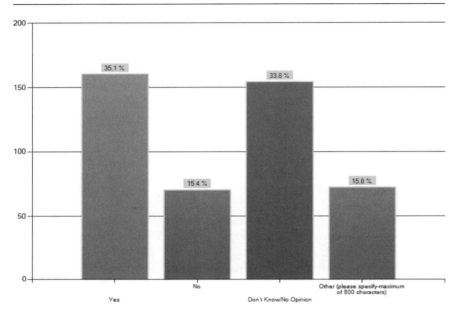

Catalogers (and others) are nearly split on the utility of FRBR: 35 percent find it is useful, but 34 percent don't know if it is or not. Thirty-four percent represents a lot of catalogers that cannot grasp the full meaning and measure of FRBR, and its ability to meet user information needs in the web and digital environment. In addition to that, 15 percent of the respondents believe FRBR doesn't have what it takes.

There are a sizeable number of comments for this question, and they reflect these starkly contrasting views:

- I would like to see how it functions in a public library OPAC. Will users EASILY be able to identify and locate the exact format of a work from all other formats?
- Looks good on paper, but will be a nightmare to implement. A lot like health care reform
- FRBR is a beginning model and needs further work and research.
- I agree somewhat, but the fact that understanding the difference between manifestation and expression can be so difficult complicates its real-life application.

- FRBR has the potential to be useful and even valuable. As presently constituted, I believe it cannot be effectively implemented by existing technology.
- The terminology is too esoteric to be easily understood.
- It is functional, but how well suited? Hard to tell—not enough examples.
- It's good conceptually, but it's useless unless ILS vendors implement it.
- It is a useful idea, but has been made too complex for easy implementation.
- It will need to change in the future.
- The library community as a whole needs to study user reaction to FRBRized data more.
- I don't believe FRBR works well for all types of items, especially serials. However, it does seem to be an attempt at grouping information in categories that users naturally conceptualize. I don't know to what extent our catalogs will ever be successful at doing this, but I do think we need to try, and FRBR is a step forward.
- I love FRBR. My issue is the *retrospective* work that needs to be done to implement FRBR/RDA. It is a classic theory versus pragmatism conflict!
- FRBR is a hard-to-understand model but it does bring things together better and will benefit users.
- To my knowledge, FRBR has never been tested to determine if it is useful and will meet user information needs. Until it is tested, we have no idea if it is better model.
- I am still skeptical about FRBR. Its rules are vague and subject to interpretation, meaning everybody will implement it differently, and the data will be less standard as a result
- I think it has great potential.
- The very few times I've encountered FRBRized practices, they have been extremely confusing and counterintuitive to a user's needs. I've never heard it adequately explained (even after taking a FRBR workshop).
- I still can't get my mind around it.
- FRBR is a horrendous mish-mash of computer-modeled data and has no place in a bibliographic universe. It is a hindrance to searching and is foolish in the extreme.
- Absolutely not. I am far more against the FRBR model as it was introduced to me than I am RDA itself.
- No, I believe FRBR is already outdated. I believe the technology that is being developed for faceted browsing will make the need for FRBRized displays of search results unnecessary.
- It's an abstract model which conforms to a view of the universe frozen in the early 1990s. It doesn't account for how people use information in the internet age. People do more than find-select-obtain-use. They want to annotate-share-repurpose. FRBR is not robust enough to model that.
- The model is useful. What we need is the GLUE to hold the pieces together, and that is dependent on ILS vendor implementation/capability.

Figure 3.24 Question 30 on survey
Have you heard from your ILS vendor about any plans and/or timeline to
redesign their systems for RDA and FRBR as well as any additional costs this
might require? (All title and copyrights in and to the Software are owned by
SurveyMonkey. Material is copyright and trademark protected.)

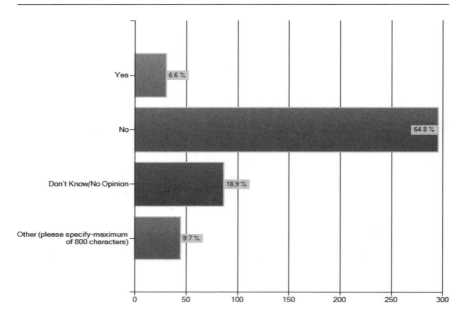

The next couple of figures discuss vendor implementation of RDA and FRBR
and funding for the cost of RDA and any ILS redesign necessary to implement
RDA and/or FRBR.

Libraries are beginning to ask ILS vendors about any plans and/or timelines
to redesign their systems for RDA and FRBR as well as any additional costs for
this. The percentages in Figure 3.24 aren't very encouraging in terms of numbers
of vendors who are working on this and communicating about it with their constituent libraries. Sixty-five percent had not heard from their vendors. Only
7 percent had heard anything (but we don't actually know how detailed the
information was). A large number of respondents, 19 percent, didn't know at
all, more than likely because they are not in the administrative or system level
loop with ILS vendors.

The comments with the highest number of respondents are listed in the first
five bullets below, and they reflect the majority of their opinions on whether
libraries have heard from their ILS vendor about any plans and/or timeline to
redesign their systems for RDA and FRBR, as well as any additional costs this
might require. The remaining comments were selected due to their mention of
specific ILS, as well as unique, contradictory, or general interest content.

- ILS vendors said they are watching and waiting, thinking of planning for FRBR, RDA: 27 percent.
- Just have heard discussion, nothing particularly enlightening or helpful, no cost information yet: 12 percent.
- In a consortia we don't usually hear: 8 percent.
- We use Evergreen open source ILS, which means our community will need to plan and pay for RDA, FRBR development, which has not yet happened—wait-and-see mode: 8 percent.
- We are doing the modifications ourselves; or, we will tweak our in-house system when the time comes: 8 percent.
- Could be two years after RDA is rolled out before ILS reworks with changes.
- I'm sure it will cost something.
- Update will be same as any other, and no additional costs are expected.
- Vendors are waiting for FRBR to be implemented before changing, and FRBR is being used in some ILS in Europe.
- Our vendor is ready for RDA, and has some FRBR, but in an expensive discovery layer, not yet complete.
- ILS vendor will implement new MARC 336–338 fields, used by RDA, but no news on making the catalog FRBRized.
- Haven't heard, but there will be a cost, as we are a LibLime Enterprise Koha library.
- III indicated they are working on RDA compatibility; I don't know about FRBR.
- Our ILS vendor already supports FRBR, but I don't know about RDA.
- I don't think our ILS will handle all of this and we don't have money for a new one.

Following the funding train of thought, Figure 3.25 queries respondents on how they might fund costs for vendor redesign of their ILS for RDA and FRBR.

Seventy-five percent of the catalogers (and others) responding have no funding (or don't know where it would come from) for a vendor redesign of their ILS (integrated library system) for FRBR RDA. The most prevalent source is the library's own maintenance and operating budget (27%). "Other source" data (3%) was not reported in any comments on the survey, so more information regarding these sources is unknown. Grant funding, always an uncertain source of funds, makes up 2 percent of the overall funding sources that respondents indicate they might use. Library fees, at 1 percent, are the smallest source that catalogers foresee being able to utilize for ILS redesign.

The remainder of the survey covers topics that are futuristic cataloging concepts, on the use of upstream data as a basis for building a cataloging record and cataloging on the Semantic Web (Figure 3.26), and a final question for respondents to offer any comments they felt necessary.

The Working Group on the Future of Bibliographic Control issued a report in 2007, "Report on the Future of Bibliographic Control," the premise of which is based on their introduction:

Figure 3.25 Question 31 on survey
Please select the method or methods your library would use to fund any necessary costs for vendor redesign of ILS for RDA and FRBR. (All title and copyrights in and to the Software are owned by SurveyMonkey. Material is
copyright and trademark protected.)

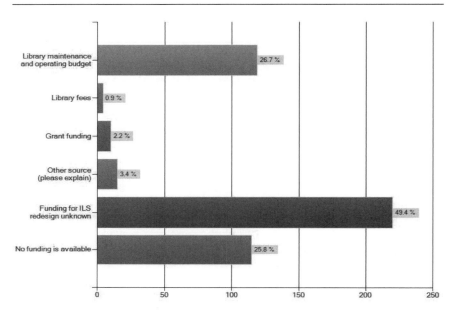

The future of bibliographic control will be collaborative, decentralized,
international in scope, and Web-based. Its realization will occur in
cooperation with the private sector, and with the active collaboration
of library users. Data will be gathered from multiple sources; change will
happen quickly; and bibliographic control will be dynamic, not static.
The underlying technology that makes this future possible and necessary—the World Wide Web—is now almost two decades old. Libraries
must continue the transition to this future without delay in order to
retain their relevance as information providers. [4]

The report has five recommendations, all of which unleashed a torrent of
controversy, anger, anguish, vision, and continuing upheaval and change in
the cataloging world. The two recommendations concerning the use of upstream
data as a basis for building a cataloging record, and cataloging on the Semantic
Web, are as follows:

1. Increase the efficiency of bibliographic production for all libraries
   through increased cooperation and increased sharing of bibliographic

records, and by maximizing the use of data produced throughout the entire "supply chain" for information resources.

2. Position our technology for the future by recognizing that the World Wide Web is both our technology platform and the appropriate platform for the delivery of our standards. Recognize that people are not the only users of the data we produce in the name of bibliographic control, but so too are machine applications that interact with those data in a variety of ways.[5]

Catalogers (and others) had many comments on the survey question regarding the use of ONIX and publisher or distributor metadata as a basis for starting a cataloging record in a shared bibliographic utility. ONIX stands for Online Information eXchange, and is an "XML-based family of international standards to support computer-to-computer communication between parties involved in creating, distributing, licensing or otherwise making available intellectual property in published form, whether physical or digital."[6] ONIX for Books[7] has many elements that are the same as, or similar to, those in cataloging records, such as title, contributor, persons and unnamed persons, edition, language, extent, illustrations, subjects, audience, and award notes. It also has much other information specific to the publisher, distributor, and retail community, as this is its prime audience and reason for being. Because of that, the bibliographic information so critical to cataloging description and access is not as high priority to those publishing and other entities that create the ONIX data, which means that the resulting data in ONIX records for these important elements is often lacking, incorrect, or not consistent in quality.

Responses were categorized into the predominant issues arising from the results. The first analysis of responses measures catalogers (and others) thoughts whether the use of ONIX and publisher or distributor metadata as a basis for starting a cataloging record in a shared bibliographic utility is a good idea, or not. The following list categorizes the responses in positive, negative, and neutral components.

- Yes, it's a good idea: 17 percent.
- Yes, it could be a good idea if publishers control quality and make the records more useful for cataloging information: 29 percent.
- No, it's not a good idea, or catalogers are skeptical and doubtful: 9 percent.
- No, it's not a good idea, as records are poor quality for cataloging needs: 21 percent.
- No, it's not a good idea, because publishers have different purposes and needs for the records than a cataloging record has: 7 percent.
- Don't know enough to respond to the question: 16 percent.
- If publishers want it to work, and think it is worthwhile to make their ONIX data useable as cataloging information, they will do so, and it will work: 1 percent.

It is interesting to note that the composite score for the positive responses is 36 percent, and the composite score for the negative responses is 37 percent. I think this may mean that catalogers know it could be a good thing if it were to work well and could create good basic records, but that in reality, publisher- or distributor-supplied records currently are not good quality, and catalogers are skeptical that this will change.

The second analysis of the ONIX and cataloging record question categorizes respondents' other comments into the most commonly repeated themes. The following list of these comments is in descending order according to percentage:

- It's better than nothing, can provide a starting point, and, if it works, the cataloger doesn't have to reinvent the wheel each time: 32 percent.
- Publishers are not the best source for metadata, as they do not have the same standards as catalogers, and errors will increase in the bibliographic utility; additionally, pre-publication data changes and data entered by publishers is not reliable: 18 percent.
- Level 3 publisher or distributor records in OCLC are poor quality, and if this is any indication of the worth of ONIX information for cataloging records, this is not a viable situation: 16 percent.
- Sharing bibliographic data across systems is a good thing to do, and increases efficiency: 7 percent.
- The idea is good in theory, but it doesn't hold true in practice, or it is not in common everyday use as of yet: 6 percent.
- Reducing duplication of work is a good thing to do, and relying on publisher upstream data could achieve this: 6 percent.
- Garbage in, garbage out: 4 percent.
- ONIX data should be used to create only minimal or core level records: 4 percent
- This is already happening: 4 percent.
- Using this data will require double work for catalogers to edit and make the records of sufficient quality, as the records are the lowest possible quality of "dumbed down" records; this, in turn, will cause many duplicate records in the shared bibliographic utility: composite of 3 percent.

These "other" comments reflect the varying thoughts on the usefulness of ONIX data for cataloging records, similar to the responses on whether it is a good idea to use them as a starting point records for a shared bibliographic utility, or not.

The second "futuristic" cataloging concept, and the last question in the survey with a specific topic, asked respondents to rate their knowledge of Cataloging on the Semantic Web. As previously noted, this was one of the recommendations of the Library of Congress Working Group on the Future of Bibliographic Control, "Report on the Future of Bibliographic Control: Draft for Public Comment."

Figure 3.26 Question 33 on survey
Please rate your knowledge of Cataloging on the Semantic Web. (All title and copyrights in and to the Software are owned by SurveyMonkey. Material is copyright and trademark protected.)

33. Please rate your knowledge of Cataloging on the Semantic Web, using the scale of 1-5, with 1 as the lowest: 1 "No knowledge" and 5 as the highest "Expert knowledge."						
	1 No knowledge	2	3	4	5 Expert knowledge	Response Count
Rate your knowledge of Cataloging on the Semantic Web.	56.3% (258)	24.0% (110)	14.2% (65)	5.0% (23)	0.4% (2)	458

Position our technology for the future by recognizing that the World Wide Web is both our technology platform and the appropriate platform for the delivery of our standards. Recognize the people are not the only users of the data we produce in the name of bibliographic control, but so too are machine applications that interact with those data in a variety of ways.[8]

Figure 3.26 presents the data gathered from respondents on their knowledge of this topic.

Cataloging on the Semantic Web is a very difficult concept to understand.

The Semantic Web, representing Berners-Lee's initial vision of the World Wide Web (Web), is an extension of the Web where "information is given well-defined meaning, better enabling computers and people to work in cooperation" ... The goal is to construct a network of structured, sharable semantics that is accessible, understandable, and manipulable by computer agents. Computer agents (Semantic Web agents), acting on behalf of people or other computer agents, will traver[se] the semantic network, find and manipulate information, perform desired tasks, and offer services.[9]

For bibliographic data and cataloging records, this means the disassembling of the record into discrete elements and marking it up to provide permanent and unique links, or identifiers, to this data across the Internet. When the data is searched, the computer agent uses the identifiers, assisted by network structures and standards, to find and gather the matching text associated with the link or identifier, and generate some kind display of all linked elements to represent and/or actually "be" the desired item. I hope that's right—that's what it seems.

It's no wonder that 56 percent of the cataloging (and other) respondents indicated that they have no knowledge of cataloging on the Semantic Web. Some do have some knowledge (24%), and it's good to see that almost 20 percent have average to expert knowledge. This is a theoretical concept, and has no immediate, live, holistic, and active cataloging application in our present time, so it remains to be seen if it will become a necessary concept to learn in the future.

CONCLUSION

I need to reiterate that the survey itself was not "professionally" created—it was just written by me, a practicing cataloger. I tried to not be too biased in its questions, but I received several responses about my negative attitude toward RDA and my AACR2 slant. I did try to include questions that would bring out everyone's comments, no matter what cataloging code they were leaning toward. I hope that I haven't squelched or diminished anyone's opportunity to participate and have his or her say because of the format of the survey. Catalogers are a passionate, dedicated, intense bunch who know what is right, but also know that the world has a lot of ambiguous gray, too. I hope the results of the survey will offer the light of ideas and sharing of knowledge to help us all in this most unsettled time, to find our way.

NOTES

1. RDA Scope and Structure, 5JSC/RDA/Scope/Rev/4/1 July 2009, to Joint Steering Committee for Development of RDA from Alan Danskin, Chair, JSC, 1, http://www.rda-jsc.org/docs/5rda-scoperev4.pdf (accessed May 27, 2010).

2. RDA—Resource Description and Access: Objectives and Principles, 5JSC/RDA/ Objectives and Principles/Rev/3 1 July 2009, to Joint Steering Committee for Development of RDA, From Alan Danskin, Chair, JSC, http://www.rda-jsc.org/docs/5rda-objectivesrev3.pdf (accessed May 27, 2010).

3. All material is copyright and trademark protected. All title and copyrights in and to the Software are owned by SurveyMonkey. All title and intellectual property rights in and to the content which may be accessed through use of the Software Application Services is the property of the respective content owner and also may be protected by applicable copyright or other intellectual property laws and treaties. The Company contact information is as follows: SurveyMonkey.com, Portland, Oregon, USA; author and owner, Ryan Finley.

4. Library of Congress Working Group on the Future of Bibliographic Control, "Report on the Future of Bibliographic Control: Draft for Public Comment," 1, November 30, 2007, http://www.loc.gov/bibliographic-future/news/lcwg-report-draft-11-30-07 -final.pdf (accessed May 28, 2010).

5. Ibid., 1–2.

6. ONIX FAQs, http://www.editeur.org/74/FAQs/#q1 (accessed May 28, 2010).

7. EDItEUR, Jointly with Book Industry Study Group, New York and Book Industry Communication, London, "ONIX Books Code Lists, Issue 11, for Release 3.0, March 2010," http://www.editeur.org/files/ONIX%203/ONIX_Code_Lists_Issue_11 _for_Release_3.0.pdf (accessed May 28, 2010).

8. Library of Congress Working Group on the Future of Bibliographic Control, "Report," 1, http://www.loc.gov/bibliographic-future/news/lcwg-report-draft-11-30-07 -final.pdf (accessed May 28, 2010).

9. Jane Greenberg, "Advancing the Semantic Web via Library Functions," *Cataloging & Classification Quarterly* 43, no. 3–4: 203–4.

II

VISIONS: NEW IDEAS FOR BIBLIOGRAPHIC CONTROL AND CATALOGS

4 A SYSTEMS LIBRARIAN'S CATALOGING DAYDREAM

Jon Gorman

INTRODUCTION

There are many daydreams. Some revolve around sipping a drink with an umbrella on a sandy beach. Others center on an amazing achievement such as an Olympic victory. This essay is an exploration of a favorite daydream of mine: What if we had the chance to build a new cataloging workflow, using technologies from scanning efforts and information retrieval to assist us? Variations on this question have lead to many engaging conversations with colleagues here at the University of Illinois and with members of the Code4Lib community. For those who do not know, Code4Lib is a loosely assembled group of people involved with library technologies who gather and communicate about their shared interests in a variety of ways. These ways include, but are not limited to: an IRC chat room, e-mail lists, conferences, and even a journal. There is no formal Code4Lib organization or Code4Lib membership in a traditional sense; instead, it is just a group of interested people who share knowledge. If you want to find out more about Code4Lib a good place to start is the Code4Lib Web page, http://www.code4lib.org.

However, back to the daydream. In order to make this daydream less abstract, let us use a setting where this new cataloging process would take place. So, come along on the tour of the facility of the fictional catalog agency known as YAMCA (Yet Another Midwestern Cataloging Agency). This agency serves a wide range of libraries and consortiums.

YAMCA PROCESSING PHASES

YAMCA processes the material it receives in three phases. Each type of material, such as print monograph, print serial, CD, or digital resource, will go through the three phases, although details of the workflow might differ somewhat for each. The phases include:

1. *Initial Processing*: This stage consists of at least limited digitization and minimal gathering of bibliographic information, with some material being fully digitized. The focus of the minimal bibliographic data is "seed information." "Seed information" is information that can be used to get more information in step 2, Data Harvesting.

2. *Data Harvesting:* The Data Harvesting stage uses the "seed information" from the previous Initial Processing stage, such as ISBN or title/author combinations, to look up information from both internal resources like authority records and external resources such as Syndetics (a company that provides title page images and more), Internet Movie Database, and Wikipedia. For fully digitized content, software will be run to try to extract information such as geographic places, names, and citations. All information gathered in this stage will be stored for possible later use in catalog indexes, record display, and to assist the cataloger in stage 3.

3. *Cataloging and Classification*: Specialized tools will allow the cataloger to interact with the information gathered in the above stages to determine the final bibliographic content associated with the material being processed.

Information gathered in each of these phases is recorded in a database and displayed via interfaces for the operator and the cataloger. An identifier is attached to physical items by a barcode or some other means when they are received by shipping. For digital information, an identifier will be added when the item is downloaded and packaged in something like BagIt[1]—a packaging format for exchange of digital content. There will not be an actual cataloging record created until stage 3, Cataloging and Classification.

We will begin the tour in the room centered around the first activity: Initial Processing. It should be stated that YAMCA provides metadata and records to its member libraries but does not actually own any of the material. New materials might be purchased out of member funds and distributed to member libraries, or material might be delivered first to YAMCA and then to the purchasing organization.

YAMCA INITIAL PROCESSING

The impression I received, when I was learning cataloging, was that it was a solitary activity. You are handed a book, and either you find a matching record on OCLC to modify, or you start original cataloging. In practice, I found that cataloging is not truly a solitary activity, but rather a process of multiple stages requiring many resources and people. Some of the earliest cataloging is done at the point the item is acquired, even if it is a short record useful for bookkeeping and routing the material to the appropriate places.

The goal of the initial processing stage at the YAMCA agency is to gather the information needed to start making connections for harvesting data from external resources in the second phase, and to assist in the analysis of materials in the cataloging phase. How the material is processed depends largely on its format. Sample workflows for the acquisition and processing of monographic materials, print serials, media, and digital materials are explained in the following sections. However, no matter what the format, data acquired for this stage will be accessible later in the Data Harvesting and Cataloging and Classification stages. Data is mostly bibliographic with captured elements that can include (among many others):

- Author and other names
- Title
- Edition
- Identifiers (ISSN, ISBN, LCCN, UPC and "disc ID" for CDs)
- Extent of item or technical specifications for digital resources, including size (height-width-depth) and weight, if applicable
- Series title

Workstation Setup

The Initial Processing phase largely revolves around different types of workstations set up for different material formats. Some of these workstations look much like the typical cataloger's workstation, with a desk, keyboard, monitor, and computer. Also available is a small flatbed scanner, which can be used for scanning album covers, included booklets and other related items. In addition, there are stations for material such as CDs, DVDs, and "born-digital" works. For all these workstations, there is a specialized interface for recording some basic bibliographic information that will be described later on.

Print material requires a different workstation configuration. Each print workspace is built around a cradle scanner with a nearby touch-screen monitor and a keyboard. Cradle scanners are not your typical consumer flatbed scanners on which you lay a book with the text facing down like a copy machine. Instead, a book is laid on its back and spine in an adjustable V-shaped cradle, with the text facing up toward one or more digital cameras overhead. A "scan" consists of having these cameras take pictures of the item in the cradle. This scanning setup is a common approach in digitization processes, since it is typically faster and less stressful on the book. There has been some exciting progress in making cradle scanners cheaper and more accessible. Some hobbyists have managed to create setups with high-quality scanners costing only a few hundred dollars. For these reasons, they are a logical choice for YAMCA's workflows.[2]

YAMCA Print Monographic Materials

Initial Scanning

When a monographic item is received by an operator of the scanning station, the YAMCA operator will scan in several random pages of the text, table of contents, title page, verso (back) of the title page, and the cover (front, spine, and back). The touch screen will display each image and allow the operator to assign a name or tag, such as title page, to the image. The computer will run optical character recognition programs optimized for each page type to attempt to discern information such as title and author. It will also attempt to automatically determine the language of the text from the randomly sampled pages first, as this will affect the optical character recognition.[3] The computer will prompt the operator with the guess of language and allow the operator to correct it if the operator knows what the language should be. The set of images created from these scans will also be kept for later internal use at YAMCA to be available for catalogers at member institutions, so that they can compare the item to their own material or perform a lightweight cataloging review without having the item in hand.

Gathering Limited Bibliographic Information

After the initial scanning is finished, the YAMCA operator is presented with a form for some minimal data entry, including, but not limited to, identifiers such as the ISBN or LCCN, the title, and names associated with the work with the addition of a drop-down menu to assign roles such as author, editor, contributor, and so on. This form would not be blank as it would have been pre-populated by the results of optical character recognition programs optimized for each type of page, such as title page and table of contents. Optical character recognition occurred as soon as the operator identified the page image types on the limited set of scanned pages, so the operator would only have to add what was missing, or correct errors made by the program.

The information gathered on the form is "seed information," information useful for identifying the work for use in later stage 2 lookups. These types of lookups will be described in more detail later, but an example would be using the ISBN of a work to query LibraryThing to see if the monograph has been identified as being part of a series. If it is in a series, the system can alert the cataloger in stage 3 that the work is part of a series, and can suggest the appropriate cataloging changes as well as any links to bibliographic records in the series, or to a serial record, if it is an analytic.

It is important to note that in the Initial Processing stage (stage 1), the operator is just transcribing bibliographic data based on the piece. There is no authority work done at this stage. The operator would likely not be a trained cataloger, but rather a paraprofessional trained to work with basic bibliographic identification and the operation of the hardware and software.

Physical Description

The scans also provide valuable physical information. There is no need to measure height, width, and depth, as border detection algorithms using the edges of the cover allow an estimate of size. Rulers built into the scanner allow the operator to sight check and verify accuracy. A scale next to the scanner will record the weight of the book. The idea of weighing books like cuts of meat might seem odd, yet this information is relatively easy and inexpensive to obtain. In an age of robotic arms and high-density storage areas, the cumulative weight of a box of books might be important. If nothing else, it can be used to reassure architects that their newest library building will not become an actual manifestation of the sinking library urban legend.[4]

Full-Scale Scanning

Full-scale scanning is done on certain selected items. The goal of these scans will be to run optical character recognition for data harvesting through textual analysis in the Data Harvesting phase. After that is done, the scans and the produced text would be destroyed due to copyright concerns. While I'd like to see every item be scanned in this way, even this daydream needs a hint of practical reality. The time and expense required to scan a book means scanning all print material is impractical. Instead, full-scale scanning would be based on a combination of factors determined by YAMCA staff, such as the number of libraries that are planning on purchasing the book, the number of existing citations it has, and the number of requests that have been received for the book.

The actual images of the pages are not meant to be displayed to the public, though, as their purpose is to serve as source images for optical character recognition.

Summary of YAMCA Monographic Materials Initial Processing Workflow

So, for a print monograph, the item will go through limited scanning: title page, verso of title page, cover (front, spine, and back), table of contents, and several random pages of the text. Optical character recognition programs optimized for extracting information from these pages would attempt to extract bibliographic and physical information about the book. This would then be presented on a form on the operator's touch screen monitor. The operator would correct mistakes in the form and add information that was not extracted through the scans. The information would center on key identifiers and search terms useful for doing lookups in other systems, such as ISBN, title, author, and publication date. Physical dimensions and other properties would also be captured via automated means and inserted on the form for the operator to double-check. No authority work or extensive cataloging work would be done at this point.

YAMCA Print Serials

Serials workflow in the YAMCA Initial Processing phase would proceed much like the monographic materials workflow above, with an initial scanning of the cover (front and back, spine if possible), title page (if one present), table of contents, and any page with information on the serial. The bibliographic information that is gathered is also similar to that for books, such as an ISSN if one is present, instead of the ISBN. Also transcribed will be any title and chronology information. Again, no cataloging is done at this stage. Typical cataloger work with serials, such as trying to determine if there has been a title change for an existing serial, if holdings need to be modified, or if the frequency of the serial has changed, will take place at stage 3, Cataloging. At this Initial Processing stage, the goal is to add information that will help with performing automated lookups within the existing catalog and in external resources.

YAMCA Media Materials (Covering Examples of CDs, DVDs only)

The Initial Processing stage for audio CDs is a bit more complicated. The container for the CD will be scanned, as will any included booklets. CD covers and booklet materials do not really have as well established an order of information as print housing does, and they are visually complicated, which greatly decreases the accuracy of optical character recognition. Instead, more of a focus at YAMCA is the use of embedded metadata contained in audio CDs. This embedded metadata can be included in the CD in the form of CD-Text, which could include the album name, song name, and artist (http://en.wikipedia.org/wiki/CD-Text), or the subcode channels, which might have the Media Catalog Number (MCN), and the International Standard Recording Code (ISRC) with year of publication, owner rights, country of origin, and so on (http://en.wikipedia.org/wiki/Compact_Disc_subcode).

The most important information to gather at the initial processing stage for audio CDs are the identifiers. Three types of identifiers can prove useful: the UPC barcode, the disc ID, and the International Standard Recording Codes (ISRCs). The software will attempt to recognize the UPC barcode on the package and extract it. In addition, the software will create a disc ID for the CD. Disc ID is an identifier generated by taking the number of tracks, the running time of each track, and some other information, which is then run through an algorithm to create a number (http://wiki.musicbrainz.org/Disc_ID_Calculation). A disc ID is not unique, but a single disc ID typically only has a few corresponding CDs, and the correct one can be determined by supplying the band or album name. Disc ID was created to allow automatic retrieval of album and track information from the Compact Disc Database, now known as Gracenote, which continues to be used by other services.

The final identifiers we are concerned about, International Standard Recoding Codes (ISRC), actually identify the individual recordings (on each track), not the overall CD. The overall set of ISRCs could identify a CD, but the main advantage of ISRC is that it is granular enough to connect the same recording being used on different albums. The ISRCs will be embedded in the subcode channels mentioned above and can be automatically extracted if present.

All of these identifiers will be extremely useful in stage 2, Data Harvesting. Indeed, automatic retrieval of CD information using these identifiers has been used by almost every software-based media player to display track names and album information. Just as the print stages take random pages for later textual analysis in stage 2, for audio CDs, random short samples will be extracted for use in stages 2 and 3. In addition, the software will record the number of tracks and the duration of each track.

Finally, the operator will be presented with a form where he or she will be able to fill in some basic bibliographic information, such as artists, bands, orchestras (and so on) that are involved in the work, track titles, and publication date.

As for DVDs, while containers and accompanying materials can also be scanned, initial records for DVDs are likely to require YAMCA operator manual transcription for a while yet due to artistic styling of the housing. UPC codes can be obtained from the barcode on the housing, similar to the process described above for audio CDs. However, there are serious obstacles to using software to automatically extract parts of a DVD. Any software that reads a DVD requires a software license to bypass the Digital Restriction Management system built into the DVD standards.

For media with closed captioning, tools to capture the closed captioning of videos and speech-to-text technologies could be used to create transcripts for the Data Harvesting phase, which follows the Initial Processing phase. While closed caption is actually a text stream, subtitles in DVDs are a stream of images. There are programs, such as SubRip, that can be used to extract these images and run optical character recognition to produce a text file for the textual analysis of stage 2 (http://www.divx-digest.com/software/subrip.html). More study needs to be done to determine both the frequency of the subtitles actually corresponding to dialog in the film, quality of the extraction, and possible legal issues due to license restrictions.

YAMCA Digital Materials

Textual digital materials, such as PDFs or even JPEG images of pages, remove the requirement of actually physically scanning the items. Depending on the format though, optical character recognition may still need to be applied. In either case, the workflow is the same as for the print material, minus the physical steps of scanning. The operator will have the interface showing the images that make up the file. He or she will select title, title verso, and table of contents. There's no need to select random pages as the software can do that. If optical character recognition needs to be performed, it will be. After that, the software will attempt to extract the metadata from text in order to populate the limited bibliographic detail on the form. Identifiers for digital textual objects would also include the DOI, or Digital Object Identifier, used to uniquely identify a digital object.

A goal of YAMCA would be to work with the publishers to obtain the digital masters for books and journals. This would save the costly and labor-intensive scanning steps of the regular workflow and allow the material to be immediately introduced into the initial processing workflow, without human or scanning intervention.

Web sites, PDFs, and other digital content may never be published in print or physical media forms. However, some libraries do add these materials to their catalog, which requires that they go through the initial processing phase. YAMCA could create a browser plug-in that would work similar to Zotero, which would look for embedded metadata in the page using microformats and also would download the appropriate files into the YAMCA system.

An interesting development in digital resources is the rise of material that acts like digital continuing resources, such as blogs and podcasts, and which uses syndication formats that would allow automatic updates to be incorporated into the YAMCA catalog. Once a record for a blog, podcast, or videocast was created using the plug-in, the plug-in could also note the presence of any RSS or ATOM Web feeds that enable programs to check for Web page updates. This would be an automated method to keep content up to date in the catalog for these digital resources.

YAMCA DATA HARVESTING

This is the second phase of processing, coming directly after Initial Processing. The Data Harvesting phase is entirely automated. Physical items are transferred to a temporary storage area until the harvesting window is finished, which would probably be a few hours at most. One could imagine the most sensible workflow would be to do all the initial processing during regular work hours, and then have the computers working on the data harvesting during the night hours when no initial processing is done. The goal of the Data Harvesting phase is to gather as much information automatically in order to be able to present it to the cataloger at the final phase, Cataloging and Classification. Data harvesting performs two actions: it extracts additional information from the digitized content, whether full or partial; and it uses the "seed information" gathered in Stage 1, Initial Processing, to query external resources for additional information.

Harvesting Information from Scans and Textual Analysis

After the Initial Processing stage has received the material and created the "seed information," the resource moves to the Data Harvesting stage. This next stage in the YAMCA processing workflow adds more information regarding the work into the database for its eventual destination and use in Cataloging and Classification. Data harvesting relies on automated data gathering, from two sources. The first is internal, from further textual analysis of the text produced by optical character recognition. The second is external to the material, using programmed search and retrieval of related data from YAMCA's catalog and on-line bibliographic services or databases. By identifying, extracting, and inserting reliable content and descriptive information found in external services into the record prior to cataloging, the cataloger is given additional valuable information, such as:

- Reviews
- Series
- Lists of related topics
- Bibliographies
- Social networking tags
- Table of contents
- Cover images
- Geographic locations related to works
- Possible matching authority records and other information about a resource that can be presented and made ready for the cataloger in the third stage of the process, Cataloging and Classification

By the time a book, serial, media, or digital resource reaches most libraries there is a wealth of information that exists in external resources. This is true for YAMCA materials, as well. Some information is available through services that provide reference information, such as Wikipedia, Dictionary of American Biography, Musicbrainz, Discogs, LibraryThing, Google Books, and the Internet Movie Database. Other information could be gleaned from Web sites that commonly discuss and describe or evaluate books, such as publishers' Web sites, newspapers, and the Web pages of academics. Only some of these services provide ways for software to automatically query or connect to them, and not all are free. Licenses similar to most electronic resources would be required to utilize these services. Sadly, many good resources as of yet have no easy way to integrate with automatic searches. A concentrated effort by libraries and organizations, including YAMCA, might be able to persuade these publishers and entities to provide interfaces that programs could use, as well as the licenses to do so legally. It sometimes seems that libraries are more than willing to spend money to obtain licenses for online resources, but will not extend the same funding for their own internal use. Reusing the technology behind federated search systems might also allow us to use the already-gathered seed information to perform some automatic searches of collections like EBSCO, JSTOR, and other online resources, in order to find related works and have the results summarized for the cataloger in phase 3, Cataloging and Classification. So, let's start first with the internal data harvesting from the material itself.

Internal Harvesting—Limited Scanning of Monographic Material

The limited scanning of a monographic work can still provide some useful information that can be extracted and stored about an item. Most of the information derived at this part of the phase will be the result of textual analysis, but there is still a part of the physical description that can be created at this point. Image processing of the cover scans could create a breakdown by percentage of the colors used in the composition of the image. Adding this information to a search index gives librarians at member institutions the ability to finally answer questions, such as, "I want to find a book I read as a kid. It had a blue cover with some sort of yellow bird on it." Now, YAMCA's specialized cover search interface would allow searching for covers with specified colors—in this case, lots of blue with some yellow colors. Automatic object detection is gaining more ground and perhaps someday could also be added to this part of the process to automatically identify the objects in an image, such as the bird on the cover. In the meantime, there's promise of using a database of manual cover descriptions that will be explored in the section on data harvesting from external resources.

Textual Analysis—Reading Level and Statistically Significant Words

From the randomly sampled pages that the YAMCA operator scanned, the software can derive reading level. There are actually several existing libraries for various programming languages that can perform this type of analysis, given a block a text, and return the reading level using various metrics such as Fog, Flesch, and Flesch-Kincaid.[5] Even with the limited samples, some attempts at pulling out statistically significant words can be useful for later automatic suggestions for subject analysis.

Internal Harvesting—Full Text Analysis

Having an entire digital copy of the work along with text derived from optical character recognition gives the ability to extract even further information to be used by the cataloger in stage 3 for subject analysis, adding to indexes for the catalog search, and for inclusion in the catalog display. This process would assemble the previously mentioned information gathered in cases of limited scans, cover colors, and reading level, and would still be connected with the extracted full text. Indeed, the reading level is likely to be more accurate with the additional data to work with.

Information retrieval has a large literature base for analyzing a text and determining useful properties that distinguish it from other texts. We can use the same algorithms and techniques to extract frequently used words and phrases in the work, statistically unusual words and phrases when compared to the other works in the collection, and perhaps even details such as the longest word in the book. This type of information can be useful for adding to the indexes for searching, but it can also be useful in public displays, to give people a better idea of the material.

Citation recognition software run on the full text would attempt to extract citations to other works. This could later be displayed to the cataloger in stage 3 with the section of the original citation in the original digital image, and the citation text for sight double-checking. This would allow the addition of generated notes in the display record, such as, "This book cites . . .," and would also search for the work cited in the cataloging database to add a corresponding entry in the record of the cited book, "This book is cited by . . .," thus linking intellectual works together in YAMCA's online catalog for enhanced patron access. At this point, it would also store, for later cataloger review, books that exist in the catalog that might cite the currently examined work.

Proper nouns would be extracted from the full text and inserted into the "seed information." The "seed information" will be used in the later part of this stage for harvesting from external resources. At least for English materials, proper nouns are pretty easy to extract because English capitalization rules make them easy to identify.

Dates would also be straightforward to extract as dates follow conventions such as May 11, 2009; 04/02/2010; 2009; and so on. Dates could be useful to help the cataloger in finding chronological subject headings. They could also be used in the catalog display in the form of a timeline, which could be a valuable guide for readers to understand the coverage of the book. The timeline can show both the range of years mentioned in a text, shown on the x axis; and the frequency that the year is mentioned, shown on the y axis.

External Resources—Data Harvesting

The seed information gathered in the previous processing phases in YAMCA's workflow would be used to find possible matching authority records, subject headings, classification, and information from external databases. The information gained from this harvesting can be broken into a few rough categories: additional information that might be useful for the cataloger and for the catalog display, links to other records both within and outside of YAMCA's catalog, and keywords for harvesting.

Covers and External Resources

Earlier in this stage, the YAMCA software extracted the percentages of colors that made up a cover. This information will be destined for a specialized search interface for covers. While object recognition is still tricky, there is an external resource that promises to be almost as good. This is the exciting work being done by LibraryThing called "CoverGuess." It is a game where people can see covers and attempt to describe those using tags. People get points for how many tags they use in describing a cover, which match tags that other people have used for that same cover. These tags could be acquired in the Data Harvesting phase and added to the cover search to allow both searching by color and also by terms.

Proper Nouns and External Resources

The proper nouns identified in the full-scale scanning done in the earlier part of the Data Harvesting phase can now be coupled with use of external data sources and software to separate out the proper nouns into lists of geographical locations and names. For example, YAMCA's catalog software could compare proper nouns identified in the resource against gazetteers and atlases for geographic information; and a variety of sources for names could be used to retrieve authoritative name data for the cataloging record being created: YAMCA's own authority records, the character information stored in LibraryThing, Wikipedia biographical entries, American National Biography, and many others.

These lists will be presented to the cataloger in stage 3, Cataloging and Classification. The cataloger will then be able to review some of the nouns and resolve possible ambiguities, such as if "Dallas" means a person, a place in Texas, a TV show, or perhaps a small town not in Texas.

Data Harvesting of Reviews, Table of Contents, Covers, and Social Networking Tags

Amazon seems to have licensed several of what they call "editorial" reviews from various journals and magazines, including *Library Journal*. There is a certain irony that a *Library Journal* review is seldom found inside the actual record of a library catalog, but they appear on just about every Amazon record. I am noticing more and more services that link resources to reviews from other sources. This is very good news for enhanced cataloging records in YAMCA's online catalog. For example, LibraryThing for Libraries incorporates the tagging and reviews created by bibliophiles around the world. Syndetics offers links to table of contents, reviews, covers, and more. These services have potential, but they are introduced at the wrong point of the process, after cataloging and indexing have already occurred. They typically use JavaScript and Web technologies to add information to the catalog display based on an identifier in the page such as LCCN or ISBN. Reviews linked or shown in this manner are not part of the actual bibliographic record or the indexes created by OPAC software, but are only links to external information sources with the required matching content.

Why does the fact that reviews and tags are not present in the actual record matter? One extremely valuable aspect of reviews is they often describe a work using words and terms not found in a bibliographic record and sometimes not even in the work itself. If these descriptions were included in the record, they could be used in producing index terms for keyword searching. Users of YAMCA's online catalog would find this very helpful. Imagine a user trying to find *Our Gods Wear Spandex: The Secret History of Comic Book Heroes* by Chris Knowles. Let us imagine that the YAMCA cataloger used the following subject headings:

- Comic books, strips, etc.—History and criticism.

- Heroes in literature.
- Myth in literature.

A user of the catalog incorrectly remembers the title as "Our Heroes Wear Capes." After failing at that title search, he tries some variations of hero, superheroes, and other items worn by superheroes. Indeed, the word "superhero" would mislead anyone looking for this book in some catalogs, as the word doesn't appear in the title, subtitle, or in any subject headings. However, it is frequently used in reviews of the book and would make it possible to retrieve this book in a member library by searches such as "history of superheroes."

For information where YAMCA does not have a license for its use, say, reviews found via a Web search, they can still harvest the keywords for inclusion in the database. The database can keep track of what citations provided which keywords. The YAMCA catalog display would show the matching keywords followed by a citation and link to the original Web page. This would be automatically created by the data harvesting software.

Data Harvesting of Series, Bibliographies, Lists

Series, bibliographies, and lists are available in various sources and provide more information in the YAMCA catalog regarding the resource. Imagine that YAMCA's online catalog had the ability to import and sort different types of lists from sources, such as Amazon lists or LibraryThing collections. The YAMCA catalog could even have a feature that would allow users of the catalog to create the lists themselves, using imported data in ways of their own choosing.

Lists are useful for YAMCA because if works show up on a list, they are likely to be related in some way to the other material on that list. Frequently, the title of the list might itself provide some clues for genre headings for the cataloger in stage 3. Think of "Top 10 Science Fiction books," or, "My favorite books featuring Greece."

Series lists, in particular, can be particularly useful in identifying and finding titles in fictional series. While current cataloging can often describe the publication number sequence of a series, it does not typically convey the chronology used in the overall story arch by the creators of the entire fictional work. Authors and publishers will sometimes create a book that takes place earlier in the storyline than the previously published books, also known as a prequel. For example, the *Star Wars* film series first had three movies detailing the rebels versus the Empire. However, the last three movies in the series produced actually create the story of the *initial* rise of the Empire and the emergence of the character of Darth Vader, several decades earlier in the chronology of the "Star Wars Universe" than the first three movies. Fans have created lists on sites such as Amazon and other social networking sites that outline the order the movies were created, and also outline the order of the overall story chronology. Not only that, some fans have attempted to create different lists of the overall chronology of the "Star Wars Universe" by having lists of both *when* the various *Star Wars* material was originally published and *where* the individual stories take place in the overall fictional chronology, an example of which is on Wikipedia (http://en.wikipedia.org/wiki/Chronology_of_Star_Wars). The harvesting of these lists would enable the cataloger in stage 3 to make additional bibliographic records if needed, or to add the lists to YAMCA's own listing capability, and create a link in the catalog record.

Bibliographies are also an interesting possible source for automatic harvesting. Increasingly, savvy academics and others are starting to include Linked Data via microformats in Web pages.[6] By using a Web crawler, YAMCA regularly scans academic Web sites and other Web sites that might contain bibliographies. If a bibliography is found, at first an attempt is made to find a microformat containing linked data. What this means is, while the page looks like a normal Web page, it is really set up in such a way that a software program can easily extract a citation. If this is not possible, the same software that attempts to find citations in the OCR text can be used, although the accuracy will not be as high. Bibliographies are good sources for finding works that are likely to be related, and these harvested citations will be used in stage 3 by the cataloger.

Retrieving Music Information

As mentioned in the media section of the Initial Processing phase, there are a lot of resources out there for automatic lookup of information related to audio CDs, and the technology has been carried into many common digital formats such as MP3s. Some resources for doing lookups by id for information include sources like last.fm (http://www.last.fm), Discogs (http://www.discogs.com), MusicBrainz (http://musicbrainz.org), freedb (http://www.freedb.org), and Gracenote (http://www.gracenote.com). These services can offer a wealth of information and frequently offer a machine-accessible way to access their information. By using the identifiers gathered in stage 1, the YAMCA data harvest programs will attempt to pull in some basic metadata such as track titles, band name, and composer, but will also attempt to get information such as genre classifications, similar music and bands, remixes, and other albums containing the same song. This information should help the cataloger in creating the table of contents for the album as well as assigning genres. The program will also be able to suggest links to other records in the YAMCA database from the harvested information.

Similar Records in YAMCA's Catalog—Data Harvesting

The full text, and the matched words in common that were previously extracted, can also be compared to records for existing documents in the YAMCA collection in an attempt to come up with some possible related works, subject headings, and classification numbers based on classification used for these works with similar words. Words like "elves" and "dwarves" might indicate a fantasy element, while frequent mentions of "Jedi" and "Sliths" almost certainly indicate Star Wars. Another example would be that words like "Vietnam," "Johnson," and "protests" might indicate history of the United States during the Vietnam War. So, in addition to finding classification numbers, YAMCA's software would identify common subject terms in records for these works and match them with closely related indexes and shared common words, thus facilitating the suggestion of subject headings to be used in stage 3, Cataloging and Classification.

YAMCA CATALOGING AND CLASSIFICATION

All this accumulated stage 1 and 2 information is presented to a YAMCA cataloger who will make the final determination on what information is to be used and included in the cataloging record for the resource. The software that allows the YAMCA cataloger to review and use the stage 1–transcribed and scanned information and the harvested information collected during processing stage 2, in order to ultimately create the final cataloging and classification information and descriptive record, is something I will refer to as the Integrated Cataloging Environment (ICE).

Since a traditional MARC record would not be able to hold all the information that has been gathered in stage 1 and 2, the ICE would provide an interface to the YAMCA database containing this information. Certain information, such as lists for example, would be put into a designated locally used field when the cataloger exported the record as a MARC record. Other information would be inserted into local 9XX fields for member libraries who wanted to import the information and index it in their own catalog system. YAMCA's online catalog also allows member libraries to add their holdings.

YAMCA's ICE, or, Integrated Cataloging Environment

The idea of an Integrated Cataloging Environment (ICE) for YAMCA is inspired by what programmers call an Integrated Development Environment (IDE). Like modern cataloging, modern software development frequently involves many small, interrelated parts. In order to make software development easier, the IDEs offer a suite of tools, with which a programmer can view multiple parts of the project in different ways. The programmer might see a program as an outline, where large parts of the software code are collapsed, in order to view the overall flow. Or, the programmer could cause colors to appear in the margin to indicate sections of code lines that contain mistakes. Using another method, the programmer could cause a red dot to appear next to a line missing a required semicolon at the end of the line, or a yellow dot to act as a warning that a variable is being used that is not yet defined. Many such quality control possibilities can be programmed in the IDE, which could be translated to the YAMCA Integrated Cataloging Environment.

ICE Quality Control

ICE system software for YAMCA's integrated library system could be developed in a similar fashion to IDE. There would be data and structural quality control components and tools that allow the cataloger to insert, review, and perform quality control for stage 1 and stage 2 data, while finalizing the cataloging record. These would include automatic keyword selection, classification, and subject analysis and selection of subject headings, all performed using information supplied from stage 1 and stage 2 data.

For example, during creation of the final cataloging record, an ICE might warn YAMCA catalogers if they are entering a language code in the MARC 041 language code field that does not correlate with the selected language in MARC 008/35-27, which is the fixed field language code in the MARC record. Another quality control example would be an ICE-generated warning to alert the unaware YAMCA cataloger that an authority string had been entered in the record that did not match anything in the authority files. Yet another case might be a warning displayed if the cataloger erroneously used a second indicator of 4 in the 245 title field, which causes the computer to skip over four characters in the indexing of the title (to ignore initial articles in filing and indexing), but subfield $a in that same 245 field did not contain a leading article in the language of the material. In addition, a very beneficial quality-control IDE feature, potentially of use in cataloging at YAMCA, would be the autocomplete feature for subject heading entry. One could imagine that as the YAMCA cataloger adds a new subject heading in the record, autocomplete would be used to show what subject headings could complete the line, to assist in selection and to head off typographical errors.

Stage 1 and 2 Data Integration Using ICE at YAMCA

Since most catalogers would be more comfortable editing in the MARC view, let's describe how a cataloger using an ICE program might see and use ICE in a MARC edit view. At this point, the cataloger has started her ICE program and is beginning to review the results of the first two stages. A MARC record is shown with information pre-populated from these phases. For example, the size information in the 300 $c subfield would be derived from taking the height, weight, and depth measurements after the appropriate, matching AACR2 rules for this physical description have been applied. A corresponding local 930 field (for example) would contain the original complete measurements. The 245 title field is somewhat more straightforward to apply, and ICE would have pre-populated this field quite easily from data obtained in stage 1.

A box to the right of the record would have an outline showing general *groups* of all extracted information. By clicking on an individual group, it would expand to an outline, allowing the cataloger to move up and down within the entries. For example, there might be a group called "people." Clicking on that would show a list consisting of: Roles added at Initial Processing, Possible matching Authority Records, or, Names from the Data Harvesting stage. Clicking on any individual category would show the names, and dragging an individual name to the appropriate part of the MARC record would insert it.

Basically, the ICE interface at YAMCA would include as many tools as possible that allow the cataloger to integrate all the bibliographic information gathered in stages 1 and 2, including size, titles, names, subjects, reviews, lists, series titles, and the many additional bits of bibliographic and other information listed in these prior stages. Authority information could be integrated, too. One idea to automate the YAMCA authority-control process, for example, would be to display an ICE-generated list with a summary of possible authority records that were similar to or matched the stage 1 and 2 data. This would occur as the cataloger moved the mouse over the name and subject section of the record that had already been populated with the preliminary stage 1 and 2–supplied possible authority and subject headings. Each entry in the list would offer information to help guide the cataloger to books with similar names and subjects that were already linked to the authorities and cross-references, to assist the cataloger with classification, additional subject analysis, access points, and description.

In a similar vein, harvested reviews and Web sites acquired in stage 2, that might be connected to the content of the resource, could be shown to the YAMCA cataloger in a summary view. Then the cataloger could pick several promising reviews, highlight a section, and right-click to "import into record index" in order to add them as "keywords," that partially describe the resource. Another option might allow adding a link into the record itself to connect the resource directly to the reviews.

ICE and Classification, Subject Analysis at YAMCA

The interface for both subject analysis and classification in the ICE would use a display that is called the Taxonomy Browser. This would allow the display of a controlled vocabulary, thesaurus, and similar systems in a graphical manner. When the cataloger is ready to classify a book, he or she selects this tab and a search box is shown, as well as some sort of data structure for browsing the subject or classification system. If the system contains a hierarchy, like Dewey, it might display a tree interface. A tree interface is often seen in Web forms, where you have "parent" nodes that you can expand or collapse, and each parent node can have children nodes below it. Each node of the tree interface is a subject heading, with the broadest headings at the top and the narrower ones branching off from these. Each node, or subject heading, also has a description. Filling in search terms in the search box above the tree interface "collapses" the hierarchy so that only nodes that match are displayed.

Database Management of YAMCA's Online Catalog

ICE and the YAMCA's catalog utilize one other powerful concept that has emerged from the software world. Software, as mentioned before, has certain parallels to bibliographic information. There are many interrelated documents that are changed by a large number of people, and it is frequently possible two people might try to change the same file at the same time. Different approaches have been used to help reduce confusion and error, which occur when two people open the same file and the last person to save "overwrites" the other's work. Some approaches tried to control who could edit the "master files" or implemented a locking scheme so that only one person could edit a file at a time. However, this continues to prove ineffective.

The solution that has been applied to this problem for YAMCA's ICE is what is called a version control system. There are several different systems out there, some of the popular ones these days being Subversion, Mercurial, and Git. Wikis actually use version systems to keep track of changes to their Web pages. This is what allows people to step back through all the changes made to a wiki page and see who modified what.

The basic concept is as follows. There is a "master copy" of the file on the version control server. This server has the original version of each file involved in the project and is responsible for recording the changes made over time. Each developer will have his or her own copies of all these files as well, typically called a "working copy," and a version control client program that communicates with the server. Periodically, a developer will decide that the changes to one or more files in the "working copy" need to be saved in the master copy, and will issue a "commit" command. This creates a set of files called a "change set" that describe, in a machine-readable way, the difference between the last version of the files and the ones in the working copy. Developers also will periodically issue an "update" command, which downloads from the master copy all the change sets that have been committed since their last update, and attempts to apply them to the developer's "working copy." However, the version control may not always be able to apply these changes as it checks to make sure that the developer hasn't modified the same section of the file that would be updated. If this situation occurs, the version control program would then warn the developer, who can manually reconcile the change. Also, the tools that generate the change set can also be used to do things like reverse changes by doing the same comparisons but reversing the order in which the files are evaluated.

Version control would allow changes to be accomplished, or reverted back to, even though update changes were created by another updating mechanism such as global replace, a current database management function in online catalogs. Here is an example that might occur in any library organization. A cataloger is working on an authority record for an actor, whose heading currently is Nobody, M., $d 1912–. The cataloger needs to add a death date, to change the heading to Nobody, M., $d 1912–2009. The cataloger decides to do this via global search and replace, in order to make sure all the bibliographic records with this prior heading will be changed to have the new heading with the death date added. However, the cataloger didn't actually copy the correct authority string to use as the replacement text, and instead used Nonamous, Anne, $d 1969–, which causes the entire set of records with the Nobody, M., $d 1912– heading to be changed to Nonamous, Anne, $d 1969–. The mistake wasn't noticed until weeks later, and it is no longer possible to do a global search and replace, because the original Nonamous, Anne, $d 1969– entries are correct. Without version control functionality, this situation would lead to a complicated process whereby records that were changed by the global search and replace would need to be identified and probably manually corrected. A version control system would make it far easier to revert just that one change across all the files without impacting changes made after that mistake, and without a large amount of manual fixing.

Most modern IDEs provide several different graphical tools that allow interaction with the version control system. Most provide a history function, allowing browsing logs to see what, who, and when a group of files were modified. There are also individual file-level tools, such as a diff tool or file comparison utility program, which allows you to see two versions of a file side by side, and changes are color-coded. This allows for rather rapid comparisons.

Without getting too detailed, the latest trend of version control systems is more complicated than the above model with one "master copy" and several working copies. What is emerging now is a way to have a hierarchy of version servers, so that there can be layers of "master copies." In practice, in the software world the one "master copy" ran into issues of control and access. The question of who was allowed to commit changes up to the "master copy" became a large issue. Many open-source projects, because of their decentralized organization and distributed nature, would have a core group of people who were allowed to make commits, and the change set would be given to them if someone wanted it added to the project. They would review this change set, called a patch, and if approved, they would issue the commit command. There are a couple of drawbacks to this. One obviously was that folks who became used to being able to make many small commits would have to establish their own version server and proceed with the difficult task of trying to keep their developments in synch with the "master copy," while making commits to their own version server. Other folks who purposefully wanted to keep a slightly modified version of the software would have to take a similar approach, creating their own version server and trying to keep synch with yet another master. Distributed version control tools and systems have started to emerge where one can have a "local" master that keeps track of revisions done locally, while also pulling in from a higher-up "master copy." These systems make it far easier both to track a local set of changes (such as your own 9XX fields) and to work with an ultimate master system. In the case of YAMCA, this would allow member institutions to keep track of local changes, but also to submit changes up to the master record at YAMCA for approval by a local cataloger, or perhaps to be accepted automatically if they've been given permissions to be a committer at that level. The learning curve for distributed systems is higher, but the payoffs of being able to track local changes, and submit changes that might be useful for all consortium members back up to YAMCA's master copy, is more than worth it. In fact, that is the path that YAMCA has chosen.

Those who want to pursue this idea further might want to read Galen M. Charlton's article "Distributed Version Control and Library Metadata."[7]

ICE Beyond the Individual Record Workflow at YAMCA

The ICE should also be able to work on a more general scale than just an individual record. An imaginary scenario involving the Food Network demonstrates this possibility. Imagine that you are a special library for the Food Network. After many complaints from Chef Morimoto and Alton Brown, you decide LCSH is just not detailed enough to use as a basis for determining classification. Luckily, you just read, in the latest *Cataloging & Classification Quarterly* issue, that a researcher has created a very detailed and structured taxonomy for food terms. You download a file from the researcher's Web site that describes this taxonomy in a machine-readable way. You then load this taxonomy description file into your ICE. Fortunately for you, the researcher has also made a file available that has a list of ISBNs and other identifiers, and how the books corresponding to those identifiers were classified in the new food taxonomy. So, you also download this file into your ICE. To complete the process, and make the new food taxonomy available for users, you do a bulk load that adds each of these subject headings to any records in your system that have an identifier that matches records in the researcher's file. Now you have plenty of examples of the taxonomy and can begin adding your own (if you dare) using the Taxonomy Browser feature.

ICE and the Future: Trends in Current Cataloging Systems

There are some promising trends in current cataloging software that make me hopeful that an ICE-like system, such as that envisioned and demonstrated here for YAMCA, could be created. Terry Reese's MarcEdit, biblios and the associated biblios.net, and the effort of Koha and Evergreen to develop new open-source interfaces to cataloging are all impressive pieces of software, which can be utilized to envision and perhaps develop a system similar to the ICE presented in this essay.

CONCLUSION

So, daydreams are nice, but are these daydreams practical? I do not believe the technology I have described is beyond the abilities of current research efforts and organizations like the Internet Archives, Open Content Alliance, OCLC, or even commercial companies like Google and Amazon. Many of the cataloging tools I have described in the imaginary YAMCA workflow do not yet exist, but the concepts and generic tools do already exist in other fields and are serving the needs of programmers and other data professionals.

As for the reality of YAMCA, the actual creation of a unique organization like the large Midwestern cataloging agency I describe does seem unlikely due to high initial costs. There is also the limitation that the organization would have to work very fast and keep almost no backlog of uncataloged materials. If this wasn't achieved, there would be many works that individual libraries would receive long before the central organization had created cataloging records for them. Some of this might be dealt with by providing many of the ICE tools that allow local catalogers to merge records. There are other time-saving steps that could be utilized from the ICE workflow so that more cataloging data would be acquired at the beginning of the acquisitions process, and the cataloging done at the end would be a matter of verifying and organizing the data already existing, rather than creating a record from scratch.

What is more likely than the creation of a complete ICE integrated library system as detailed in this essay is that bits and pieces of this daydream will become true. I could see more companies coming into existence that gather some of the metadata mentioned through various means, such as direct user input, scanning, and data harvesting. These organizations would resell their services down the line or perhaps even to upstream creators of bibliographic data, such as publishers themselves. As I wrote this essay, OCLC announced an initiative to do something similar for publishers, called the Enhanced Metadata Service for Publishers (http://publishers.oclc.org/en/metadata/default.htm [accessed August 30, 2010]). Although there doesn't seem to be a lot of details, it seems that OCLC would let the publishers pull information about subject headings and the like from OCLC, for their own internal databases.

As for the ICE tools, I think they are possible. I hope that the renewed competition in the library software community will be a useful catalyst for change and will spur ILS vendors to improve their cataloging interfaces. These vendors would do well to pay attention to the emerging research within the computer science community and libraries regarding linking data and resources throughout the Web. Just search for terms such as "linked data" or the "semantic web," and you will find an amazing amount of research and initial real-life applications.

More ways will emerge to link together large quantities of existing data, and I suspect this will be done by organizations like the Library of Congress, OCLC, and other large organizations that can handle these technologies. My hope is that we can leverage the expertise of catalogers to integrate this information into the record and provide a better searching experience for our patrons.

NOTES

1. University of California, California Digital Library, "BagIt," https://wiki.ucop.edu/display/Curation/BagIt;jsessionid=0AEF0355141743A0A9BACC05891DBBFC (accessed May 5, 2010). BagIt is a hierarchical file packaging format for the exchange of generalized digital content. A "bag" has just enough structure to safely enclose descriptive "tags" and a "payload," but does not require any knowledge of the payload's internal semantics.

2. Eric Hellman, "The Revolution Will Be Digitized (By Cheap Book Scanners)," Go to Hellman blog, October 13, 2009, http://go-to-hellman.blogspot.com/2009/10/revolution-will-be-digitized-by-cheap.html (accessed May 5, 2010).

3. A. Lawrence Spitz, "Determination of the Script and Language Content of Document Images," *IEEE Transactions on Pattern Analysis and Machine Intelligence*, 19, no. 3 (March 1997): 235–45.

4. "That Sinking Feeling," Snopes.com, http://www.snopes.com/college/halls/sinking.asp (accessed May 5, 2010).

5. Kim Ryan, "Lingua-EN-Fathom-1.12," in CPAN, the Comprehensive Perl Archive Network, a large collection of Perl software and documentation. This module analyses English text in either a string or file. Totals are then calculated for the number of characters, words, sentences, blank and non blank (text) lines and paragraphs. Three common readability statistics are also derived, the Fog, Flesch and Kincaid indices. http://search.cpan.org/~kimryan/Lingua-EN-Fathom-1.12/lib/Lingua/EN/Fathom.pm (accessed May 5, 2010).

6. Patrick Hochstenbach, "Linked-Data in the Academic Bibliography," TekTok-Digital Library Technology Blog, October 7, 2009, http://lib.ugent.be/tektok/2009/10/test.html (accessed May 5, 2010).

7. Galen M. Charlton, "Distributed Version Control and Library Metadata," *Code4-Lib Journal*, issue 3 (June 23, 2008), http://journal.code4lib.org/articles/86 (accessed May 5, 2010).

5   A QUESTION OF IDENTITY: THE ROLE OF IDENTIFIERS IN LIBRARY CATALOGS

Ed Jones

INTRODUCTION

In one sense, identifiers have been around since the dawn of language. To name something is in essence to identify it, and human beings have been naming things pretty much nonstop since we first acquired the ability.

But in this essay, I'm interested in identifiers in a narrow sense, in a cataloging sense. More precisely, I'm interested in identifiers in terms of the 2009 *Statement of International Cataloguing Principles* (ICP).[1] Because of this particular focus, readers will have an easier time if they are comfortable with the terminology of the ICP, especially as it applies to the entities and user tasks elaborated in *Functional Requirements for Bibliographic Records* (FRBR) and *Functional Requirements for Authority Data* (FRAD).[2]

The ICP defines identifier as "[a] number, code, word, phrase, logo, device, etc. that is uniquely associated with an entity, and serves to differentiate that entity from other entities within the domain in which the identifier is assigned."[3]

According to this definition, an identifier must satisfy three criteria: It must be assigned (which assumes an assigning authority), the assignment must occur within the context of a recognized domain (the object to which the identifiers are being assigned must conform to a definition), and it must be uniquely associated with an [instance of an] entity. To take a mundane example, the California Department of Motor Vehicles is authorized to assign identifiers—California driver's license numbers—within the domain of the driver's licenses it issues, and each California driver's license number is uniquely associated with one of these licenses, that is, there is a one-to-one correspondence between the two:

no license bears more than one number, and no number applies to more than one license.

FRAD elaborates the ICP definition slightly by explicitly excluding "record numbers assigned to authority records," a class that would otherwise seem to fit the definition of identifier.[4] For purposes of this essay, however, this exclusion will be interpreted narrowly to apply to numbers used solely within a local system and not to numbers that are in common use outside their local system and may even have associated XML (Extensible Markup Language) namespaces, such as Library of Congress and OCLC control numbers.[5]

In the following sections, I'll examine the role identifiers have played throughout the history of cataloging, beginning with their modest role in manual catalogs (book catalogs and card catalogs) and proceeding via the introduction of the MARC (Machine Readable Cataloging) formats to our current online catalogs, interacting more and more with the wider World Wide Web.

IDENTIFYING

In the beginning, there were manual catalogs, clunky from a twenty-first-century perspective but often cutting edge in their own time. In these catalogs, identifiers were few and far between, functionally limited to identifying resources, usually in a very specific context. Among nineteenth-century cataloging codes, identifiers first show up in Charles Cutter's 1876 *Rules for a Printed Dictionary Catalogue*, in an example under rule 20, showing how to identify rare and old books by reference to entries in an authoritative bibliography (e.g., "Hain no. 16128").[6] An additional class of identifier appears in the 1904 fourth edition of Cutter's rules, in the additional rules for music by O. G. Sonneck, where rule 367 states that "[f]or purposes of identification, the publisher's number [for printed music] should always be entered" in a note.[7] These two uses of identifiers are noteworthy if only because Cutter was parsimonious in his use of notes, feeling that they drew attention to books and this might not always be a good thing. Cutter felt that in a catalog "[d]ull books and morally bad books should be left in obscurity."[8]

This was pretty much where matters stood until the mid-twentieth century, when LC (the Library of Congress) introduced a number of identifiers for its own use and for the use of its cooperative cataloging partners. For example, LC assigned their own identifiers to books and serials acquired abroad under U.S. Public Law 83-480 for subsequent distribution to other U.S. research libraries (e.g., "PL 480:I-D-E-524").[9] Similarly, LC sometimes included an identifier specifying the entry in a foreign national bibliography on which a bibliographic description was based (e.g., "B68-07112" for an entry in the British National Bibliography), enabling subsequent consultation of the source bibliographic description should questions arise. Although it might have been useful to provide added entries under these new identifiers to facilitate their retrieval, the cost would have been prohibitive. Such functionality would have to await the development of the MARC format.

FINDING AND IDENTIFYING

"In 1964, the Council on Library Resources, Inc., (CLR) awarded a contract to Inforonics, Inc., for a study of the possible methods of converting information on Library of Congress catalog cards to machine-readable form for the purpose of printing bibliographical products by computer."[10] From this study emerged the MARC Communications Format (as it was initially called), the antecedent of today's MARC 21 Bibliographic format.

The original (experimental) MARC I format carried two identifiers: the Library of Congress catalog card number (now called the LC control number) and, when a description was based on an entry in a foreign national bibliography, the national bibliography number of that entry. MARC I was succeeded in 1968 by MARC II and two more identifier fields were added: for the Standard Book Number (SBN, the precursor of the ISBN or International Standard Book Number) and for the PL480 number (see above). While these identifiers were primarily of interest to LC cataloging and acquisitions staff, as well as technical staff at other libraries using the format, they could now be used by those staff to query the system—to find bibliographic records in terms of the FRBR user tasks. Of course, in those early days, the query was likely to be submitted on a punch card, and the response was likely to come in the form of a lengthy printout.

With the advent of online cataloging systems such as OCLC, at first heavily dependent on the MARC records supplied by the Library of Congress, technical staff at other libraries began to actively use these identifiers to find online cataloging copy, expediting their own acquisitions and cataloging. The first identifiers to be indexed in systems such as OCLC were the LC catalog card number (LCCN) and the ISBN, one or both of which frequently appeared on the verso of a book's title page. Ironically, the LCCN, once used to order card sets from LC, was now used to avoid ordering card sets from LC. When used as a search argument, an LCCN or ISBN would typically return a single record, and the ISBN quickly became the preferred index for batch retrieval of catalog records.

The start of the CONSER (Cooperative Online Serials Program) Project in 1975 introduced serial catalog records to OCLC and a new identifier, the International Standard Serial Number (ISSN). Whereas the ISBN had been introduced within the publisher community as that community automated many of its internal processes, the ISSN was different. It arose not within a producer community but within a consumer community, from efforts by the International Council of Scientific Unions (ICSU) and UNESCO to create a central database of information on scientific and technical serials (later extended to all serials) and their coverage by abstracting and indexing services.[11] Because producers have different priorities from consumers, uptake of the ISSN within the producer community has been a lengthy and arduous process, but Bowker assigned them en masse to entries in their two annual bibliographies, *Ulrich's International Periodicals Directory and Irregular Serials and Annuals*, and their 1950–1970 cumulation of *New Serial Titles*. Armed with these, the ISSN was an immediate hit with serial catalogers, especially for differentiating among serials with "generic" titles such as Bulletin, Journal, and Annual Report, which would otherwise be irretrievable given the primitive search arguments available at the time.

So matters stood on the eve of the Online Public Access Catalog (OPAC). While identifiers were exploited by technical staff to find appropriate cataloging copy, they were used by the general public—whether in catalog cards, printed book catalogs, or microform catalogs—solely to identify. But with online catalogs—available at first only locally, but later worldwide via the Internet—this changed, if only because it was comparatively easy to extend public access to indexes that were already being routinely exploited by library staff. For example, a 1998 directory of Internet-accessible online catalogs revealed that public access via ISBN, ISSN, and even LCCN, while not universal among the listed catalogs, was a common practice.[12]

These early online catalogs were at first accessible only via computer terminals on the library premises, and typically included only materials cataloged since the local introduction of MARC records (perhaps a decade or two earlier). Remote access to these catalogs, when available, was initially by means of dialup connections and via online connection over the Internet, using the telnet protocol and related terminal emulation software. Though still clunky—and initially a dubious improvement over the manual catalogs they were replacing—these catalogs trumped their predecessors in terms of timeliness and remote access. For the first time, both librarians and the general public could instantly search a wide variety of online catalogs located all over the world. What once was exotic was about to become familiar.

With the growth of the World Wide Web during the 1990s, the potential of the Internet for commerce became increasingly apparent, and more identifier schemes were introduced to the online world. At the product level were new schemes like the International Standard Music Number (ISMN, analogous to the ISBN, but for scores and parts) and existing ones such as the International Article Number (EAN) and its North American analog, the Universal Product Code (UPC). At the level of intellectual property (IP) were schemes such as the International Standard Recording Code (ISRC), the International Standard Musical Work Code (ISWC), the International Standard Text Code (ISTC), and the International Standard Audiovisual Number (ISAN). To accommodate the proliferation of these schemes, the handling of identifiers in MARC 21 was modified so that elements for new schemes were not intrinsic parts of the format but instead extrinsic, maintained in a separate code list for identifier schemes and codes referenced by use of a generic identifier field (024, formerly reserved for the ISRC) with a "source" subfield ($2) for the code of the associated scheme. Libraries could choose which of these schemes to index in their online catalogs. On bibliographic records for component parts (works that are part of larger works), provision was made for identifier schemes that focused on that level of analysis, such as the new Digital Object Identifier (DOI) and the older Serial Item and Contribution Identifier (SICI).

Curiously, despite the fact that indexes for various identifiers have long been present in OPACs, no Anglo-American cataloging code, including the code in force at the time of this writing, has ever made provision for such indexing. Nevertheless, FRBR singles out identifiers as attributes of bibliographic resources that can be used to find those resources (i.e., as index terms).[13]

But if identifiers now satisfied two of the user tasks set out in FRBR (find and identify), with the growing integration of OPACs into the World Wide Web, they would soon satisfy all four (find, identify, select, and obtain).

FINDING, IDENTIFYING, SELECTING, OBTAINING

With their emergence onto the World Wide Web, library catalogs acquired the potential to interact with other Web-enabled databases. Identifiers in catalog records could link to related records in other databases and even to representations of the resources described by those records. If a Web browser was enhanced by library-specific add-on software such as Virginia Tech's LibX, identifiers in Web objects might trigger an identifier-based search of the library's online catalog or, if journal- or article-based, of the library's OpenURL resolver. These searches might, in turn, lead the user directly to the resource. This is a revolution with which libraries and librarians are still coming to grips.

Formal access from catalog records to external Web data had been available since the addition of field 856 (electronic access) to the MARC format. The field was typically used to link to the resource described or to a publisher-supplied table of contents, brief description, or author biographical data. These were static connections requiring a specific URL (Uniform Resource Locator) in subfield $u of the 856 field. But things changed once catalogs and library tools could incorporate application programming interfaces (APIs) in their Web pages. APIs could be designed to make on-the-fly connections between resources in different domains. For example, such Web pages could incorporate an API to search Google Books for data relating to the resource described in a displayed catalog record (and often the resource itself, either in whole or part), by using an identifier (e.g., ISBN, LC control number, OCLC control number) present in the catalog record. Ideally, the link would appear only if associated data were present in Google Books. Such links greatly expanded the data to which a user could connect from a catalog record, though they were dependent on an identifier being shared between records in the two systems. For Google Books, this identifier might be extracted from metadata supplied by a partner library in one of its mass digitization programs, or by a publisher whose ONIX metadata had been enhanced with Library of Congress or OCLC cataloging metadata.

Links might also be made from outside systems into library catalogs, either via an intermediate Web site such as OCLC's WorldCat.org, or directly via a library-specific Web browser plug-in (see xISBN Bookmarklets below). In the former case, the WorldCat Search API would be embedded in third-party Web pages such as those of Google Books (when an appropriate identifier is present in the Google Books metadata), or ERIC (when an ISBN or ISSN is present in the ERIC metadata).

Beyond such manifestation-to-manifestation linking, more sophisticated linking was being enabled by Web services such as OCLC's xISBN and xOCLCNUM services. Using the ISBNs or OCLC control numbers recorded in WorldCat's bibliographic records, these services applied the OCLC FRBR Work-Set Algorithm, which clusters bibliographic records according to the FRBR conceptual structure, in this case linking manifestations to works. In terms of FRBR user tasks, invoking the xISBN or xOCLCNUM services allowed Web applications to generate approximate manifestation-to-work linking, thus enabling users to select among related manifestations.

Finally, Web browser plug-ins, such as OCLC's library-specific xISBN Bookmarklets and Virginia Tech's LibX plug-ins, enabled library-specific linking by principally using ISBN pattern recognition in targeted Web pages. This triggered an xISBN search of a given library's online catalog, typically resulting in a single match. LibX also used ISSN and DOI pattern recognition on Web pages to trigger searches of a given library's OpenURL resolver, but that lies outside the scope of this essay. The one drawback of browser plug-ins was that they needed to be explicitly downloaded and installed by the user to be enabled.

This is the state of the identifier in library catalogs today, supporting all four FRBR user tasks: finding, identifying, selecting, and obtaining. The future, like the past, is a foreign country, but one possible future holds particular appeal to librarians and researchers: the Semantic Web.

ONE POSSIBLE FUTURE: IDENTIFIERS AND THE SEMANTIC WEB

Tim Berners-Lee, the father of the World Wide Web, introduced the idea of a Semantic Web in 1998, in the form of a "road map" for discussion within the Web community.[14] Along with James Hendler and Ora Lassila, he subsequently introduced it to the broader public in the May 2001 issue of *Scientific American*.[15] The Semantic Web, as Berners-Lee, Hendler, and Lassila envisage it, is to be a place where online objects are marked up, not just to enable a pleasant reading and navigating experience for the human user, but also to enable reading and navigation by what are called "intelligent agents"—programs that users, desktop applications, etc., can unleash on the Web to answer a specific query or to gather and organize materials relevant to various information needs. The travels of the intelligent agents will be facilitated by a network of structures, including metadata, ontologies, ontology description languages, and Web services.

In the Semantic Web, communities (e.g., libraries, publishers, museums) are able to create metadata structures appropriate to their own online resources, and other communities may borrow whatever parts they find useful for their own structures. This is done within the overarching framework of a general-purpose language known as the Resource Description Framework (RDF) and associated vocabularies and ontologies, the details of which lie blessedly outside the present discussion.[16] Within the digital library community, Dublin Core (DC) is an example of a community-specific vocabulary whose elements can be expressed in RDF and used by other communities.[17] Further vocabularies are being prepared to accommodate the structures and elements of FRBR and of the new cataloging code, Resource Description and Access (RDA). Beyond these specific structures, the British JISC (Joint Information Systems Committee) Infrastructure and Resources Committee has created a Vocabulary Mapping Framework (VMF) to support interoperability across the publisher/producer, education, and bibliographic/heritage communities, creating a superset of the elements used in the major vocabulary standards of those communities and a related RDF/OWL (Web Ontology Language) ontology.[18]

Within all these existing and emerging structures, identifiers are key. For example, identifiers can be used to find and select metadata about a given resource, and—via linked identifiers—metadata about related entities, potentially ad infinitum. In one scenario, an ISBN could be used to find and extract bibliographic and holdings data from WorldCat (possibly including related editions identified by the xISBN or xOCLCNUM services). At the same time, it could find and extract pertinent data (summary, table of contents, reading level, cover image, etc.) from a publisher's or producer's database; and find and extract price, availability, and delivery data from one or more online sellers. Similarly, one of the purposes envisaged for an International Standard Name Identifier (ISNI)—an identifier for what are called "public identities"—is to facilitate the extraction of metadata on persons, corporate bodies, etc., from stores such as the Virtual International Authority File (VIAF). Assuming robust IP rights identifier systems (ISWC, ISTC, ISAN) and a widely accepted public identity identifier system (ISNI)—both admittedly big assumptions—metadata could be extracted from multiple other stores, then combined by the software agent and arranged for concise presentation to the user.

Of course, questions remain about whether the Semantic Web will be able to do this, especially whether it will be able to successfully transition from the relatively protected environment of the few well-defined data stores where its transactions currently tend to take place, to the more exposed environment of the open Web, where numerous uncertainties come into play.[19] But the benefits that would accrue to all parties from a well-structured Semantic Web suggest that ways will be found to overcome such obstacles.

What would the local library catalog look like in this particular future, where the human searcher has been supplanted in most instances by his or her software agents? It is conceivable that in this future, the local catalog record will consist simply of one or more widely recognized product identifiers (ISBN, ISMN, etc.) or an OCLC control number (OCN) linked to local management data relating to holdings, location, availability, etc.[20] A software agent seeking a particular library resource would send its requirements out across the Web as a query to WorldCat or some other designated store of multi-institutional catalog data, selecting this store on the basis of the local institutions at which the user had borrowing privileges. Targeted data stores would return availability data and might even initiate a transaction if certain user-defined conditions were met.

The agent would already know the user's authorization data and institutional borrowing privileges, as well as a hierarchy of document delivery preferences and conditions. Such a world would save the time of the reader (to cite Ranganathan's fourth law) on a scale never before imaginable.

From the end user's perspective, the local library catalog in such a world would have ceased to exist. From the librarian's perspective, it would in fact have completed a long odyssey from a world in which identifiers were rare and of only occasional interest—the long-ago world of manual catalogs—to one in which they were in some ways all there was, a world in which the local catalog had functionally become absolutely and exclusively dependent on them for its continued existence.

NOTES

1. *Statement of International Cataloguing Principles* (n.p., 2009), http://www.ifla.org/files/cataloguing/icp/icp_2009-en.pdf (accessed November 10, 2009); "IME-ICC: IFLA Meetings of Experts on an International Cataloguing Code," http://www.ifla.org/node/576 (accessed November 10, 2009).

2. International Federation of Library Associations and Institutions (IFLA), "Functional Requirements for Bibliographic Records: Final Report, as Amended and Corrected through February 2009" (n.p.: IFLA, 2009), http://www.ifla.org/files/cataloguing/frbr/frbr_2008.pdf (accessed November 10, 2009); "Functional Requirements for Authority Data: A Conceptual Model," draft, April 1, 2007 (n.p.: IFLA, 2007), http://archive.ifla.org/VII/d4/franar-conceptual-model-2ndreview.pdf (accessed May 10, 2010).

3. *Statement of International Cataloguing Principles*, 11, http://www.ifla.org/files/cataloguing/icp/icp_2009-en.pdf (accessed November 10, 2009).

4. "Functional Requirements for Authority Data: A Conceptual Model," 14, http://archive.ifla.org/VII/d4/franar-conceptual-model-2ndreview.pdf (accessed May 10, 2010).

5. "The LCCN Namespace," Network Development and MARC Standards Office, Library of Congress, November 2003, http://www.loc.gov/marc/lccn-namespace.html (accessed November 10, 2009); "The "info" URI Scheme for Information Assets with Identifiers in Public Namespaces," Network Working Group Request for Comments: 4452, April 2006, http://www.ietf.org/rfc/rfc4452.txt (accessed November 10, 2009).

6. Henry Stevens, *Catalogue of the American Books in the Library of the British Museum at Christmas MDCCCLVI* (London: Chiswick Press for Henry Stevens, 1856), ix–xxv, http://books.google.com/books?id=nIUYAAAAMAAJ (accessed November 10, 2009); Charles C. Jewett, *Smithsonian Report on the Construction of Catalogues of Libraries and their Publication by Means of Separate, Stereotyped Titles*, 2nd ed. (Washington, DC: Smithsonian Institution, 1853), http://books.google.com/books?id=ONIWeyTN_CMC (accessed November 10, 2009); Charles A. Cutter, *Rules for a Printed Dictionary Catalogue* (Washington, DC: GPO, 1876), http://books.google.com/books?id=rj-f4-Ps-AkC (accessed November 10, 2009).

7. O. G. Sonneck, "2. Music," in Charles A. Cutter, *Rules for a Dictionary Catalog*, 4th ed., rewritten (Washington, DC: GPO, 1904), 138–40 (rule 367), http://books.google.com/books?id=X078UC_a7IIC (accessed November 10, 2009).

8. Cutter, *Rules for a Printed Dictionary Catalogue*, 65 (quote), 80 (rule 205).

9. John G. Lorentz et al., "The Library of Congress Abroad," *Library Trends* 20, no. 3 (January 1972): 548–76, http://www.ideals.uiuc.edu/bitstream/handle/2142/6637/librarytrendsv20i3i_opt.pdf (accessed November 10, 2009).

10. Henriette D. Avram, *The MARC Pilot Project: Final Report* (Washington, DC: Library of Congress, 1968), 3, 9, http://www.eric.ed.gov/ERICWebPortal/contentdelivery/servlet/ERICServlet?accno=ED029663 (accessed November 10, 2009).

11. M. D. Martin and C. I. Barnes, *Report on the Feasibility of an International Serials Data System, and Preliminary Systems Design* (London: INSPEC, 1970), 1.1–1.2, http://www.eric.ed.gov/ERICWebPortal/contentdelivery/servlet/ERICServlet?accno=ED061954 (accessed November 10, 2009).

12. Bonnie R. Nelson, *OPAC Directory 1998: A Guide to Internet-Accessible Online Public Access Catalogs* (Medford, NJ: Information Today, 1998), xiii.

13. IFLA, "Functional Requirements for Bibliographic Records: Final Report," 80.

14. Tim Berners-Lee, "Semantic Web Road Map, September 1998," http://www.w3.org/DesignIssues/Semantic.html (accessed November 10, 2009).

15. Tim Berners-Lee, James Hendler, and Ora Lassila, "The Semantic Web," *Scientific American* 284, issue 5 (May 2001): 34–44; Karin K. Breitman, Marco Antonio Casanova, and Walt Truszkowski, *Semantic Web: Concepts, Technologies, and Applications* (London: Springer, 2007).

16. "RDF Primer: W3C Recommendation 10 February 2004," http://www.w3.org/TR/rdf-primer (accessed November 10, 2009); "SKOS Simple Knowledge Organization System Primer: W3C Working Group Note 18 August 2009," http://www.w3.org/TR/skos-primer (accessed November 10, 2009); "OWL 2 Web Ontology Language Primer: W3C Recommendation 27 October 2009," http://www.w3.org/TR/owl2-primer (accessed November 10, 2009).

17. Dublin Core Metadata Initiative, "DCMI Metadata Terms," http://dublincore.org/documents/dcmi-terms/ (accessed November 10, 2009).

18. "Major Content Vocabularies to Be Mapped" (June 15, 2009), http://www.doi.org/news/VMF_project_announcement_090615.pdf (accessed November 10, 2009).

19. "Uncertainty Reasoning for the World Wide Web: W3C Incubator Group Report 31 March 2008," http://www.w3.org/2005/Incubator/urw3/XGR-urw3 (accessed November 10, 2009).

20. Janifer Gatenby, "Identifiers and GLIMIR. OCLC Symposium for Publishers and Librarians, 18 March 2009," http://www.oclc.org/multimedia/2009/files/GatenbyJ-Identifiers_GLIMIR.pdf (accessed November 10, 2009).

6 NF: A NEW FORMAT FOR METADATA

Bernhard Eversberg

WHAT IF WE HAD TO START FROM SCRATCH AND CREATE A NEW FORMAT (NF) FOR METADATA?

MARC (Machine-Readable Cataloging) can and will evolve to contain bibliographic description and provide access for new formats of publications. But how long can this effectively be done? What if we started from scratch to create a new bibliographic record structure with none of MARC's weaknesses, and with more flexibility and ease of use for computerized catalogs and future forms of digital data? This essay seeks to formulate design goals and principles that try to avoid some of the weaknesses and faults inherent in the MARC structure. Whereas in practice there will be no way to introduce a new format on a large scale, it can be instructive and helpful to see what might be envisioned in order to possibly accommodate today's objectives and necessities. I have translated this vision into a new record format and structure, which I call NF, or New Format. It has been implemented with the *allegro* software package, my own development, to demonstrate simpler, less restrictive bibliographic and authority data formats. Examples of different types of records formatted in NF, that can be compared to MARC format, can be found in a sample database of over a million records located on the Internet at: http://www.biblio.tu-bs.de/db/a30/neutral.htm (a Flash-based application). Screenshots demonstrating how to access these examples are at the end of this essay.

WHY A NEW FORMAT?

The purpose of a new format is not a pointless attempt to replace existing formats like MARC, whose structure and usage are firmly established. Instead, it may be considered for new metadata projects, which sometimes have requirements that for MARC21 or other communications formats (with all the historical baggage they carry) are perhaps inappropriate, much too complex, or not flexible enough for the intended use.

MARC and other communication formats come, in reality, in more than one flavour. There are versions for bibliographic resources, for personal and corporate name authority data, for holdings, for subject authorities, for classification, and for community information. For static, analog publications, and for data exchange, this works well; however, for online digital resources and integrated online catalogs, this static and rigid multiplicity is less appropriate.

In the real world of library metadata, MARC serves many purposes with diverse requirements—some of which are very specific, and some of which are obsolete, harking back to functions and necessities (like card production) of times long past. This NF record structure alternative was therefore developed to work with current evolving standards that are meant to provide description and access to the newer digital resource universe. These standards include FRBR (Functional Requirements for Bibliographic Records), RDA (Resource Description and Access) and DC (Dublin Core), to name just a few.

Nevertheless, NF can be no more than an exercise. To start a new record format from scratch like this, with a new design based on a body of experience rather than merely theorizing like the early DC community, might provide some food for thought or bits of new insight. For those who do not believe MARC can or should live forever, and if that is the reality, it means that sooner or later there will have to be a new format. NF is one possible idea in this direction. Much more work waits to be done.

PRINCIPLES AND STRUCTURE OF THE NF

NF was created using the *allegro* software package which I developed for the Universitätsbibliothek Braunschweig (see http://www.allegro-c.de), so a little understanding of *allegro*'s format is helpful to introduce NF. NF was not, however, designed specifically for *allegro* but was instead created for general library catalog or database applicability in mind. And, very practically, how better to check if and how NF works than by doing an implementation in some real software? Relational database systems are not optimal for the NF, as is the case for metadata management in general. Just as with MARC, *allegro* is decidedly non-relational. It can be called "object-oriented," although that term has a much less standardized meaning than "relational." Using *allegro* as the platform, I have created NF as a bibliographic and authority control database system with much of the elements of MARC, but with more flexibility and open-design.

ELEMENTS OF THE NEW FORMAT

The following tables demonstrate NF's structural elements and principles.

- Table 6.1: General database design principles
- Table 6.2: Fixed fields
- Table 6.3: Variable fields and data elements
- Table 6.4: Tags
- Table 6.5: Indicators
- Tables 6.6 and 6.7: Subfield design principles and codes
- Table 6.8: Authority fields
- Table 6.9: Bibliographic main record groups
- Table 6.10: Most important bibliographic record fields

The information in these tables constitutes the basic NF record. Not every component of NF can be addressed in this essay, however. For a complete list of field definitions, tags, codes, examples, and more, go to http://www.allegro-c. de/doku/neutral/tab.htm.

Table 6.1
Basic Design Principles for Metadata Records (Both Authority and Bibliographic)

Design Principles	Description and Values
Record syntax: No ISO2709	Other than MARC, NF data are not supposed to be embedded in the arcane ISO2709 wrapping. A record can be thought of like a piece of structured text.
Reasonable compatibility with MARC	Full compatibility with MARC should not be expected, for if this were required, then why not choose and use MARC itself and just do some improvements? *Reformatting* of essential content, however, from and into MARC is easily done with *allegro* export and import parameterization, or similar tools. Much the same holds true for DC (Dublin Core) export, i.e., output of data with XML or similar tagging structures using DC element names.

Design Principles	Description and Values
Simplicity of structure, or, "Scalable complexity"	Simplicity is important for the most frequently occurring cases and purposes of records, such as plain bib records for small databases. Those who want very simple, basic cataloging should not be overloaded with detail that may be necessary only for sophisticated applications. The structure of a simple record might be a record with brief but necessary information, and with no indicators or subfields.
Character encoding for exchange and internal use	No option seems more acceptable these days than UTF-8. It is now the most widely used Unicode standard on the Web.
Non-sort control characters: for marking initial articles and other parts to omit in filing	These can be applied everywhere, in any position of all fields and subfields, using the ´ character (ASCII 96). The MARC non-sort indicator is too limited and awkward.
All fields are optional; an application may only use what is really needed	Mandatory fields, as well as formal validation, are left to local programming. (Experience has shown that the usefulness of general specifications like these is limited.)
Letters used as codes in fields and subfields	When used for fields and subfields, letters have been chosen to be *mnemonic* (in English).
No data typing as part of the format (the format doesn't say what kind of data a field may hold: numbers, dates, time, text)	Every field's content is to be considered variable-length text. This does not mean that implementations may not use verification routines wherever they are useful. If in an application it is vital that a field holds a correct structure of, e.g., a date, the implementation should provide a routine to check this upon input—it is not the job of the format itself.
No terminating punctuation at the ends of fields or ending subfields	Punctuation will have to be entered manually *inside* fields or subfields. A period at the *end* of a field or subfield text is to be entered only if it terminates an abbreviation. Punctuation in displays or outputs is left to be inserted by software. (MARC requires many field contents to be terminated by a period or other ISBD punctuation. This was done to ease catalog card production.)

(continued)

Table 6.1. (*continued*)

Design Principles	Description and Values
Part=>Whole relationship	The Part-to-Whole work relationship is indicated by using identifiers (record numbers or URIs) by which a part record points to its parent record, but not the parent record pointing to all its parts because software can take care of that. Hierarchically structured records are also possible (stored contiguously: parent record plus attached part records). Multiple levels of hierarchy are structurally possible though not recommended.

Table 6.2
New Format Fixed Fields

Fixed Fields	Description and Values
Fixed-length elements with position-dependent information	There are *no* fixed-length elements with position-dependent information as, for example, in the MARC "Leader" or 008 field. Application-specific definitions of specific field contents can, however, use such designs if necessary, and do their own checking on these contents.

Table 6.3
New Format Variable Fields and Data Elements

Variable Fields, Data Elements	Description and Values
Order of data elements	There is *no* fixed order of data elements. The arrangement of fields within a record should be semantically insignificant. In some MARC systems, the sequence of notes, for example, carries meaning, but other MARC systems sort fields in numeric order, thereby destroying this significance. This has often been seen as a flaw of MARC as used in practice. (The order of field definitions in an *allegro* database configuration can be changed at any time without affecting the data already stored but also without imposing a specific meaning.)

Variable Fields, Data Elements	Description and Values
Field names	Every field has an English and German BriefName (containing no spaces). Internally, for the storage of data, however, nothing but the language-independent tags are to be used. This way, the brief names are not fixed forever. Preferred terms are the Dublin Core Names (http://dublincore.org/ documents/dces), for these may well be the most commonly known and most widely accepted data element names. Their semantics were discussed and agreed upon by several important communities. Still, we do not consider these brief names themselves to be tags. In other words, data tags as parts of records do not have textual designators.
DC-element names: the names defined by the Dublin Core Metadata Initiative (DCMI)	Some of these are the logical headlines of the *main parts of the format* (Titles, Subjects, etc.). These main elements enable a reduction of complexity (so-called "dumbing down"), which may be a requirement in some applications. There are, of course, numerous additional elements that, although not covered by DC, will probably be needed in many applications.
Like elements	Like elements are handled in the same way. This is important for indexing. (MARC is a little less rigorous: it doesn't handle all titles in the same way, it separates the first and subsequent creators into different areas.)
Field repetition	Multiple occurrences of a particular field come in two equivalent techniques: • Repetition of the field tag, and adding a digit or a letter at its end. This makes it look like a MARC indicator. Normally, there is only one space between field tag and contents. This space position is then used for the repetition code. For example: 500 First subject term 5002Second subject term • Separation of multiple content within one field by the | character. This method may be the preferred one for simple and short data elements. The | may be replaced by a line break or a semicolon in data display functions. Each one of the multiple field contents may contain all the subfields that are defined for the field tag. For example: 500 First term | Second term

Table 6.4
New Format Field Tags

Tags	Description and Values
Tags (content designators)	Tags have three characters and consist of digits and (sometimes also) letters (MARC has only digits).
Textual designators: labels verbally designating field content	Tagging has no textual designators, in order to avoid language-dependence and outdated and obsolete words, or terms.
Local extensions for tags: third digit of a variable field tag	Implementers may easily define their own extensions. In all groups, the value of "9" is used as the third digit of a tag to remain available for local definitions. This also applies to capital letters in the same position, as well as the subfield codes B, C, E, and all the others not defined in the subfield list. This allows local extensions to always be easily recognizable.

Table 6.5
New Format Indicators

Indicators	Description and Values
There are no indicators	There are no control fields to make an additional statement about the content of a particular field, which is quite different in MARC. Most indicators in MARC, though, are obsolete anyway since they relate to card formatting. When there is a need to make an additional statement about a field's content, the standard NF $T is the option to use.

Table 6.6
New Format Subfield Design Principles

Subfield Design Principles	Description and Values
Subfields not normally needed	Field contents in many cases need no subfields. Different from MARC formats, there is no mandatory $a for the *main content* of a field—it just starts right after the field tag, like #100 *Title*

Subfield Design Principles	Description and Values
Data elements that belong together	Where data elements are not meaningful when separated, they are not specified as two or more fields but rather subfields of *one* field. In other words: There is no semantics in any pairing or tripling of fields or subfields. This way, easy and unambiguous *repetition of multipart fields* is ensured. (This is something that had already been understood in MARC design, but see "standard subfields" below.)
Subfields defined only when useful	Subfields have been defined only where they really seem pragmatically useful. Well-established and unambiguous punctuation has in some cases been preferred and found sufficient, for example: "Title : Addition" where the ": "sufficiently marks the beginning of the addition, or "Lastname, First-name" instead of a subfield code for the Firstname.
13 Standard Subfields (see Table 6.7)	These are denoted by capital letters that may be used as part of any field. Besides $Y, for example, there's $Z, the field-specific note; this saves a long list of specific note fields that exist in MARC21 and that relate only to the content of (other) specific fields. In the examples in the demo database (see directions to the database at the end of this essay), there are some subfields not explained in this paper. Let this not distract you; for space limitations, this paper can not contain the entire format definition with all the subfields.

Table 6.7
New Format Subfield Code Table

Alphabetical Code and Abbreviation	Code Description
$A FldAbbr	Abbreviated form of the field content
$D FldDate	Date related to field content
$I FldID	Source +IdNr for field content, e.g., authority record number

(*continued*)

Table **6.7.** (*continued*)

Alphabetical Code and Abbreviation	Code Description
$L FldLang	Language and script of field content
$N FldNum	Numbering, if a number is significant part of field content
$P FldPre	Prefix: to be displayed in front of the field content
$R FldRule	Rule or standard the field content conforms to
$S FldSpell	Different spelling of field content or parts (for indexing)
$T FldType	Specifies if field content can be of different types
$U FldURI	URL or URN relating to field content
$X FldNNote	NonPublicNote: additional text, not to be displayed
$Y FldText	Text to be displayed instead of field content itself (e.g., transcribed text), i.e., if a differing transcribed form is required for display, it goes into the universal subfield $Y, which can be part of every field.
$Z FldPNote	PublicNote: additional text for public display

The thirteen standard subfields; these can occur in every field, whereas small-letter codes are mostly field-specific.

INDEXING

The main field content is to be understood as suitable for indexing (Principle: *access* is more important than *description*). Indexing, in the *allegro* system for example, is the task of so-called Index Parameters—it is not a part of data definition but specified in a separate file. Implementers can therefore index the data in whichever way they find necessary or useful, without a need to restructure any data. This is not to say one would not need guidelines or even rules (as part of a cataloging code) for indexing! In fact, interoperability of systems and efficient cross-system searching (federated searching) will always be suboptimal without such rules. It is unfortunate that RDA doesn't seem to recognize this but continues in the AACR tradition of not bothering with filing. In any event, indexing is not a part of the format definition but is a function of any system that uses the content of formatted records.

DISPLAY

It is important to note that display is no business of the format. The NF therefore does not refer to "display constants" (like MARC). If there are display conventions or "best practices" used for OPACs, then it is the task of implementations to create the display out of the content of the NF records. Different catalog systems can choose different display structuring and wording.

LAYOUT OF NF AUTHORITY RECORDS

NF Authority records share a common structure, as they all use the same three-character tags #n00–#n98, i.e., the first character of the tag is always the n,

Table 6.8
New Format Authority Fields (Just the Most Important Ones)

Field Tag	Definition
#n00	IdNumber (of the local system)
#n08	*International Authority Number*
#n10	Authority type (e.g., p = Person, . . ., t = topical term)
#n30	Preferred form
#n31	Alternative forms
#n35	Preferred textual form (if #n30 is a code)
#n40	"Used for" forms (or "also known as, etc . . . .")
#n50	Dates
#n60	Geographic designation
#n80	General notes
#n85	Scope notes
#n90	Free for local use

Table 6.9
New Format Bibliographic Record Main Groups

Group	Purpose
#0 Codes, Numbers, Identifiers, Dates	Identifying and typing
#1 Titles	Naming the object
#2 Personal names	Naming persons involved in the object's creation
#3 Corporate names	Naming bodies involved
#4 Relations, Context	Referring to larger objects containing the one described
#5 Subjects, verbal	Indexing by verbal terms
#6 Subjects, classes and codes	Assigning the object to classes
#7 Sources	From where or what does the object originate?
#8 Physical description	Describing physical properties
#9 Local data, copy information	Describing the object's location, and how to get it
#9x Application specific data	Serving housekeeping and related local tasks
#n Authority data	Authority records for standardization of names, terms, classes, etc. Use of these fields is restricted to the authority records, which in turn use none of the other fields.
Implementations can define additional fields	

followed by two digits. In this way, there are no field tags with two or more meanings (as in MARC, where 500 in an authority record (personal name see also reference) is not the same as in a bibliographic record (general note)). Note that authority records use *only* these fields, and no bibliographic fields, to avoid confusing the two record formats.

LAYOUT OF NF BIBLIOGRAPHIC RECORDS

NF Bibliographic has eleven main groups, each starting with an **x00** tag, as shown in Table 6.9. These eleven groups form the structure of the authorship, description, classification, subject analysis, copy information, identifiers and coding, local data, and authority data for the work represented.

MOST IMPORTANT FIELDS IN NF BIBLIOGRAPHIC RECORDS

The most important fields are displayed in Table 6.10, and the simplest implementations may probably need little more than these, with no subfields. The fields and tags in Table 6.10 correlate to their broader values in Table 6.9, or bibliographic main groups, but are expanded to include more specific data, as necessary for the work. These fields relate, broadly, to the original fifteen DC terms, the names of which appear *italicized*.

Table 6.10
Overview of New Format's Most Important Bibliographic Record Fields
(Fields Are Repeatable as Needed)

Field Tag	Definition
#000	IdNumber (of the local system)
#020	*Relation* (typically: link to the higher unit)
#030	**Content Type** (MARC 336: text, performed music, moving image)
#03g (the "g" comes from the former GMD)	**Media Type** (relating to type of equipment required, MARC 337: audio, video, unmediated)
#03s (the "s" comes from the former SMD)	**Carrier Type** (physical material substrate, MARC 338: audio disk, video disk, sheet)
#040	*Date* (of publication, production . . .)
#050	*Language* code (of textual content)
#060	*Country* code (*of publ.*)
#070	Electronic *Identifier*, normally URI
#080	Other *Identifiers* (e.g., ISBN, ISSN)

(continued)

Table 6.10. (*continued*)

Field Tag	Definition
#100	*Title*
#200	Personal names (**Creators**, **Contributors** and others)
#300	Corporate names
#360	*Publisher*
#400	*Relation* (for example, a Series title)
#500	*Subject* term (verbal)
#560	Geographic *coverage*
#600	*Subject* as Class notation
#700	*Source*
#750	Event (e.g., Conference, exhibition)
#800	*Format*
#810	Extent (e.g., pagination)
#830	SMD (carrier detail, more specific than #03s)
#860	Imprint (conventional, descriptive) and/or #360 Publisher (authority form)
#870	*Description* (Abstract, ToC)
#8r0 "r" means rights	*Rights*
#900	Local Call number. There may as well be local holdings or copy records, linked to the bib record, carrying an item call number
#9zx several application or system specific codes for z and x may be defined	Record-related metadata (e.g., #9z0 Record type) These are system specific! Not expanded here

EXAMPLES OF DIFFERENT TYPES OF NF BIBLIOGRAPHIC AND AUTHORITY RECORDS

Sample records are available for view in the *Allegro* Neutral-Format (New Format) Demo Database search screen, located at: http://www.biblio.tu-bs.de/db/a30/neutral.htm. Preformatted examples are also available at: http://www.allegro-c.de/doku/neutral/example.htm.

Records are shown in an OPAC display mode as well as in the actual NF coding, so that record tagging can be analyzed and compared to MARC records, if so desired. The display will typically not show the entire record content. It is important to realize that the format is not designed with one specific form of display in mind, like ISBD, so please do not be irritated by the displays. Display ought to be a matter of programming; logically, it ought not to be mixed up with internal formatting. This is arguably the biggest flaw of MARC: it is deeply intertwined with the obsolete LC card format. Clearly, not every field needs to be shown in a catalog display, but any field *might* be shown if found useful. The display examples given are thus *not* intrinsically tied in with the NF design.

The reader is invited to open the Neutral-Format (New Format) Demo Database, using any Internet browser, in order to review several kinds of records. Figures 6.1 through 6.5 demonstrate how to do this.

Figure 6.1
First screenshot of *allegro* Neutral-Format (New Format) Demo Database. Click on "Menu" (tab to left of "Search" tab) for the next screen. (Courtesy of B. Eversberg.)

Figure 6.2
Second screenshot of New Format database. Click on "Examples" to obtain a
list of record samples for viewing. (Courtesy of B. Eversberg.)

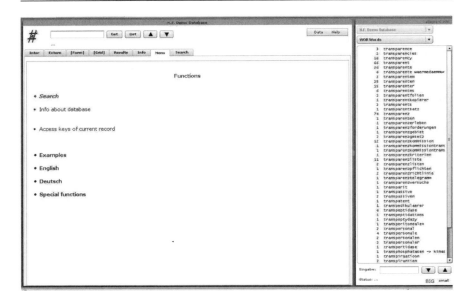

Figure 6.3
Third screenshot. Click on a desired record format or type of entity to view it in
the PAC display format of the New Format database. (Courtesy of B. Eversberg.)

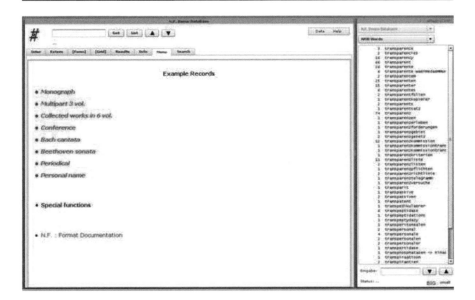

Figure 6.4
Fourth screenshot represents the PAC display of the selected monograph record example. The coded display is available by clicking on the "Inter" tab (left of "Extern" tab). (Courtesy of B. Eversberg.)

Figure 6.5
The New Format internal or coded display of the selected monograph record example (try the "Edit+" button to see a labeled display with the internal field names). (Courtesy of B. Eversberg.)

CONCLUSION

There has been a lot of talk in recent years about the necessity of improving, transcending, abandoning or even killing MARC. Not much, however, has happened. New suggestions very often focus on XML (Extensible Markup Language) as a syntactic paradigm. But although XML has been around for quite a while, we still have no convincing XML schema for bibliographic data, let alone an implementation that would demonstrate its power or efficiency. This essay and the NF design do not look toward the XML way, but rather explore a route that, while avoiding many of MARC's deficiencies, still preserves the approach that has ensured the success of MARC to this day: its economy.

The MARC economy lies in its brevity, its conciseness, its precision of expression, and in achieving this in a language-neutral way, with tag numbers and codes. This is in sharp contrast with the XML "philosophy," which is strongly based on "natural language" (meaning English). MARC has achieved what English tags couldn't have done: it has become the very language of catalogers' everyday talking the world over. The necessity of such a language must not be overlooked, and MARC has provided it. If this sounds as if we might just as well stay with MARC forever, then there are still all the flaws and historic baggage that were exposed in the first part of this essay. Eventually, sooner rather than later, something ought to be done about them. A new design, like NF, can hopefully make a contribution to this process. The full specification of NF *does* contain brief names, without spaces, for every element, which may be used in XML schemas for communication, should this be needed.

The economy of MARC must not be sacrificed, or the production of good metadata will no longer be feasible. Therefore, we may be either stuck with MARC forever, or there will eventually be reformed MARC that gets rid of historic baggage, like indicators, fixed fields, and many subfields, thereby achieving even more brevity, conciseness, and precision. The appearance will likely not be spectacularly different—as you easily perceive in the NF design—but appearance is certainly not what counts the most.

7 THE SINGLE SHARED CATALOG REVISITED

Martha M. Yee

Ten years ago, I wrote a short piece in the *ALCTS Newsletter* called "One Catalog or No Catalog?"[1] In it, I suggested that if we did not find a more efficient way of sharing the intellectual labor of authority control, we were in danger of losing our catalogs altogether. Ten years on, we can see two possible scenarios for creating a single shared catalog that we all cooperate in keeping under authority control. One is OCLC WorldCat; currently, OCLC is trying to persuade libraries to substitute OCLC access for local OPACs (Online Public Access Catalogs). The other is the nascent discussion in our field of the possibility of putting cataloging data onto the Semantic Web, connected with a new set of cataloging rules (RDA, Resource Description and Access) that claims to be RDF-ready (Resource Description Framework–ready).[2]

In this essay, I first review all the reasons why sharing a single catalog would be a good idea. Then I propose some specifications or "specs" for shared cataloging (and the resultant catalogs) in the future. Finally, I examine both OCLC WorldCat and the Semantic Web approach using RDA, enumerating the pros and cons of each approach for meeting the "specs."

BENEFITS OF THE SINGLE CATALOG APPROACH

Cataloger Efficiencies

Catalogers would no longer have to put in the time necessary to keep thousands of completely separate catalogs under authority control, nor would they have to put in the time necessary to devise and manage complicated systems of record intake and outflow, record overlay, and the like, in thousands of completely separate catalogs. It should be noted that computer algorithms for doing this kind of matching and overlaying tend to be seriously flawed and often undo the intellectual labor of catalogers by overlaying two records that are actually for different expressions, or failing to overlay two records that are actually the same manifestation.

Intellectual Work, Not Clerical Work

Catalogers, the best and the brightest of librarians, could focus their energies on intellectual work rather than clerical and managerial work. Cataloging work would become focused on entity identification and definition, i.e., on linking items to the manifestations, expressions, and works they contain; the persons and corporate bodies who created them; the subjects they discuss, illuminate, or depict; the genres or forms they exemplify; and the disciplines in which they were created. Each time such a link was made, it would be immediately available for the use of all other catalogers, thus providing further cataloger efficiencies.

More Time Available to Catalog Neglected Works

Time saved using the single shared catalog approach could allow catalogers to catalog special collections, cuts on sound recordings, poems in anthologies, journal articles, and other types of works that have been neglected or ignored in our catalogs.

Learning Efficiencies for Catalog Users

Catalog users worldwide would have to learn only one piece of catalog searching software. We could teach children in kindergarten how to search catalogs along with their ABCs, and they could use the knowledge for the rest of their lives.

More Works Linked and Available for Users

Catalog users would benefit immensely from the more efficient use of cataloger time and intelligence, since more of the world's cultural treasure would be linked into our hierarchies of works, creators, subjects, genre/forms, and disciplines.

SPECIFICATIONS (SPECS) FOR THE SHARED SINGLE CATALOG

Note that the most important prerequisite for any shared single catalog is an agreement on standards for entity definition among the catalog's constituent libraries. This is true with both methods of creating a shared single catalog: the OCLC WorldCat single catalog, or the Semantic Web approach. We need to reach global agreement on entity definition across language and cultural boundaries as much as possible for entities such as person, corporate body, work, subject, genre/form, and discipline (classification). A list of key definitions follows.

Definitions

Entity: Entity is the general term used to encompass all of the following things that could be sought in catalogs by catalog users.

Person: For person, the FRBR (Functional Requirements for Bibliographic Records[3]) definition is used, as follows:

(3.2.5): [A]n individual. . . . Encompasses individuals that are deceased as well as those that are living.[4]

Corporate Body: For corporate body, the FRBR definition is used, as follows:

(3.2.6): [A]n organization or group of individuals and/or organizations acting as a unit. . . . Encompasses organizations and groups of individuals and/or organizations that are identified by a particular name, including occasional groups and groups that are constituted as meetings, conferences, congresses, expeditions, exhibitions, festivals, fairs, etc. . . . Also encompasses organizations that act as territorial authorities, exercising or claiming to exercise government functions over a certain territory, such as a federation, a state, a region, a local municipality, etc. . . . Encompasses organizations and groups that are defunct as well as those that continue to operate.[5]

Work: For work, the FRBR definition is used, as follows:

(3.2.1): [A] distinct intellectual or artistic creation. . . . Variant texts incorporating revisions or updates to an earlier text are viewed simply as *expressions* of the same work. . . . Similarly, abridgements or enlargements of an existing text, or the addition of parts or an accompaniment to a musical composition are considered to be different *expressions* of the same work. Translations from one language to another, musical transcriptions and arrangements, and dubbed or subtitled versions of a film are also considered simply as different *expressions* of the same original work. . . .

By contrast, when the modification of a *work* involves a significant degree of independent intellectual or artistic effort, the result is viewed, for the purpose of this study, as a new *work*. Thus paraphrases, rewritings, adaptations for children, parodies, musical variations on a theme and free transcriptions of a musical composition are considered to represent new *works*. Similarly, adaptations of a *work* from one literary or art form to another (e.g., dramatizations, adaptations from one medium of the graphic arts to another, etc.) are considered to represent new *works*. Abstracts, digests and summaries are also considered to represent new *works*.[6]

Expression: For expression, the FRBR definition is used, as follows:

(3.2.2): [T]he intellectual or artistic realization of a *work* in the form of alpha-numeric, musical, or choreographic notation, sound, image, object, movement, etc., or any combination of such forms. . . . The boundaries of the entity *expression* are defined . . . so as to exclude aspects of physical form, such as typeface and page layout, that are not integral to the intellectual or artistic realization of the *work* as such. When an *expression* is accompanied by augmentations, such as illustrations, notes, glosses, etc., that are not integral to the intellectual or artistic realization of the *work*, such augmentations are considered to be separate *expressions* of their own separate *work(s)*. Such augmentations may, or may not, be considered significant enough to warrant distinct bibliographic identification. Inasmuch as the form of *expression* is an inherent characteristic of the *expression*, any change in form (e.g., from alpha-numeric notation to spoken word) results in a new *expression*. Similarly, changes in the intellectual conventions or instruments that are employed to express a *work* (e.g., translation from one language to another) result in the production of a new *expression*. If a text is revised or modified, the resulting expression is considered to be a new *expression*. Minor changes, such as corrections of spelling and punctuation, etc., may be considered as variations within the same *expression*.[7]

Manifestation: For manifestation, the FRBR definition is used, as follows:

(3.2.3): [T]he physical embodiment of an *expression* of a work. . . . As an entity, *manifestation* represents all the physical objects that bear the same characteristics, in respect to both intellectual content and physical form. . . . Whether the scope of production is broad (e.g., in the case of publication, etc.) or limited (e.g., in the case of copies made for private study, etc.), the set of copies produced in each case constitutes a *manifestation*. All copies produced that form part of the same set are considered to be copies of the same *manifestation*. The boundaries between one *manifestation* and another are drawn on the basis of both intellectual content and physical form. When the production process involves changes in physical form the resulting product is considered a new *manifestation*. Changes in physical form include changes affecting display characteristics (e.g., a change in typeface, size of font, page layout, etc.), changes in physical medium (e.g., a change from paper to microfilm as the medium of conveyance), and changes in the container (e.g., a change from cassette to cartridge as the container for a tape). Where the production process involves a publisher, producer, distributor, etc., and there are changes signaled in the product that are related to publication, marketing, etc. (e.g., a change in publisher, repackaging, etc.), the resulting product may be considered a new *manifestation*. Whenever the production process involves modifications, additions, deletions, etc., that affect the intellectual or artistic content, the result is a new *manifestation* embodying a new *expression* of the *work*.[8]

Subject: In this paper, subject is used to mean what a work is about. Thus it could potentially encompass any of the entities above, as well as concept, object, event, and place as defined in FRBR 3.2.7 to 3.2.10.

Genre/Form: In this paper, genre/form is used to mean any category that a work falls into. Examples would include novels, poetry, gangster films, or dictionaries.

Discipline (Classification): In this paper, discipline is used to refer to the perspective taken toward a particular subject in a given work. For example, the subject "water" could be discussed from the perspective of a hydrological engineer, or it could be described from the perspective of a poet.

The "specs" for a single shared catalog would include the following:

Spec 1

When a cataloger changes either an entity definition or a preferred heading for a particular entity or adds variant name access for a particular entity, it should be possible to make this change in one place rather than multiple places. In our current environment, another way to say this would be that it should be possible to change a single authority record and have the change automatically reflected in all other records that cite that particular entity, without any additional cataloger labor being necessary.

Spec 2

For any given entity, it should be possible to designate different preferred forms of heading for different languages and for different cultural settings (e.g., a public library versus a technical special library) so that computer programs can automatically supply the correct preferred forms in each different environment.

Spec 3

It should be possible to provide subject access to entities beyond works-expressions-manifestations. For example, the ideal single, shared catalog should be able to provide subject access to persons in order to allow a researcher to assemble a list of, for example, women authors of the nineteenth century who published in England, and then go from there to a list of all of the works by such authors found in the catalog. It should also be able to provide subject access to corporate bodies, to allow a researcher to assemble a list of government agencies around the world that regulate immigration, for example. Similarly, it should be able to provide subject access to proper names of geographic entities, to allow a researcher to assemble a list of lakes found in the state of Wisconsin, for example, and then go from there to a list of all works about those lakes found in the catalog.

Spec 4

When a user (or a cataloger) searches for an entity in such a way that there are multiple potential matches, it must be possible to display an alphabetical list of results consisting of the entities matched, with the list containing a single heading for each entity matched. In other words, the same entity should never appear in the list twice under two different forms of name. Ideally, this heading would be the "name commonly known" for each matched entity in the language, script, and/or transliteration desired by the user (or cataloger).

Spec 5

When a user (or a cataloger) searches for an entity using one or more keywords, all entities described by those keywords should be produced in the search results, even when the keywords appear in variant name fields for the entity, such as cross-references in authority records or variant title fields in bibliographic records. This is particularly critical for work searching. A user (or a cataloger) should be able to search for a work combining a variant name for the author and a variant title and still succeed in retrieving the work. This does not happen in any current systems.

Spec 6

All hierarchies should be made available to users (and catalogers) for exploration. These include the following:

- o Classification hierarchies
- o Broader, narrower, and related term hierarchies in subject headings
- o Cross-references to main headings (corporate names, personal names, subject headings) should be shown to any user whose search matches the variant form of the main heading plus a corporate subdivision, a subject subdivision or work title appended to a personal name, or a subject subdivision
- o Work-expression-manifestation-item hierarchies for any work, expression, manifestation or item desired by a user

Spec 7

Once a user (or a cataloger) has chosen a particular work of interest and wishes to survey the available expressions, the user or cataloger should be able to request an arrangement of the available expressions in any of the following orders or suborders:

- ○ Alphabetical by language
- ○ Alphabetical by surname of editor
- ○ Alphabetical by surname of translator
- ○ Alphabetical or numerical by edition statement
- ○ Alphabetical by publisher
- ○ By initial publication date in ascending or descending order

Spec 8

If the user (or the cataloger) interested in a particular work wishes to survey works related to that work, it should be possible for the user to request an arrangement of the available related works subgrouped by media, e.g., motion pictures based on the work, television programs based on the work, plays based on the work, etc.

For more detailed specs, please see my earlier work, *Principles for the Display of Cataloger-Created Metadata.*[9]

OCLC WORLDCAT

Unfortunately, in many ways, the choice of OCLC WorldCat as presently constituted would amount to the "no catalog" rather than the "one catalog" choice presented above, for the following reasons:

1. OCLC WorldCat is not under authority control. Many entities are represented by more than one form of heading in OCLC WorldCat.
2. Users (non-catalogers) are not even allowed access to the cross-references and scope notes found in authority records, let alone given default (or any) searches that match on authority records.
3. Users (non-catalogers) are not allowed to browse headings; only a key-word search of bibliographic records (i.e., manifestation records) is allowed.
4. It is not possible to search for a particular work using variants of both the author's name and the title, with matching being done on authority records; and then to display works matching the search query in order by work identifier (main entry).
5. The default display for large search results is, from my point of view, in "no discernible order," which OCLC inexplicably calls "relevance" order. Whatever the order is, it has no relevance to me! There is limited sorting capability as an option. However, the user must choose to sort search results either by author or by title; a work sort (main entry, author-title sort) is not an option.
6. Uniform titles are not used to organized displays.

7. In search result displays for a particular work, expressions of the work are not differentiated from works that are about that work, or works that are related to that work.
8. Users are not shown important expression information in bibliographic record displays. Part of this is OCLC's fault for truncating displays of individual records, but part of it is the fault of OCLC-contributing libraries. Many OCLC-contributing libraries (especially public libraries) operate under the theory that users just want works and aren't interested in expressions, so they leave expression-identifying information out of their cataloging records. Examples of expression-related data that is often missing from the bibliographic records themselves include illustrator, translator, and editor statements of responsibility, series, and edition statements.
9. OCLC requires that a new record be made for every manifestation change (format change or change in distribution information); the problem with this is that there is no way for a computer to tell when a new record has been made for a new expression and when it has been made for a new manifestation that is an exact copy of another manifestation in the catalog. As a further complication, OCLC now even encourages making a new record for the same manifestation of the same expression of the same work for each different language of cataloging. Paradoxically, despite this worship of the manifestation, the record-merging algorithms that are applied to the batchloading of records ignore expression and work identification data in bibliographic records to such an extent that two different expressions of the same work, or even two different works, can easily be merged.

It is a real shame that the developers of OCLC have so far failed to mine the treasure to be found in our records, particularly in our authority records, but also the expression information to be found in bibliographic records. There are signs that this might be changing. The WorldCat Identities project begins to demonstrate what OCLC could accomplish if it figured out better ways of providing users with access to authority records first (instead of the current emphasis on bibliographic records). After all, the entities of most interest to users (works, persons, corporate bodies, subjects, genre/forms, and disciplines [classification]) are all represented by authority records, not by manifestation-based bibliographic records. In this connection, it should be noted that in the list of the OCLC Top 1000[10] (the works held by the most libraries), none are single edition works by single work authors.

RDA/SEMANTIC WEB

The Semantic Web with RDA cataloging rules is the second potential method that might eventually be used to create a single shared catalog. All assertions below concerning RDA should be accompanied by the following caveat.

The last draft of RDA released for the review of the cataloging constituencies in November 2008 was subsequently modified by the JSC (Joint Steering Committee for Development of RDA) before being submitted to the publishers, and the true final draft as submitted to the publishers is currently not accessible to anyone other than the RDA developers themselves. My assertions below are based on the November 2008 draft[11] and may be inaccurate concerning the draft finally published.

The premise of the Semantic Web seems to be that we would assemble records—or, more accurately, perhaps, displays and indexes—from bits of data scattered throughout the Internet. Can this work? Is the Internet fast enough to do it? RDA seems to take it on faith that a huge increase in granularity is a good thing without any prior experimentation to demonstrate how these tinier and tinier bits of data will be reassembled into coherent displays and indexes.

It appears that RDF resists hierarchy. Hierarchy is one of our main tools for allowing users to navigate vast amounts of information efficiently. RDF-based RDA, for example, expects relationships to be demonstrated by means of one-to-one links (no hierarchy) rather than one-to-many (hierarchical) links. With our current cataloging rules (AACR2), when we catalog a parody, we link it up to the work it parodies, but we don't make a link in the opposite direction. Currently, when a person searches for the work, it is possible to display all the parodies of that work by means of this one-to-many link. In RDA, not only will we link a parody to the work parodied, we will also be required to make a link to the parody from every manifestation and expression of the work parodied that we have already cataloged. Thereafter, every subsequent manifestation and expression of that work must have a link inserted that leads to the record for the parody. This hierarchy-resistant approach is simply not efficient for either the cataloger or the catalog user.

I fear that RDF not only resists hierarchy, but may also resist the provision of ordering of elements. It is clear that RDA completely removes display from the rules. Since, from the catalog user's point of view, cataloging *is* display design, RDA seems successfully to have removed cataloging from the cataloging rules. Everything we call cataloging (effective indexing and effective displays) is pushed out of RDA and into "application" or "implementation."

I also fear that RDF resists linking related data elements, such as all of the data elements (place, publisher, date) pertaining to the publication and/or distribution of a particular manifestation, or such as the data elements (number, type of instrument) pertaining to instrumentation of musical works or arrangements. For example, we may need to associate one place of publication with the publisher and another place of publication with the distributor. In order to deal with this, RDA has become more granular, defining place of publication separately from place of distribution and place of manufacture. It now also requires that all resources be given information about publication, even those that are not published, such as motion pictures. Even with this solution, there are still problems when a piece of data is repeatable and another piece of information needs to be associated with it, as when there are two publishers, each with its own place of publication.

As another example, to express a complex instrumentation for a particular musical work, we may need to associate more than one number with more than one instrument, e.g., 2 two organs and 5 accordions (not 2 accordions and 5 organs). If number cannot be linked to type of instrument, the user interested only in music for 2 accordions might have to retrieve and look through music for some other number of accordions and 2 organs, pianos, violins, etc. RDA development constantly ran into problems caused by the inability of the RDA model to allow linking of related data elements such as these. This cannot be seen as simply a "display" concern, when failure to solve it will prevent the design of effective display. Rather, this is a concern with the model itself, which does not reflect the reality of what a catalog is, what kind of intellectual work it does, and what function it serves.

I have been assured that RDF does not prevent collecting the same piece of data in two or more different forms, e.g., a transcribed form for the publisher, a controlled form for the publisher, and a supplied note explaining something about the publisher. I am still skeptical about whether this is possible, though, partly based on the fact that RDA seems to avoid collecting the same piece of data several different ways. In fact, RDA is completely ambiguous about the function of a particular piece of data. Will this data function as a note, or will it function as an access point (i.e., a heading in an index)? We frequently cannot tell from the rules themselves. RDA's excuse is always that this is a "display" concern, and RDA does not deal with display. Because RDA does not deal with display, examples initially provided in the first drafts of RDA were unreadable and had to be converted to ISBD before any of the constituent reviewers could make any sense of them.

Can all bibliographic data be reduced to either a class or a property with a finite set of values? Can everything that catalogers do be reduced to a set of pull-down menus? Cataloging is a discursive art, a kind of descriptive writing. It is not simply the coding of data.

Skepticism is critical; we *cannot* adopt Semantic Web standards such as RDF until there have been demonstration projects that show it is possible to take RDF data and produce a catalog, with effective indexing and effective displays, according to our specs (above).

That said, the idea of converting our current shared creation of manifestation-based bibliographic records into shared creation of entity definitions (URIs, or Uniform Resource Identifiers) is very appealing. The URI for a particular entity such as a work, a person, a corporate body, a subject, a genre/form, or a discipline (classification) could then be used as a node for all variant names for that particular entity in every known language and script. This, in turn, could enable designers of indexes and displays to build in features that would allow users to select a particular language, script, even educational level or disciplinary perspective (e.g., kindergartner versus physicist), which could then determine what forms of name are preferred for that user in displays of multiple matched entities. Users could be allowed to search directly for the entities they seek, such as a particular work or a particular creator, unlike the current situation in which catalog systems force users to search for particular manifestations (no matter what their actual entity interest); and unlike the current situation, in which users' searches fail when they do not choose to search under the variants that happen to appear on a particular title page for a particular manifestation that is in the system being searched.

Perhaps we need either to adapt RDF or to spearhead a more sophisticated way to encode data on the Internet in order to create record-like structures, each with a URI, each representing an entity (works, persons, corporate bodies, subjects, genre/forms, and disciplines), and each clustering together all of the information we want to collect about that entity, including variant names. Admittedly, I'm feeling my way in the dark here, though, in an effort to provoke true RDF/Semantic Web experts to suggest solutions to the problems I'm identifying.

ADDITIONAL RDA PROBLEMS

There is one way in which RDA (and FRBR before it) imposes a rigid hierarchy that does not correspond to bibliographic reality and that, contrary to what Tom Delsey claims, I don't believe is required by RDF. Both FRBR and RDA make the assumption that each element of the bibliographic description should correspond to one and only one level of the FRBR Group 1 (work-expression-manifestation-item) hierarchy. Subsequently, adjustments had to be made to this assumption. For example, it is patently clear that a manifestation can have a different title from its expression, and an expression can have a different title from its work. The model underlying RDA is still riddled with problems due to this flawed reasoning. One example lies in the rules on relationships that assert that a film work can have a director, but only a film expression can have an editor. As another example, any data that is transcribed from a title page is linked only to manifestation, despite the fact that most of the elements of the bibliographic description were put there originally because of their value in differentiating expressions. Examples of transcribed statements and other manifestation-linked data that should be linked to expression include statements of subsidiary responsibility, such as illustrator and editor statements; edition statements, such as 2nd rev. ed.; and statements of extent, which have proven in past experiments to be one of the most reliable indicators of content change between expressions. These are all rigidly linked to manifestation, rather than expression in RDA (following FRBR's tables, which do not correspond to FRBR's own definitions of the group 1 entities). As an aside, in the latest RDA-FRBR mapping table,[12] there does seem to be some wavering with regard to extent, which is linked to "manifestation/expression," with a question mark, but in the structure of RDA itself,[13] extent is still covered in the "describing carriers" chapter.

RDA has completely turned its back on the opportunity to call for identifying entities by the name commonly known in the community of the catalog, e.g., English in the United States, Russian in Cyrillic in Russia, and Chinese in the vernacular in China. In the past, we thought we had to impose foreign names on English-speaking users in order to share our cataloging internationally, even though that practice violated the principle of using the "name commonly known." Now, however, we are closer and closer to having a linked international authority file that would allow the sharing of cataloging internationally without requiring the violation of cataloging principles. VIAF[14] (Virtual International Authority File) gathers together the authority records from many different national libraries, and links together the authority records that pertain to the same entity. Currently, its function is primarily to serve authority-control librarians, but it could potentially support a system to serve catalog users directly.

Because of this missed opportunity in RDA, U.S. users will not only have to find works by and about the KGB under the Russian name, as they do now, they may now have to find it under the Russian name in Cyrillic (depending on decisions made at the Library of Congress about "the preferred script of the agency creating the data" (RDA 9.2.2.5.3[15] and 11.2.2.12[16])). They may now have to find works by and about Mao Tse-Tung under his name in Chinese characters.

RDA does have room for rules governing subject headings, genre-form headings, and classification, but these have not yet been developed, so we can't see yet how well RDA will be able to satisfy our "specs" in this regard.

One of the main recommendations made in Toronto at the launch of the project to transform AACR2 into RDA was that RDA be designed to solve the multiple-version problem by providing at least the option of creating an expression-based record from which manifestation records could be hung. At the end of all these years of development, we can see that RDA looks exactly like AACR2 in this regard, with a manifestation-based bibliographic record containing elements that describe both manifestation and expression, and with no attempt to tease these two very different types of data apart so that computers could compose hierarchical displays of all of the expressions of a work, and all of the manifestations of an expression.

It appears that the designers of RDA have completely forgotten about the necessity for a catalog to provide the catalog searcher with lists of matched entities to browse through. The cavalier statement that the scenario 1 (relational, object-oriented database) implementation of RDA can be done with no access points whatsoever[17] implies that the problem of designing displays of multiple matched entities is being completely ignored by RDA. This kind of approach assumes that every user can design a search that produces one and only one entity. It totally ignores the reality on the ground of users with incomplete and inaccurate information, faulty memories, and vague descriptions. It completely ignores the problems we are all having now in systems like Google that produce millions of hits and then cannot organize these hits into any useful order. For this reason, the specs in this paper prominently require the ability to create ordered displays of multiple entities using names commonly known. For both OCLC and RDA to ignore this user need is scandalous.

CHANGE OF NAME IS CHANGE OF IDENTITY?

I'd also like to raise the following question: Our current principle is that "change of name is change of identity." Recent changes in pseudonym rules (via LCRI (Library of Congress rule interpretation) 22.2 and RDA itself) are fragmenting the person entity further and further. There is no research to indicate that this principle corresponds to the way library users perceive the entities they seek, and much anecdotal evidence suggests that it runs counter to their perceptions. Show me a biography or corporate history that is about a "bibliographic identity" rather than being about a person or corporate body across any name changes that might have occurred (e.g., marriage, change in stage name, trial-and-error attempt to create a more distinctive pseudonym, change in corporate name over time, etc.).

Of equal importance, this principle surely makes it more difficult to share entity definition across language and other cultural boundaries. There is no guarantee that a change of name in one language will be mirrored in every other language. If we want to let users choose language and script, surely it would be more efficient and more logical to group all variant names for an entity together and then characterize them as to language, script, user community, etc.

The reason behind the principle was never user need (other than the temporary convenience of public library users who don't want to be bothered by having to know about the writer behind a pseudonym on a work of pulp fiction), but was always for the convenience of the cataloger. Ironically, online systems already automatically provided users with the ability to search under the forms of name on title pages, since the default search in most online systems is a keyword search of bibliographic records. Instead of using authority records and uniform headings in bibliographic records to provide an alternative kind of access that collocated works regardless of forms of name on the title page, we foolishly decided to duplicate the effect of title page keyword searching in our authority records. The excuse was that users interested in collocation could use the "see also" references in authority records to carry out collocation. However, most current systems never provide users with access to authority records or to the "see also" references at all. Thus, collocation of all of the works of a given author is removed as an option from most current systems.

In order to have a future, it is crucial that we libraries differentiate ourselves from Google, Amazon.com, and similar commercial outfits. We offer intellectual lumping (gathering together and ordering) of everything having to do with a given entity, as opposed to Google's and Amazon's destructive splitting of everything under the language used in the documents indexed.[18] This gathering and ordering function is one of the primary things we have to offer society. If we start splitting in imitation of Google, we are offering no added value, and we are much more expensive.

If we maintain the transcription principle, it ought always to be possible to use free text searching to search for forms of name on items, leaving entity records free to group everything by or about an entity together regardless of form of name on particular items. Perhaps it is time to reexamine this principle?

WHAT WILL WE NEED TO AGREE ON IN ORDER TO SHARE A SINGLE VIRTUAL CATALOG?

I would say that much of the current chaos evident in OCLC is due to our inability to agree on common standards for naming and identifying works, expressions, and manifestations. Although we do have standards for naming works that are either anonymous classics or works of single personal authorship, other works are not consistently named. The object of a bibliographic record, which in the nineteenth century would have been an expression, in the twentieth century became either a manifestation or an expression, without much theoretical consideration on our part.

Some of those in our field who welcome the Semantic Web seem to think that it will be enough just to throw bits of data onto the Internet. I don't see how this can work to create the hierarchical displays our users need unless the bits of data are rigorously tied to FRBR entity levels. In order to share a single virtual catalog, surely we will need to agree with each other on entity definition. In the past, our de facto entity definition could be deduced by our practices regarding the object of a record. Most of the FRBR entities are represented by authority records (works, persons, corporate bodies, concepts, objects, events, places). The object of a bibliographic record, which used to be an expression, became willy-nilly the manifestation in the twentieth century, when various reproductive techniques became common. Semantic Web designers insist that records will not exist on the Semantic Web. If that is the case, I fail to see what the bits of data on the Semantic Web can cluster around if not the FRBR entities. What are catalog users seeking in the Semantic Web if not bibliographic entities such as authors, works, and works on a subject? What will we display to them if not clusters of data that represent a sought entity? If the Semantic Web allows us to do that more effectively than we have been doing heretofore, I doubt we will regret the loss of the "record." It may even have the salutary effect of refocusing catalogers' and system designers' attention on the entities users are most interested in (works, authors, and subjects) and away from the entities that have dominated our attention heretofore (physical manifestations acquired, paid for, and shelved in libraries). In effect, the display to the user of the data pertaining to the entity of interest will become the record. If we cannot agree on entity definitions that match the entity definitions of our users, however, it is hard to see how we can provide any kind of coherent display of these bits of data to our users.

In addition, in order to provide users with browsable displays of all of the entities that match their search queries, surely we will also need to agree on names commonly known in the different language and cultural contexts from which catalog users come. Otherwise, we will not be able to provide a name for each entity matched in the form of a browsable list.

CONCLUSION

I believe society will benefit immeasurably from having one catalog to search, as opposed to having no catalog to search. The benefit will be considerably weakened if that one catalog is not a good catalog, however. We library catalogers have more than a century of experience with cooperating. Surely we could cooperate to devise electronic solutions to the problem of building a single user-friendly virtual catalog over the Internet, the maintenance of which we could then share.

NOTES

1. Martha M. Yee, "Viewpoints: One Catalog or No Catalog?" *ALCTS Newsletter* 10, no. 4 (1999):13–17, http://repositories.cdlib.org/postprints/3084/ (accessed May 11, 2010).

2. Martha M. Yee, "Can Bibliographic Data Be Put Directly Onto the Semantic Web?" *Information Technology and Libraries* 28, no. 2 (2009): 55–80, http://repositories.cdlib.org/postprints/3369 (accessed May 11, 2010).

3. International Federation of Library Associations and Institutions (IFLA), "Functional Requirements for Bibliographic Records: Final Report, as Amended and Corrected through February 2009" (n.p.: IFLA, 2009), http://www.ifla.org/files/cataloguing/frbr/frbr_2008.pdf (accessed May 10, 2010).

4. Ibid., 25.

5. Ibid., 25–26.

6. Ibid., 17–18.

7. Ibid., 19–20.

8. Ibid., 21–22.

9. Martha M. Yee, "Principles for the Display of Cataloger-Created Metadata, February 15, 2002 Draft," http://www.slc.bc.ca/yee.pdf http://slc.bc.ca/yee.pdf

10. "OCLC Top 1000," www.oclc.org/research/top1000/default.htm (accessed May 10, 2010).

11. "RDA: Full Draft, 11/24/08," RDA: Resource Description & Access Toolkit, RDA Constituency Review, http://www.rdatoolkit.org/constituencyreview (accessed May 5, 2010).

12. "RDA to FRBR Mapping, 5JSC/RDA/RDA to FRBR Mapping/ Rev/3, 1 July, 2009," http://www.rda-jsc.org/docs/5rda-rdafrbrmappingrev3.pdf (accessed May 10, 2010).

13. " RDA Prospectus, 5JSC/RDA/Prospectus/Rev/7, 1 July, 2009," http://www.rda-jsc.org/docs/5rda-prospectusrev7.pdf (accessed May 10, 2010).

14. "VIAF: the Virtual International Authority File," http://www.viaf.org (accessed May 10, 2010). See also Janifer Gatenby, "Identifiers and GLIMIR. OCLC Symposium for Publishers and Librarians, 18 March 2009," http://www.oclc.org/multimedia/2009/files/GatenbyJ-Identifiers_GLIMIR.pdf (accessed November 10, 2009).

15. "RDA: Full Draft, 11/24/08," "9. Identifying Persons. 9.2. Name of Person. 9.2.2. Preferred Name for the Person. 9.2.2.5. Different Forms of the Same Name. 9.2.2.5.3. Names Written in a Non-Preferred Script," 10.

16. Ibid., "11. Identifying Corporate Bodies. 11.2. Name of the Corporate Body. 11.2.2. Preferred Name for the Corporate Body. 11.2.2.12. Transliteration," 21.

17. Association for Library Collections and Technical Services, Cataloging and Classification Section, Committee on Cataloging: Description and Access, "Minutes of the Meeting held at the 2008 ALA Midwinter Meeting in Philadelphia, Pennsylvania, January 11, 12, and 14, 2008," http://www.libraries.psu.edu/tas/jca/ccda/docs/min0801.pdf (accessed May 10, 2010).

18. "Lumpers and Splitters," Wikipedia, http://en.wikipedia.org/wiki/Lumpers_and _splitters (accessed May 10, 2010).

8 ROLE OF THE ILS AND HOW LIBRARIES WILL PURCHASE AND MAINTAIN THEIR SYSTEMS, INCLUDING INFORMATION FROM A VENDOR PERSPECTIVE

Scott Piepenburg

Books, computers, librarians. We take all three for granted in today's modern library, and while there are still some libraries, mostly school and smaller rural libraries, that have no automation system, the integrated library system (ILS) is as much a part of our library operations as the reference desk or the coffee bar in the lobby. For the most part, we don't pay any attention to the library system until it goes down, is updated with new and strange features we don't understand, or it doesn't give us the information we want when we want it. The term "systems librarian" more often than not refers to a computer professional, one who is more "computer geek" than librarian. This is a switch from just a few years ago, when the "systems librarian" was frequently a cataloger pressed into service to "take care" of the library system, or, as they have been called, "the accidental system administrator."

This article is not intended to be a comprehensive history of library automation; others, such as Marshall Breeding, have thoroughly covered that ground. However, if we are to look ahead at what the future may bring, then we need to look back. It is always dangerous to try to predict the future, and no attempt will be made here to divine what the future holds for library systems; rather than looking at the technology and computers of the future (which would be a lot of fun since I'm a firm believer that biological computers will someday overtake electronic computers), let's take a look at what the future holds for the automation business, for libraries, and most importantly, for our funding agencies.

Library automation is a relatively simple activity. At the 2008 TLC (The Library Corporation) user's conference (LiSA) held in Charleston, South Carolina, Tim Heishman, vice-president of operations for TLC, said that when he came to TLC, he could not understand what was so hard about library automation—books were checked out, and then checked back in. What's hard about that? At a staff meeting in my own district a year ago when we were discussing library automation, our departmental webmaster couldn't understand why our ILS was so expensive. "It's nothing that a simple SQL (Structured Query Language) database couldn't do. It would take me just a few days to create it." A former roommate of mine who was a programmer and had just started with Follett Software, the automation company I used to work for, was mortified by this "MARC" (Machine-Readable Cataloging) thing that libraries used; how inconvenient, dated, and inflexible it was. The first automation system I was exposed to had a field of twenty-four characters for the title of the book, the ISBN, and a barcode; it was designed to run on an Apple IIe and used floppies for storage. Really wealthy libraries, or libraries with large collections, dispensed with the floppies and used "siders," 5 or 10K hard drives that attached to the computer.

Of course, large universities had long since adopted much more powerful systems. Large mainframes and the advent of time-sharing had enabled libraries to tap the power of the university's computer center for library automation. Working with staff programmers, many colleges and universities developed their own systems. Two such systems, one developed at Virginia Tech and another at Northwestern University, evolved into commercially viable systems, VTLS and NOTIS, respectively. Others saw these systems and, rather than develop their own, offered to purchase the software and share in their development; the age of the commercial ILS vendor was born. Other companies, seeing the large base of nonautomated libraries, entered the fray. Even the cataloging powerhouse OCLC offered its LS2000 stand-alone system. On the small system side, Follett spun off their product from the book company division, which was initially designed to help sell more books. Mandarin, a Canadian company, entered the market, and some "purpose-driven" companies, those dedicated exclusively to library automation systems, like DRA, offered systems. Not content with what was out there, some colleges continued to develop their own systems (no doubt a little ego was involved in some of these decisions).

This was the heyday of library automation. Companies were aggressively competing with one another for the next sale, demonstrating the next great thing, each vendor staking out its areas of expertise; VTLS and NOTIS courted the academic world, DRA was big in the public library market, and Follett and Winnebago focused on the school market. Of course, each vendor had customers outside of their niche, but the respective products were developed for their target market. A lot of "making it up as we go along" was occurring, with some vendors perplexed by terminology when they ventured outside their target market. During a visit to DRA in the early 1990s, a data technician there asked me, confidentially, what the heck "microlif" was and why it was on floppy discs instead of 9-track tape. It seems that they were bidding on a consortial contract which included some school libraries, libraries that received their cataloging from vendors on floppy disks in the new "microlif" format.

As with all products, the market started to mature. Vendors, which for so long had been making money off of their retrospective conversion operations (a labor-intensive but very profitable operation if managed properly), now were faced with the task of supporting, developing, and enhancing their product with support fee revenues. One company, Biblio-Techniques Library and Information Systems (BLIS), attempted to take the Washington (and later Western) Library Network system, drop it onto the ADABAS database management system, and develop it as an "open" system. The plan was to take the best that was offered by the various vendors in the business and tie them all together into the ultimate system. Library literature from the 1980s and early 1990s discuss this idea, called the X.12 protocol—a seven-layer concept that encompassed everything from cataloging, to circulation, to OPAC and acquisitions. In X.12-compliant systems, a customer could select the acquisitions module from one vendor, the cataloging module from another, and the circulation module from a third, and rest assured that they would all seamlessly work together. This promised to break down the "lock" that a vendor had on a system, a "take it all or leave it all" approach.

While elegant and attractive in concept, it never came to fruition. There were many reasons, but two were that vendors could not agree on data standards (presaging some of the Z39.50 problems) and that vendors were hesitant to "unbundle" their products. Even with "standards," there are various "flavors" of standards. Z39.50, while a "standard," came with its own set of problems, just as federated search engines would face the problems of searching multiple databases and multiple indexing schemes. Still, others continued to dream of being able to take the best of the different systems and integrate them together, or at the very least, getting a system custom-written for their needs at costs that were closer to "volume" pricing.

Consolidation ultimately occurred. Sirsi purchased DRA and then Dynix, Follett purchased Winnebago, and TLC purchased CARL. To the outside observer, it seemed like a slam-dunk market; create a simple database product, check items out and in, offer some search options, and wait for the money to roll in. As we have seen, the perception is different from the reality. There was always a desire for one more feature, one more function, more reports, more screen displays, and new functionality. There was no pot of gold at the end of the rainbow, as companies such as Ameritech (one of the early regional Bell operating companies, or RBOC) discovered before selling off their ownership in Dynix.

Today, many would consider the library automation business a "mature" industry. Some libraries are into their third- or fourth-generation system, and vendors are working hard to hold on to their established customer base while trying to develop the next great thing—vying to be the information portal to the world. New companies are advancing themselves as an alternative method for information discovery. Federated search was heralded as the next best thing, something that everyone would want, until we looked behind the curtain and saw that the wizard was not all that powerful, and that he had his shortcomings, too. Automation vendors responded by attempting to place their products as information portals. Products like SirsiRooms offered users a directed, focused search product; TLC has integrated multiple database searching into its PAC through negotiated licensing agreements; Follett has offered database enrichment to validated and maintained Web sites; while other vendors have moved into the area of content management.

Initially, networks were a new and awe-inspiring thing. In the early 1990s, the Dallas Independent School District (Dallas ISD) created a shared bibliographic database of over 200 schools; every student had equal and consistent access at any school, a boon to education and bibliographic instruction. In Wisconsin, the idea of federated systems took off, with users able to go to any library in the federation to check out and return items seamlessly. Indiana offered shared networking via a hosted system; libraries no longer had to have staff dedicated to the system, as a central network system administrator and management structure would take care of the system. Many of these networks only hinted at the possibility of resource sharing. With the advent of the Internet and a new crop of budding programmers, the game changed again.

At its inception, the Internet was predicated on sharing. Some of the first functions developed were intended to move files, or programs, around, such as the file transfer protocol, or FTP. A new type of computer geek or programmer was emerging. These people did not have the baggage of mainframe systems, of file structures, or of batch programs. The new game in town was to write a program that did something, *anything*, and then go on a bulletin board and tell everyone how cool it was. If anyone was interested, he or she would download and use it, maybe making some changes to it if they felt it could be improved, and then *they* would make it available to others, and the cycle would continue. "Shareware" and "freeware" was the new thing. Libraries could be a part of this new concept by buying software that they could circulate to patrons who could take it home, load it onto their computers, and do what they would with it. Even new operating systems, such as Linux, became "open" to all, with the code freely shared to anyone who wanted to use it. Some enterprising people would take some of these products, package them, and sell them to less computer-savvy people, offering "technical support" or help desk functions if required; all for a fee, of course.

Ultimately, this new wave of thinkers turned their attention to the library world. To them, library automation seemed fairly straightforward: create a database of information that you could search. "MARC" and "cataloging" and "OPAC" were foreign words to them; they would create a database structure, plug in information, and then see what they could do with it. Some libraries leveraged the skills of these people to create a "homegrown" system; if something went wrong or they wanted a new feature, they would ask "the kid" to take care of it. "The kid" was frequently a student at a college or vocational-technical school, or just some "geeky" person in the community who thought it was kind of fun to write software—that, and getting first crack at the books or the promise of a few bucks for each project. For the most part, these systems were simple and served their purpose. They couldn't import MARC records, but who cared? Users could search the database, administration could keep track of items, and there was very little expense.

In 2005, Tim Spaulding developed LibraryThing, which Wikipedia describes as "a social cataloging web application for storing and sharing personal library catalogs."[1] Now everyone can be a cataloger/librarian and share their collection with the world at no cost (for up to 200 items). The library catalog was no longer the domain of the educated professional librarian, and now everyone could be their own librarian, describing items as they saw fit and, more importantly, seeing who else had collections like their own.

Just before the turn of the century, an open-source product, Koha, was made available to the world. The idea was that a user could take the software, download it, install it, and have his or her very own library system. It was not geared toward the individual as LibraryThing was, but it utilized servers and more formal programming to be considered a full library system. In 2005, LibLime was established to support Koha. What sets the idea of open-source software apart from the traditional model is that anyone with the requisite skills is free to create whatever changes or add-ons they want, provided that they have the skills to do so. The concept was to free the library from the whims or restrictions of the vendor and allow each site to make the product "their own." Users were encouraged to share their developments with "the community" so that all could benefit from the work of someone else, thereby spreading the costs. For those projects and enhancements of a larger scope, such as MARC record support, a library or group of libraries could sponsor development of a particular feature, which would then be shared with the community as a whole.

Large consortiums and state agencies started taking notice. In an era of reduced funding, it now became feasible for the state or other funding agency to buy "the package" for its members and then offer whatever support or development was needed through its own in-house staff. As with any centrally operated process, there was a loss of local control, but to some this was fine as they were freed from the maintenance, and cost, of an ILS. Georgia is well known for its PINES project, which is still one of the largest open-source projects around. Indiana is moving toward an open-source solution, and Wisconsin is considering it for all the state-supported schools. Not all are happy with this, as the director of one of the state schools shared with me during a conversation; they fear that if the product is purchased by the state and mandated to all sites, then the two largest schools in the state will drive development and functionality of the system, since they will have the programmers.

While it would seem that open source is the perfect solution, there are a few misconceptions. On May 8, 2009, Gar Sydnor, senior vice president of TLC, posted an open letter on the company's list about open source, with the facts and fallacies, and some things for libraries to consider before going that route. Most importantly, while the software may be free, there are installation, data migration, training, and maintenance costs. If one has qualified people on staff, then that may be all well and good; but how long will it take, what are the implications for users, and just how functional will the end product be? "Free" may be "free" to get the software, but maintenance and development over the long term are other issues entirely. One school district in Texas went with an open-source solution to save money. Save money they did, but at the tradeoff of functionality and development. When our district (Dallas ISD) went out to bid on a new ILS, we received only three bids, none of which offered an open-source solution. One can speculate as to the reason, but it is possible that the RFP (Request for Proposal) process may have been a bit daunting for them. Most importantly, before going down the open-source path, users should be fully cognizant of what they are getting into in terms of short-term and long-term costs. Mr. Sydnor of TLC, mentioned above, encouraged libraries to make their state library systems aware that TLC could beat open-source costs over the long haul, and that any statewide vendor selection process should be open, transparent, and competitive. This was posted to the company's knowledgebase on May 8, 2009, and is entitled "TLC and Open Source software." It was also posted to the company's discussion list, but both are internal documents.

Talking with vendors, I can see a new model emerging, one that uses the concepts of open source married to the dream of X.12. For a specified amount of money, a library can select various functions. This should not be confused with modules, such as a booking module, an acquisition module, etc. These options would be much more granular. For example, a library may opt for cataloging, circulation, and OPAC modules, and within each of those modules, they could select up to twenty-five or so features from a list; if you want twenty-six, then the cost would go up. Obviously, this would place a new challenge on software companies to develop software that can be integrated to such a level, but given time and programmers, anything is possible. As Tim Spalding noted during a presentation at the 2008 ALA Annual Conference in Anaheim, as long as the programmer is paid, you can get whatever is desired in your library system, Web page, or database. One legacy vendor, Innovative Interfaces, uses incremental charges based on how many indexes you wish; this is only an extension of that concept. Perhaps this will create a community of "haves" and "have-nots," and some libraries may never get the functionality or features they desire (short of paying a custom programming fee if the vendor doesn't think it is marketable to large enough base of customers), but the model does permit a library to get a system and support at a price they feel is affordable, with the tradeoff of some functionality.

Honestly, if one thinks about it, how much of your ILS's capabilities do you actually use? Why pay for functionality and features that are of no interest to you? SirsiDynix uses the "voting" model of software development, but even then, they have been known to say that they cannot provide a particular feature since it would mean altering the baseline code. In the 1960s, we saw the unbundling of hardware, operating systems, and software. In the very near future, we may see vendors unbundling their own products, allowing a user to select the functionality they want, or can afford. No doubt open-source concepts will play a role in this, and the modularity of its concept becomes even more critical to the business model. Some ILS vendors currently use "off-the-shelf" utilities to accomplish programming and functionality goals; agility and selectivity will be the name of the game in the future. Which legacy systems can adapt to this model, and whether open-source vendors will be agile enough to respond to that threat, remains to be seen. Perhaps in response to this new competitive model and pressure there will be a "Liblime clients only" version of Koha, a process called "lockin and a fork." Only those customers who pay a development fee will have access to company-sponsored or tested enhancements; no pay, no play. The "sharing" is gone for some; you get a few of the enhancements, but if someone paid for it, you don't get it unless you also pay for it, very similar to the "legacy" model. For more on this topic, Roy Tennant has written an interesting analysis of what this bodes for libraries.[2]

So, back to the future: what does this mean for us as librarians? In my opinion, I think we will see new products come more quickly from companies using agile development processes, and the "waterfall" release model (where one gets a big enhancement and update package at infrequent intervals) will be a thing of the past as libraries will now have more but smaller upgrades and enhancements during the year instead of one or two big upgrades every twelve to eighteen months. Prices may not fall, but they will become steadier. Vendors will be looking for either long-term commitments so that they can amortize development costs over the long term, or they may offer short-term, pay-as-you-go options so that libraries can get what they want, when they want it. There will be no model that is correct for everyone; the marketplace will be certain to reward those who develop a product that works at an affordable price, and penalize those who don't respond to market conditions. This is called free market, and it's a great thing for libraries.

NOTES

1. "LibraryThing," Wikipedia, http://en.wikipedia.org/wiki/LibraryThing (accessed May 7, 2010).

2. Roy Tennant, "LibLime to the Koha Community: Fork You!" Digital Libraries blog, in Libraryjournal.com (Sept. 15, 2009), http://www.libraryjournal.com/blog/1090000309/post/1050048905.html (accessed May 7, 2010).

III THE CATALOGING WORLD IN TRANSITION

Catalog and Metadata Librarian: A Foot in Both Worlds
Lynnette M. Fields

Facing a Time of Change
Halvard (Hal) Cain

Judgment and Imagination: Carrying Cataloging Through Times of Change
Jay Weitz

Cataloger Survival in a Sea of Change and a Surfeit of Acronyms
John F. Myers

Changing Mind-set, Changing Skill Set: Transitioning from Cataloger to Metadata Librarian
Christine Schwartz

Realities of Standards in the Twenty-first Century
James Weinheimer

9 CATALOG AND METADATA LIBRARIAN: A FOOT IN BOTH WORLDS

Lynnette M. Fields

Catalog librarians are trained to make description and access decisions about materials and information. Currently, these decisions are based on the Anglo-American Cataloguing Rules, second edition (AACR2) and MARC21. Metadata librarians also make description and access decisions, and even though the decisions are based on different standards, they require some of the same thought processes. This essay will focus on the challenges I faced as a long-time cataloger transitioning into a metadata librarian, while retaining catalog librarian responsibilities. It can be difficult doing both, especially when dealing with the unfamiliar procedures and the proliferating standards involved in creating metadata, but there are also advantages. A strong understanding of the basic concepts of cataloging can be very helpful when trying to learn the basic concepts of metadata creation; and understanding metadata creation can inspire a cataloger to take a look at traditional cataloging workflows with a different eye.

My experience as a cataloger encompasses over twenty-five years. This tenure includes ten years managing a cataloging department, teaching cataloging as an adjunct instructor and as a cataloging trainer for a private company that provides MARC training, software, and database processing services for catalogers, libraries, and library vendors. Throughout my career, I have kept up with cataloging standards and cataloged materials in all formats.

In January 2009, I began my current position as a catalog and metadata librarian at Southern Illinois University–Edwardsville (SIUE), a medium-sized Midwestern university. The primary responsibilities of the job are original and adaptive metadata creation and cataloging in all formats, including serials, utilizing OCLC, CONTENTdm Digital Collection Management Software and Voyager, focusing on serials, nonprint, and special-format materials. While confident of my cataloging skills, I approached the metadata aspect of the new position with trepidation. Dublin Core and metadata workshops provided a cursory introduction to the subject but I had only ever cataloged using AACR2 and MARC.

SIUE first began thinking about creating digital collections in 2007, and hired their first catalog and metadata librarian that same year. She, too, had no metadata experience, and had to learn everything on her own. Her expertise proved invaluable in my efforts. One of the first things I did to kick-start my journey toward becoming a metadata librarian was to take Steven Miller's online course, "Metadata for Digital Collections."[1] The course provided a firm foundation on metadata, but more importantly, it helped me begin to build my "metadata vocabulary." When you begin your cataloging career, you must learn "cataloger-speak," or how to think and speak AACR2 and MARC. The same holds true with creating metadata. Until a librarian has a firm grasp of "metadata-speak," it's very difficult to understand the core concepts involved, or even to be able to vocalize questions.

As a cataloger, I catalog something that already exists. As a metadata librarian, I often have to create the collection before addressing the metadata needs. High-quality digital collections don't just happen; they require careful planning and collaboration among subject specialists, metadata librarians, and digitization specialists, from the moment a project is identified to the day that the collection is finally unveiled to the public. Working with a digitization specialist, I help make important digitizing decisions from the very beginning of a project (e.g., on the method of scanning, and the types of files and names of files to be used). The more planning that is done at the beginning, the smoother the entire process will be, and the better the finished product will be.

Again, as a cataloger, I begin with deciding "what" I am describing. Under current AACR2 rules, that description represents a carrier (e.g., a book or a video recording). As a metadata librarian, I have to describe both the carrier (e.g., the digital photograph) and the content of the carrier (e.g., an architectural feature that is the "purpose" of the photograph). The cataloging rules (and sometimes even more importantly, the underlying *principles* of the cataloging rules) are used to provide the information to describe the digital carrier.

However, when dealing with metadata, I am on my own when it comes to figuring out what information to provide about the details of the content of the carrier. This is where working with the person who has proposed a digitization project and with subject specialists is very important, because these experts often have a specific vision for their project. As the project metadata librarian, it is my job to interview and brainstorm with those experts until we can, together, identify and organize the elements of metadata information that will make their vision a reality.

As a cataloger, once I decide "what" it is that I am describing, AACR2 provides a comprehensive guide for describing the thing, and providing access points for that description. As a metadata librarian, I also provide bibliographic description elements (e.g., title, creator, publication information). That bibliographic information is then enhanced with specific information about the "carrier," such as type and format of the image, date digitized, etc.

One of the first decisions to be made when beginning a new digital project is the level of description and subject analysis. The CONTENTdm software allows for three different levels of description and access: collection level, object level, and page level. At the collection level, descriptive information, subject terms, and other access points are applied uniformly to all of the objects in the digital collection. At the object level, I supply different descriptive information, subject terms, and other access points that apply to each of the objects in the collection. Finally, at the page level, I supply the descriptive information, subject terms, and other access points that might apply only to specific portions (or pages) that make up the object. In traditional cataloging, we make those same types of decisions (i.e., cataloging something as a collection, or analyzing each resource within the collection, or cataloging something as a serial or a monographic series). As a metadata librarian, I have been able to apply my understanding of cataloging principles to the concept of providing data about a collection, and its contents, at the three different levels.

As a cataloger, I know exactly the tool that I am going to use to store my bibliographic information in—a computer record to be used in a library catalog: MARC 21. As a metadata librarian, I have a plethora of metadata structure standards from which to choose: Dublin Core, MODS (Metadata Object Description Schema), METS (Metadata Encoding and Transmission Standard), VRA (Visual Resources Association Core Categories), etc. Choices also have to be made between different software for digital text and image storage and access, metadata creation, and the Web interface functionality that will make the digital collection searchable, browsable, and navigable by users. Some institutions choose to create their metadata in a program such as Microsoft Access and link it to a searchable Web interface using something like Adobe ColdFusion.[3] Other institutions choose "out-of-the-box" solutions, such as CONTENTdm, that provides modules for both metadata creation and a Web interface. As a member of CARLI (Consortium of Academic and Research Libraries in Illinois), we did not have to make these decisions at SIUE because CONTENTdm had already been chosen by the consortium. CONTENTdm provides for digital text and image storage, metadata creation, and Web-interface functionality; is an all-in-one package; and does not require programming knowledge. Although CONTENTdm is not very flexible and does not allow for much customization (beyond the choice of the labels for our metadata fields), for us, the benefits of a stable product that doesn't require programming knowledge, and the support we get from CARLI, far outweigh its weaknesses.

As a cataloger, I have had to learn how to read and comprehend the sometimes convoluted documentation provided for our cataloging rules (AACR2) and coding standards (MARC 21). As a metadata librarian, this ability to understand complex documentation has definitely helped me to be able to read and interpret the Dublin Core (DC) documentation (the metadata scheme used by CONTENTdm).

One of the primary goals of the DC creators was to make the standard as uncomplicated as possible. Every DC field is repeatable and optional. Many of the DC fields (e.g., Title, Subject, Language, Creator, Publisher, Contributor, etc.) have direct correlations with traditional cataloging fields, and are easily understood by an experienced cataloger. Some DC fields (e.g., Date and Coverage) contain information that is also provided in traditional cataloging, but in a different way. For a mapping of MARC to DC see http://www.loc.gov/marc/marc2dc.html.[4] The tricky part is remembering that we are providing metadata at the three levels mentioned previously (collection, object, page) and so might need more than one type of DC date field. For example, one Date field in a project might refer to the date of the content (at the "page" level), and another date might be the date an object was digitized (at the "object" level). It is also very important that information is labeled clearly in the public interface so that users can easily understand the difference between the meanings of the contents of different fields with similar names. Moreover, because each metadata project is different, the naming conventions we use for one project may or may not be appropriate in the next project. This impacts consistency across projects.

As a cataloger, I enter my bibliographic information (as instructed by AACR2) into designated fields (as instructed by MARC 21) and leave it to the OPAC (Online Public Access Catalog) designers to design how the data will display and index in my OPAC. As a metadata librarian, I have to decide, for each project, what information to provide, the fields to use for that information, and the indexing rules and display rules for those fields.

I'm going to use two of the digital collections that have been created at SIUE to illustrate the kinds of decisions a metadata librarian must make about the fields required for a digital project. The Louis H. Sullivan Ornaments digital collection features digitized photographs of selected Sullivan architectural ornaments that are owned by SIUE, accompanied by digitized historic photographs of the buildings that the ornaments came from. This collection may be viewed at http://collections.carli.illinois.edu/cdm4/index_sie_arch.php?CISOROOT=/sie_arch. The KMOX Popular Sheet Music digital collection contains popular works that are in the public domain, dating from the early twentieth century. This collection may be viewed at http://collections.carli.illinois.edu/cdm4/index_sie_kmox.php?CISOROOT=/sie_kmox

Figure 9.1 shows a table from CONTENTdm illustrating our indexing and display decisions for the Sullivan ornament collection. Figure 9.2 shows the CONTENTdm user interface display for the Sullivan collection that is the result of the decisions made in the table shown in Figure 9.1. Figure 9.3 shows a table from CONTENTdm illustrating our indexing and display decisions for the KMOX sheet music collection. Figure 9.4 shows the CONTENTdm user interface display for the KMOX collection that is the result of the decisions made in the table shown in Figure 9.3.

Although Qualified Dublin Core fields are used as the underlying fields for both of these collections, the field labels for public display are very different. This is because the contents of an architectural ornament collection and a sheet music collection are very different, so it is very nice to be able to customize the public displays to bring out the important aspects of each collection. In our

Figure 9.1
Collection field properties table from CONTENTdm for the Louis H. Sullivan Ornaments digital collection. (©2010, OCLC CONTENTdm screen capture used with permission from OCLC. CONTENTdm is a registered trademark of OCLC Online Computer Library Center, Inc.)

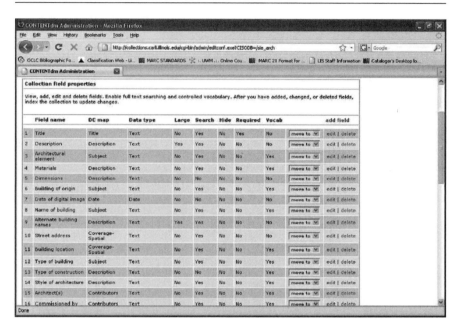

current OPACs, we cannot get this level of public display customization. For example, one library might decide to use the public label "Performer" for the MARC21 field 511 (Participant or Performer Note), and another library might decide to use "Cast"; but the chosen label will display for every 511 field in the OPAC for each library. Sometimes this works—e.g., for the video recording *Last of the Mohicans*, this makes perfect sense:

> Performer: Daniel Day-Lewis (Hawkeye), Madeleine Stowe (Cora), Jodhi May (Alice), Russell Means (Chingachgook), Wes Studi (Magua).

But for the audiobook, *Last of the Mohicans*, it does not make quite as much sense:

> Performer: Read by William Costello.

I wish that we had the ability to customize fields by format type in our OPACs, so that a MARC field could display with different labels depending on the type of material being described. However, as a metadata librarian, I wish that there

Figure 9.2
Metadata for a building image in the Louis H. Sullivan Ornaments digital collection. (©2010, Southern Illinois University Edwardsville. Used with permission. CONTENTdm screen capture used with permission from OCLC. CONTENTdm is a registered trademark of OCLC Online Computer Library Center, Inc.)

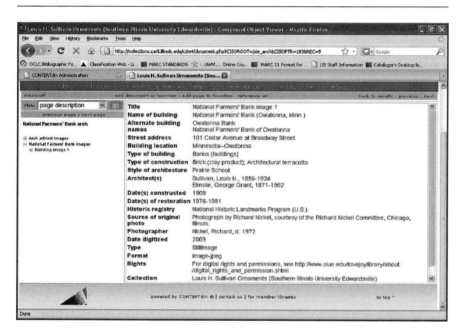

was more consistency in the choice of fields that librarians use for different projects yet similar collections.

In the Sullivan project, the DC field "Subject" did not provide us with the level of granularity that we needed, so we split that DC field into four more specific fields: "Architectural element," "Building of origin," "Name of building," and "Type of building" as shown in Figure 9.1. For the KMOX project, "Subject" was the appropriate term, so we didn't need to do any customization of the DC field for that project. As a cataloger, I sometimes feel that it would be good if we could add more granularity to the existing fields we use in a MARC record, but I also appreciate the consistency of always knowing what each MARC field will contain.

Note the column labeled "Vocab" in Figure 9.1. That column designates whether or not a controlled vocabulary is used for each field in the table. Notice that several of the descriptive fields (e.g., "Materials," "Type of construction" and "Style of architecture") use controlled vocabularies. According to ANSI/NISO (American National Standards Institute/National Information Standards) standard Z39.19-2005, "The primary purpose of vocabulary control is to

Figure 9.3
Collection field properties table from CONTENTdm for the KMOX Popular Sheet Music digital collection. (©2010, OCLC CONTENTdm screen capture used with permission from OCLC. CONTENTdm is a registered trademark of OCLC Online Computer Library Center, Inc.)

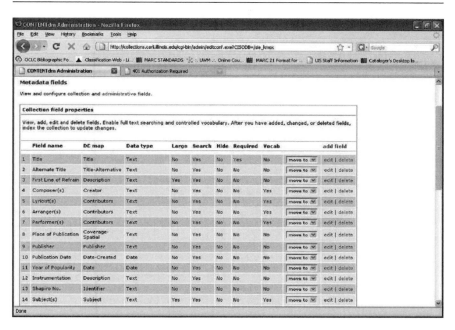

achieve consistency in the description of content objects and to facilitate retrieval."[5] Catalogers know to use authorized forms from authority records for access points (e.g., name headings and subject headings), but we do not currently use controlled vocabularies for descriptive information in our standard cataloging records. Given that using controlled vocabularies in descriptive fields ensures consistency in descriptions and aids users in searching collections, I wish we would adopt more of this controlled vocabulary approach in the traditional cataloging world. This is very important for interoperability and preparing for the Semantic Web. It is good to hear that the new RDA approach will include many more controlled vocabularies to help us both with entering and displaying data exactly as we want it to be displayed.

As a cataloger, I know that we need to use a controlled vocabulary for our subject terms for all of our digital projects. Because the Sullivan project was for an architectural collection, the Art & Architecture Thesaurus (AAT) was the logical choice as a source of a controlled vocabulary of subject terms. Fortunately, it is one of the ten controlled vocabularies that are integrated into CONTENTdm, making it very simple to choose and add appropriate subject terms

Figure 9.4
Metadata for a song in the KMOX Popular Sheet Music digital collection.
(©2010, Southern Illinois University Edwardsville. Used with permission.
CONTENTdm screen capture used with permission from OCLC.
CONTENTdm is a registered trademark of OCLC Online Computer Library
Center, Inc.)

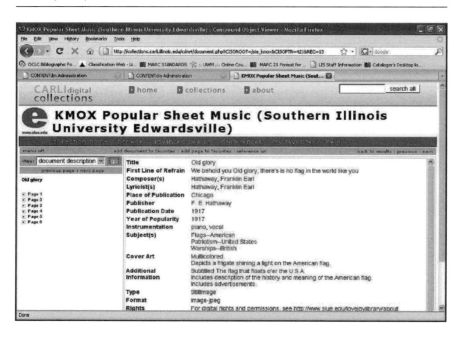

to each metadata record. If necessary, you can import a controlled vocabulary from a source that is not already integrated in CONTENTdm (e.g., subject terms from LCSH—Library of Congress Subject Headings), or you can develop your own controlled vocabulary of subject terms (very similar to creating local authority records for local subject headings).

For the Sullivan collection, as a cataloger, I also felt that it was important to provide not only AAT, but also LCSH terms whenever an LCSH term provided added value for subject searching. One of the subject fields for this project is labeled "Type of Building." Several personal residences are represented in the collection. The AAT term for personal residences is "Houses" and the LCSH term is "Dwellings." Both the AAT term and the LCSH term are used, since they are both applicable in the "Type of Building" field, and since using both adds value to the metadata. For all the "Type of building" headings, we found the appropriate AAT and LCSH terms and decided on a case-by-case basis whether to use only the AAT term, or both the AAT and LCSH terms. In some cases, it did not make sense to use the LCSH term. For example, several of the ornaments depicted are from bank buildings. The AAT term for bank buildings is "Banks (buildings)"; the LCSH term is "Banks and banking." In this particular case, the AAT term provides adequate access, and since both terms begin with the word "Banks," adding the LCSH term would not really add value to the metadata. And, really, the LCSH term "Banks and banking" does not seem applicable in a field labeled "Type of Building," as it would only lead to confusion for users.

As a cataloger, I have not been using subject terms from many different thesauri, but after working with digital projects, and having the flexibility to choose the thesaurus that works the best for a collection, I am looking at my traditional cataloging with a different eye. It might be time for us to look to other thesauri, and not depend so heavily on LCSH to provide all the subject access for the materials in our OPACs; that is, as long as we can sort out the authority control issues that will come with supplying and indexing terms from a variety of subject sources (something we do not have to think about in the metadata world, since we do not have authority control—unfortunately).

Many digital projects are visual in nature, and often use the Thesaurus for Graphic Materials (TGM) for subject and genre/format terms. TGM has "authority records" to guide the user in the proper use of the term. In TGM,

Figure 9.5
Authority record for nurses from the Thesaurus for Graphic Materials. (Courtesy of Thesaurus of Graphic Materials, Prints and Photographs Division, Library of Congress)

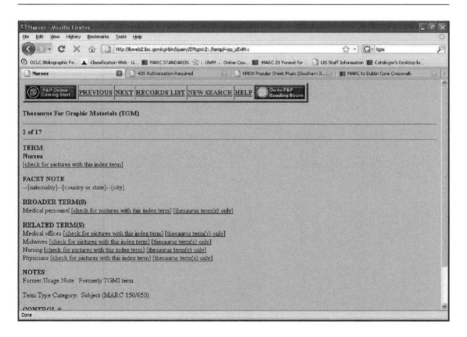

pre-coordinated subject strings can be constructed using TGM subdivisions and LCSH for geographic terms. A basic knowledge of LCSH helps with deciphering the "authority" records, and building these pre-coordinated subject strings. Figure 9.5 shows an authority record in TGM as an example.

Notice in Figure 9.5 that the TGM term "Nurses" can be "faceted" by nationality, country, or state and city. "Faceted" is another way of saying that the term can be subdivided; first by nationality (if appropriate), and then by geographic location. All geographic headings used for faceting in TGM should be used in the LCSH form. A photograph of an American nurse in Cape Town, South Africa, might have the pre-coordinated subject string: Nurses–American–South Africa–Cape Town. The metadata librarian must have a working knowledge of LCSH to be able to look at the LCSH authority record for Cape Town (see Figure 9.6) and know that the MARC authority record 781 field (geographic subdivision usage) is giving instruction on how Cape Town must be used as a subdivision (i.e., a facet). Figure 9.6 shows the LC subject geographic heading for Cape Town with geographic subdivision usage.

I diligently try to be consistent in the choice of name headings that I use in the metadata for our digital collections. Just as I do in the cataloging world,

Figure 9.6
OCLC authority record for Cape Town. (©2010, WorldCat® record, from OCLC's WorldCat® database, is used with OCLC's permission; WorldCat® is a registered trademark of OCLC Online Computer Library Center, Inc.)

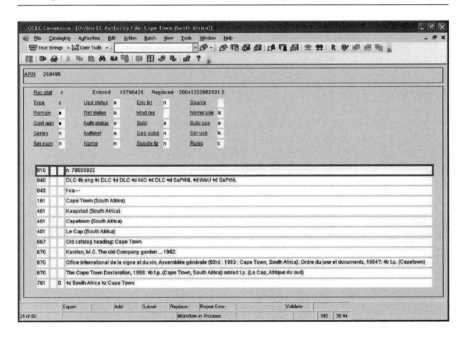

I turn to the Library of Congress NACO (Name Authority Cooperative) Authority File to try to find the established name for every heading that I add to my metadata. Unfortunately, I am often unable to find an authority record for many of the names I need to establish. When that happens, I establish the names according to the appropriate AACR2 chapters for the many forms of names, doing as much research as possible on those names. In the Sullivan collection, many of the buildings depicted not only had various forms of names, but also had different names, depending on who owned the building at a given time. CONTENTdm does not have an authority file structure; so, to compensate for the lack of cross-references that lead the user to the single authorized name, additional fields for alternate names had to be added to the metadata. If you look back at Figures 9.1 and 9.2, showing the Sullivan collection, you will notice that we have a field labeled: "Alternate building names." This field is not a controlled vocabulary field, but it is searchable to allow access to alternate names. This is by no means as efficient as using cross references in an authority record, and as a metadata librarian, I wish our metadata tools would provide that more efficient option. The metadata world currently lacks much of the "infrastructure" that we

Figure 9.7
OCLC WorldCat record for the Louis H. Sullivan Ornaments digital collection. (©2010, WorldCat® record, from OCLC's WorldCat® database, is used with OCLC's permission; WorldCat® is a registered trademark of OCLC Online Computer Library Center, Inc.)

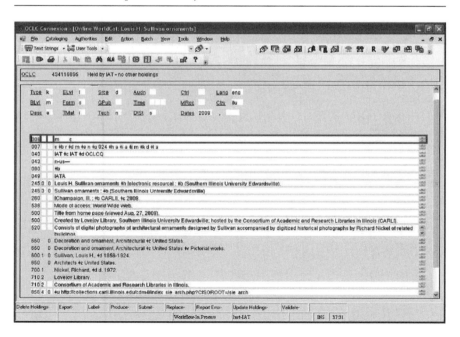

have in the cataloging world. I believe that we metadata librarians should lobby our product vendors (in my case, CONTENTdm) to access the Library of Congress NACO Authority File as a controlled vocabulary for name headings, and to provide cross-reference indexing and displays in our metadata Web interfaces, so that users of our digital collections can search cross-references, just as they can in our OPACs.

As you see in Figure 9.7, a catalog record was made in OCLC (and brought into our OPAC) for the Sullivan collection, with a link to the Web site containing the collection. The KMOX collection, and all our digital collections at SIUE, receive the same treatment. These catalog records will bring users of our library catalog and WorldCat to our digital collections, where the detailed metadata described above will provide in-depth access to the individual objects in the collections.

At SIUE we are committed to making the very best digital collections we can. We feel that by incorporating traditional cataloging standards and practices into metadata standards and practices, we are achieving that goal. I believe that a strong cataloging background, or a good working knowledge of organization of information, is necessary to provide a metadata librarian with the underlying principles to ensure that users will get the best possible access to digital collections. I'm happy to have a "foot in both worlds," and I think that straddling these worlds makes me both a better catalog librarian and, hopefully, eventually, a better metadata librarian.

NOTES

1. Steven J. Miller, "Metadata for Digital Collections" (Web site for online class registration and information), Professional Development Institute, University of Wisconsin-Milwaukee, School of Information Studies, https://www4.uwm.edu/sois/epayment/courses/index.cfm?a1=browse&notify=TRUE (accessed May 12, 2010).

2. *Anglo-American Cataloguing Rules*, prepared under the direction of the Joint Steering Committee for Revision of AACR, a committee of the American Library Association, the Australian Committee on Cataloguing, the British Library, the Canadian Committee on Cataloguing, Chartered Institute of Library and Information Professionals, the Library of Congress. 2nd ed., 2002 rev. (Ottawa: Canadian Library Association, London: Chartered Institute of Library and Information Professionals, and Chicago: American Library Association, 2002–2005).

3. Steven J. Miller, *Metadata for Digital Collections* (Milwaukee: University of Wisconsin–Milwaukee, School of Information Studies, Professional Development Institute, 2009), unit 1, p. 9.

4. "MARC to Dublin Core Crosswalk," Development and MARC Standards Office, Library of Congress, April 24, 2008, http://www.loc.gov/marc/marc2dc.html (accessed May 12, 2010).

5. *ANSI/NISO Z39.19—Guidelines for the Construction, Format, and Management of Monolingual Controlled Vocabularies* (Bethesda, MD: National Information Standards Organization, 2005).

10 FACING A TIME OF CHANGE

Halvard (Hal) Cain

Change makes us uncomfortable! Even if it does no harm to our established values and practices, we don't welcome it. As catalogers, we work to get things organized in order—we record documents which come to us in fixed forms (print or digital file or another medium), we reduce variable names, titles, and subject descriptors to fixed terms, and we classify resources so they occupy at least a relatively fixed sequence. Yet, we live in change and with change. Sometimes we seek it and welcome it; sometimes we resist. Sometimes we know it's coming, but we decide to go on doing what we've been doing all along, until change becomes impossible to disregard.

I think that is where I stand now: waiting for impending changes to become impossible to disregard; and, I think many of us catalogers are in the same position, seeing too many factors we can't control or influence. When the changes are finally here and force themselves upon me, then I'll deal with them—meanwhile, why bother, until I have to work with the new rules? I'll only forget the detail if I'm not using it!

While cataloging intakes mount and the tally of cataloging workers diminishes, we have to expect change in standards for content of bibliographic records. These changes are not always in the direction heralded by the *Resource Description and Access* (RDA) drafts[1] that we have seen and discussed. For a good many years (at least as long as I've been reading about their arrearages), the Library of Congress (LC) has used "minimal-level" cataloging standards in the struggle to reduce its backlogs. Some changes amount to cutting corners; some, such as capturing metadata created elsewhere, will reroute the whole workflow. Still, when you're being flooded, any relief helps; being flooded is what's happening to many catalogers. The LC consultants' (R2) report on the MARC market, *Study of the North American MARC Records Marketplace,*[2] reports on growing backlogs; cataloging effort is being diverted from the "mainstream" (generally commercial publications, widely available) to other projects, despite the consultants' claim that there is apparently no shortage of catalogers as such. Many libraries that have clung to revision of copy cataloging data may have to decide to abandon this practice; it would be helpful to understand better just what kinds of revision are done.

We catalogers felt we had it worked out, with standard rules for creating description, name headings, added titles, and subject treatment. Those of us who had been around for a while complained that the filing sequence of the catalog entries was an important part of how our records were connected, but the computer display had undermined that; however, we didn't complain about the cessation of card filing. Now, with Web catalogs, featuring hyperlinking of headings (allowing the user just to click to discover what other work uses a heading), the card file's primary tool of collocation by sequence of heading entries has been replicated reasonably adequately. But still, the separation of catalogers from management of the catalog itself, along with loss of a sense of enriching the existing web of connections in the catalog by inserting new data, has deadened the sense that our work builds and extends the catalog that we present to users as the key to the library collections. Now we enter data for "bibliographic control" and are liable to forget the catalog in the context of the larger database (WorldCat, Libraries Australia, whatever) against which we're working.

Change is truly all around us! As people who like stability, many catalogers feel threatened. We're facing new rules, in the shape of the forthcoming *Resource Description and Access* (RDA), to be delivered in a new mode of access—online rather than in a printed text. The value of traditional cataloging is under fire. Controlled vocabulary for subject access is under fire, too, and even the need to provide specific access terms (headings, in the terminology many of us grew up with) is called into question. The value of the standard classification schemes for resources—at least those that don't require shelving in open-access bookstacks—is doubted.

Even change for a good result brings its burdens: new tools, new rules, new frames of reference and mental constructs; and if we feel that the purpose doesn't justify the changes, and the tools aren't up to the job, we may find ourselves resisting. Yet, not all change is destructive. In 2006, LC decided to abandon series control (with qualifications). In truth, many of us who protested were upset nearly as much by LC's process as by the decision itself, without consultation, and with little attempt to argue in justification—failings LC has acknowledged. Those of us who value series control enough to continue it have filled the gap, through NACO (Name Authority Cooperative Program of the Program for Cooperative Cataloging, or PCC) or at least in our local catalogs. And the sky is still up there. But we would have benefited from a reasoned exposition of pros and cons. LC's professional leadership failed us. Naturally, LC must determine its own priorities; but when it invites us to contribute to the data it draws on—principally through the BIBCO (Bibliographic Cooperative of PCC) agencies—we expect LC to recognize the reciprocality of its relationships. After all, many of us pay for the services of OCLC, and it has avenues of communication with members and customers.

BIBCO, the Program for Cooperative Cataloging's cluster for bibliographic record production according to agreed standards, has defined a new, slimmed-down standard for cataloging, in succession to the Core record standard.[3] They call it the "BIBCO Standard Record" (BSR),[4] and it demands even less detail than Core. BIBCO has also decided that such records be coded as "full" level of cataloging, which is a most regrettable confusion of the meaning of the standard MARC 21 bibliographic-level code, and obscures the difference between base-level cataloguing and more extensive "full" cataloging as provided by the *Anglo-American Cataloguing Rules*, second edition (AACR2).[5]

There are signs that LC, traditionally considered the home of quality in cataloging, with unmatched depths of skill and subject specialization, is looking to withdraw from many of its "fringe" activities. It may decide that keyword access suffices for subject access to some resources, and that trimmed-down cataloging data (as specified for the access-level records for some serials and for monographic web resources[6]) will be declared sufficient for a range of non-mainstream data. LC's cataloging is the principal constituent of the cataloging output of North America; what LC chooses to do becomes de facto the standard other libraries follow. The recent R2 consultants' report for LC on cataloging record sources[7] (which curiously overlooks the inclusion of MARC records from extra-American sources in North American databases including OCLC) even questions the viability of the whole shared-cataloging enterprise upon which most libraries heavily rely on for our catalog data. It speculates on the effects of LC charging libraries the real cost of cataloging to obtain MARC records. While LC has legislative restraints on its ability to charge for catalog records (cost of distribution plus 10 percent), if it chooses to restrict its output or turn off our ability to download from its online catalog, we'll have to go elsewhere—and, once more, what LC does sets the standard for others to follow. In such an event we can expect "free" sources of cataloging data to dry up.

Meanwhile, new cataloging workflows are being planned to capture data prepared earlier in the bibliographic supply chain. ONIX data used by the book trade is the first target; its use is already being tested by LC[8] in preparation of cataloging-in-publication (CIP) records, and other pre-formatted electronic data supplied by publishers is already used in CIP. Well, we can only applaud efforts to get the book trade (publishers, wholesalers, and suppliers) working in closer cooperation with libraries; however, considering how often book-trade data proves unreliable when compared with the actual finished document, there's a good way yet to go. Not that the endeavor isn't worth making, but will such traditional practices as recording a title accurately (a key requirement for being able to relate a document to its record) suffer?

Some years ago we were hearing about the "dynamic record"—a pattern in which the core data is authoritatively created, and may be augmented by those who require more. This contributed to the formation of the Core standards. The concept of augmentation seems to have languished; nevertheless, we're told that the BSR is a "floor" level of cataloging, to which further data can be added as found useful. However, unless those additions are made available through the same avenues as the original record, we'll find the work being done over and over by different libraries—hardly an efficient way of employing scarce cataloging resources. Meanwhile, OCLC's rules for modifying "master" records in the OCLC database may need more sophistication. If this were done, then all OCLC participants could benefit, even more so if the types of data added can be tagged with the level of completeness in cataloging to which they pertain. This would allow libraries to be selective about incorporating additions. But not all libraries that might augment a record to enhance its value in their catalogs participate in OCLC, however. This is a limitation to record augmentation that is not often acknowledged. Augmenting dynamic records also entails consideration of how updates in bibliographic data are promulgated.

Cataloging or metadata preparation? Really, I can't see that the name to which we give the activity matters greatly, so long as the objectives of cataloging and creation of catalogs are maintained: to enable the user (including the librarian) to find, identify, select, and obtain documents and information; to follow bibliographic relationships through the catalog; and to match reliably the document in hand, the bibliographic record in the catalog, and the citation (full or incomplete) that the user brings to the catalog. It's easy, amid the technical demands of our discipline, to overlook that the user's demands are the mainspring of cataloging and catalogs. The relationship is not static, but it should be a virtuous circle: catalogers offer more, the catalog designer presents more, the user seizes on the additional facilities and goes on to demand more—not necessarily the same as has been envisaged by the cataloger.

At this point, I propose we take a different view. Instead of looking at the cataloging process and the formal output, look at the people for whose benefit we're working: the users of our catalog and the users of bibliographic databases in which our records are aggregated. Look also at the latest development, the exposure of bibliographic data directly to the Web search engines. Thanks to the ubiquitous computer, the omnipresent Internet, and the all-garnering search engine, the users of our catalogs and libraries have been changing their behavior. Whether or not we understood what they were doing before, they aren't doing that much anymore: they look first on the Web. We may deplore this, but it's a fact and won't change; it's not just a phenomenon of the "I want it now" generation, it's pervasive among all. We do it ourselves.

Relevance ranking is here to stay. Users expect the computer to list first what it identifies as "most useful" (unless they prefer to choose some other criterion, such as "most recent"). Many catalogs also provide relevance ranking, as an option or by default. So long as the catalog user can see the search results, and can opt to choose another search strategy, I see no harm.

Information specialists were prone to think of effective searching and good results in terms of complete recall (*all* the documents that match the stated search terms) and absolute precision (*only* the documents that match those search terms) with the ability to select the most useful from the results. The capacity to browse, purposefully or haphazardly, was hardly considered as a retrieval or discovery method. Dr. Thomas Mann, doyen of reference specialists at LC, gives an entertaining account of the value of shelf browsing in his recent paper, "What Is Distinctive about the Library of Congress."[9] His is an admirable exposition and defence of "traditional" full cataloging, but largely specific to LC and its particular role, and conditioned at least in part by the situation at LC, where books are not on open public access. Elsewhere, we find that the great majority of our users, apart from a few enthusiasts and some specialists, have been taking a different approach—one which in fact we all use most of the time. This approach is summed up as the Principle of Least Effort;[10] or, in familiar terms, *good enough is usually enough.*

And that is indeed something to keep in mind: when the documents we work with are or will become available on the Web (in full or in excerpt) through Google Books or otherwise, how much information really is essential? Do the guiding spirits of BIBCO perhaps have it fairly right with their reduced standard record? Before that train has gone too far down the line, let's hope for some research to test when the information is adequate, and whether more is actually required. Meanwhile, remember we aren't called upon to create perfect records: "useful" and "reliable" will suffice. For comparison, look at some LC printed cards of the 1930s and 1940s, and see what data they record that we haven't found useful (let alone necessary) for half a century and more.

In truth, most of us follow the "least effort" approach most of the time. Naturally, for some inquiries (what's my friend's home telephone number?) there is only one right answer; for many others (what's the distance from Melbourne, Australia, to New York?), it depends on the parameters, often unspoken and undetermined until we consult the results: by air, via Sydney, or direct to the United States? Via Los Angeles, then Denver or Chicago? Or round the world via the United Kingdom? Often the quickest answer that looks appropriate will be good enough, and I can proceed. Unless I happen to need the detail and precision, an answer there on my screen, without having to go out to the library, is preferable.

The Internet and the search engines meet this sort of demand perfectly. Library catalogs aren't really good tools for answering such inquiries—they never were. Much inquiry requires no more sophistication in approach. The catalog is good for inquiries about documents and the detailed content of documents. Should our ordinary cataloging be geared to extraordinary demands? Special materials, especially unique resources, may demand different treatment.

The inclusion of bibliographic information (of uneven quality, as it is) in Google may have taken some of our ground; nevertheless, the work of assembling, recording, and making resources available still relies, above all, on selection of the material to be included in our collections, and also on the selection of which data elements are important and must be recorded. Even selection of the level of descriptive treatment is appropriate. It remains very much in dispute whether increased direct access to the content is any adequate substitute for, or a better alternative to, systematic assignment of subject terms by catalogers, or even whether some classes of material are well represented by keywords, but not others. We do know that many results of keyword searching appear because the keywords have been provided by the controlled subject terms catalogers have supplied. We can't deny, though, that subject cataloging and classification are expensive, and that brings them under challenge in this era of cost reduction. New, expanded rules and data schemes seem unlikely to do much to help contain costs or increase our productivity. By the time they come to fruition, they may be largely irrelevant. After all, our managers, not we catalogers, will decide how the limited funds are to be spent—"standard" catalog records may be what we can afford, and that will be that.

A generation ago, as many of us can remember, we were moving from original in-house cataloging, supplemented by preprinted cards from the Library of Congress or other sources, plus copy-cataloging from the printed volumes of the LC catalog or NUC,[11] to copy-cataloging with shared online databases (OCLC is the most prominent and now the global survivor) and some original cataloging. In parallel, the range of resources entered in our catalogs was changing, too, as the practice of entering all resources in a single catalog gained ground: not just printed books and serials, but also microforms, sound recordings, and video recordings followed by electronic materials. We learned to deal with them. Change in the mode of our work was accompanied by change in the form of output, as computer-based public catalogs progressively superseded card catalogs. We need not fear change: we've dealt with plenty of it over the years since the original Anglo-American Cataloging Rules (AACR)[12] came our way in 1967. In my own library, the final retirement of the card catalog is only now (December 2009) being achieved. In my career, over forty-odd years, I've come from typed or handwritten cards to online networked bibliographic databases.

We need to remember that cataloging is about documents and their content, not simply about elaborating formulaic recorded data and indexing information. Among cultural institutions and information services, libraries are unique in that their ethos is built on a collection of documents: information fixed in a form and medium, which can be unambiguously described, stored, retrieved, referred to, and consulted. Documents can be specified by salient characteristics (generally title, creator, version, issuer, extent), and organized by document content in categories designed to assist retrieval. Elaine Svenonius covers the ground masterfully.[13] For physical, tangible documents, this is plain enough. The more transient kinds of digital information on the Web are the counterpart of ephemeral print material, and libraries have seldom endeavoured to collect and record more than a fraction of that material. Are transient Web sites different? There are such a lot of them, too. Retention of samples may be sufficient; maybe, apart from carefully selected resources, we should leave most of it to the Internet Archive.[14]

We may be rightly concerned to ensure that future generations will understand what this and previous ones knew—we are the memory of humankind, the "diary of the human race."[15] We should remember that libraries, even the most inclusive, have always exercised selection: by relevance, by value to users, and by practical limits. Good selection has built great libraries. As users, when faced with everything (1.5 million hits on Google, maybe?), we have to make a selection, and the library's selection provides more limited results, offered for value and relevance. The resources for compilation of our history are inherently, often haphazardly, incomplete; yet, how could it be otherwise? Should the study of a person's lifetime, or of a generation, require a lifetime for its understanding? To retain everything would be overwhelming, and our backlogs would flood our operations. Only specialist collections try to collect ephemeral publications, and they impose limits on selection. Not everything needs to be collected and retained permanently. We should participate in last-copy retention and regional storage schemes, so that we have the means to assure that the physical originals still exist for when they're required and to complement the storage of scanned images, with the originals either freely available or at a cost (it may turn out that high-quality scanned images of printed books end up costing a noticeable amount). Many of the scans by Google Books lack adequate access to illustrations and diagrams, which may be crucial portions of the content, and who can say whether or when they'll be re-digitized to capture this valuable content?

One of the keys to reliable access is, of course, controlled vocabulary. The reigning subject scheme, the Library of Congress Subject Headings (LCSH),[16] is under challenge for cost of use, slow response to change, and complexity in application. Yet no other serious general scheme seems to be emerging. If cost and development continue to be problematic, we may see LC expand its minimal-level cataloging program (eschewing LCSH terms in favour of cataloger-assigned keywords plus keywords from the descriptive data) for materials chosen to require less attention. LCSH may relax its editorial control in favour of a more cooperative management. At least until some other general thesaurus emerges, we need LCSH.

When it comes to name (including title) authorities, the scene really is changing. NACO remains the chief means of contributing authority record to the LC Name Authority File (LC/NAF at http://authorities.loc.gov). Most records are contributed through OCLC, the bibliographic utility that libraries of the Anglo-American world use and depend on. Now, alongside the NAF, we have the Virtual International Authority File (VIAF at http://viaf.org), which brings together (at present) sixteen authority files, including the LC/NAF, linked with titles of works and other data. This development is truly revolutionary (especially for those engaged with other authority files), with a wealth of verified data—not all according to the Anglo-American Cataloguing Rules, but valuable nevertheless. The revolutionary aspect of VIAF is that titles and associated data are employed to verify the matched names and establish the identities. The combined sets of data will contribute much to our name authority work, and support the development of the ISNI (International Standard Name [Party] Identifier), which is due to be released soon as ISO 27729.

In principle, there seems no reason why this kind of automated processing cannot be applied to resolving new names in current cataloging (or old names in older cataloguing where authority control has not been applied) by suggesting identities and corrections, and creating draft authority records for completion by catalogers. It might also prove feasible for libraries to use VIAF as a tool in selecting names to let pass without formally establishing authority records, saving limited time and utilizing valuable cataloger skills for the more difficult names that need attention. This would simply be formalization of the selective approach followed, in fact, by not a few libraries that catalog primarily for their own database. Meanwhile, we can reflect that the Internet and e-mail have changed authority work—authors' Web sites, institutional pages, and online resources of various kinds have made it easier than ever before to verify an author's work. The remaining improvement we need is a means by which authority data could be promulgated and loaded automatically. If it works for Internet IP numbers, why not in other kinds of data, in this case authorities? Maybe ISNI can be a way to build the road forward?

What needs to be discussed and researched is what tools libraries really need to serve their clients. I'm not confident our chiefs are any wiser about that than anyone else, but they are in a position to call the shots, as they did at LC in 2006 with cessation of series control. I fear that whatever they choose to do will be found to work, because it will be defined to be working well enough for the purposes they declare have to be served.

The patterns and constructs we're already familiar with, and have learned to exploit, naturally color our view of possible changes in cataloging. Whether or not calls for change in cataloging are justified and well founded, they aren't going to stop. The implication I see is that we catalogers, and our work, have to change, too (the unpalatable alternative being that our jobs vanish). My constant worry is that, in elaborating, consolidating, and applying new approaches, we'll find we've discarded elements that have real value for our users and ourselves, without setting in place sufficient replacement.

If only we could reach a state in which change occurs in an orderly fashion. But that's not going to happen; rather, we have to reach an accommodation with recurrent alterations of the conditions of our lives and our work—getting a grip on firm purposes, core principles, and fundamental values. For some of us (most of us, maybe), stability in our work has been a sort of compensation for instability in other areas of our lives, and as that dissolves, we need to make values and purposes clearer. Change, improvement; permanence, stability—our lives seem to be endlessly in tension between these poles.

The overall purpose of our work remains twofold: to record and to make available the materials our libraries collected, for the benefit of those who came to use them; and secondarily to answer interlibrary loan or document supply needs. But now we catalog with an eye also to the shared databases where our work is done or transmitted, and to exposure of our data on the Web. We've lived with change, any of us who've been in this game for more than a decade. It's not as if we haven't had plenty of change; however, we now have to accommodate the demands of computer processing, and of Internet search engines and global information. In addition, there is a demand that our data must be used as an asset in the competition libraries themselves face as valuable, useful, but expensive, collections of information resources that many use, even in the face of expanding data resources accessible by the Internet. Hence, most of the calls are for catalogs to change character or be replaced with new interfaces—competition where previously we had no challenger. This is genuinely a new situation for us, and there are also moves to downgrade, even abandon, libraries because "it's all on the Internet" (until one tries to find exactly the right thing and obtain access).

Change was always going on, of course: from book catalogs to card files; from handwriting to typing; from manual to electric to memory typewriters; to computer-produced cards; then to computer-based catalogs. And, of course, there were always changes of data to be made. Within the first year of my career in librarianship, I had learned to find typographical errors, filing errors, discrepancies in forms of name, and classification problems in the card catalog of the university library where I was employed. That was even before I was engaged in cataloging. But while change was something catalogers had to accommodate, it was thought to be an exception to the stability and permanence of the catalog. Making a change in a card catalog could entail serious work. "Do it once and do it right" was the slogan of the time, and it still resonates, even though our computer systems make it easier than ever before to make changes.

Our work will change, no doubt about it, but *not* the fundamental objectives and principles: to make documents and information identifiable and retrievable. If the complexities of RDA prove to be obstacles, they'll be set aside, hopefully without too much damage. Libraries are practical places, bent on getting good benefits for their money and making their resources more findable and available—with a new emphasis on unique resources. Meanwhile, consider the example data in Appendix M of the RDA draft.[17]

The traditional tools will change, and new ones will emerge. The primacy of OCLC as the global database may be challenged by others, and our reliance on the cataloging output of LC may be forced to diminish; such change will affect particularly the smaller libraries who often don't participate in OCLC or the other utilities. But cataloging will go on being done, new challenges will arise, and new ways of meeting old challenges will be devised.

Whatever the changes to be wished upon us, by the advent of RDA, metadata schemes, (which I haven't discussed), new forms of the catalog, competition with the Internet, and resources in more fluid forms than we're accustomed to, catalogers will still be pursuing their goals of description, access, and organization.

NOTES

1. "RDA: Full Draft, 11/24/08," RDA: Resource Description & and Access Toolkit, RDA Constituency Review, http://www.rdatoolkit.org/constituencyreview (accessed May 5, 2010).

2. R2 Consulting, *Study of the North American MARC Records Marketplace*, October 2009 http://www.loc.gov/bibliographic-future/news/MARC_Record_Marketplace_2009-10.pdf (accessed December 21, 2009).

3. "Introduction to the Program for Cooperative Cataloging BIBCO Core Record Standards," http://www.loc.gov/catdir/pcc/bibco/coreintro.html (accessed December 15, 2009).

4. "Implementation of the BIBCO Standard Record for Printed Books," November 23, 2009, http://www.loc.gov/catdir/pcc/bibco/BSR_ImplementationDoc.pdf (accessed December 15, 2009).

5. *Anglo-American Cataloguing Rules*, Prepared under the direction of the Joint Steering Committee for Revision of AACR, a committee of the American Library Association, the Australian Committee on Cataloguing, the British Library, the Canadian Committee on Cataloguing, Chartered Institute of Library and Information Professionals, the Library of Congress. 2nd ed., 2002 rev. (Ottawa: Canadian Library Association, London: Chartered Institute of Library and Information Professionals, and Chicago: American Library Association, 2002–2005).

6. "LC Implementation Plans for Access Level MARC/AACR2 Records," http://www.loc.gov/catdir/access/accessrecord.html (accessed December 21, 2009).

7. R2 Consulting, *Study of the North American MARC Records Marketplace*.

8. "Electronic CIP: the Cataloging in Publication Program," Library of Congress, June 9, 2009, http://cip.loc.gov/onixpro.html (accessed December 19, 2009).

9. Thomas Mann, "What Is Distinctive about the Library of Congress in Both Its Collections and Its Means of Access to Them, and Reasons LC Needs to Maintain Classified Shelving of Books Onsite, and a Way to Deal Effectively with the Problem of 'Books on the Floor,'" November 6, 2009, http://www.guild2910.org/Future%20of%20Cataloging/LCdistinctive.pdf (accessed December 15, 2009).

10. Peter Morville, *Ambient Findability* (Sebastopol, CA: O'Reilly, 2005), 55 (crediting the principle to George Zipf).

11. *The National Union Catalog, Pre-1956 Imprints* (London: Mansell, 1968–1981).

12. *Anglo-American Cataloging Rules*, prepared by the American Library Association, the Library of Congress, the Library Association, and the Canadian Library Association. North American text (Chicago: American Library Association, 1967).

13. Elaine Svenonius, *The Intellectual Foundation of Information Organization* (Cambridge, MA: MIT Press, 2000).

14. Internet Archive Wayback Machine, http://www.archive.org (accessed May 11, 2010).

15. George Dawson, *Inaugural Address of the Opening of the Birmingham Reference Library*, 1866, quoted by S. Lubetzky; recounted by E. Svenonius, *The Intellectual Foundation of Information Organization*, 8.

16. Library of Congress, *Library of Congress Subject Headings* (Washington, DC: Library of Congress, Cataloging Distribution Service, 2009).

17. "RDA: Full Draft, 11/24/08."

11   JUDGMENT AND IMAGINATION: CARRYING CATALOGING THROUGH TIMES OF CHANGE

Jay Weitz

Most catalogers working in the United States today have labored under one or both of the editions of the *Anglo-American Cataloguing Rules*. Published in 1967, the first edition, AACR1, gave way to the second edition, AACR2, in 1978. The longevity of the AACR canon over more than forty years offers an illusion of stasis and stability. But any cataloger familiar with the evolution of AACR through that period knows that those rules never stopped changing, any more than the world of things to catalog stopped changing.

This whole notion of dealing with inevitable change was actually built into the rules, thanks to the foresight of the rule makers. AACR2 in particular not merely allows, but actually forces itself to evolve constantly, pushed both from within and without.

The rules changed from within thanks in part to the concept of "cataloger's judgment" built into AACR2's foundation and given fullest voice in Rules 0.7 and 0.9.

> **0.7:** Some rules are designated as *alternative rules* or as *optional additions*, and some other rules or parts of rules are introduced by *optionally*. These provisions arise from the recognition that different solutions to a problem and differing levels of detail and specificity are appropriate in different contexts. Decide some alternatives and options as a matter of cataloguing policy for a particular catalogue or bibliographic agency and, therefore, exercise them either always or never. Exercise other alternatives and options case by case. All cataloguing agencies should distinguish between these two types of option and keep a record of their policy decisions and of the circumstances in which a particular option may be applied.[1]

0.9: These rules recognize the necessity for judgement and interpretation by the cataloguer. Such judgement and interpretation may be based on the requirements of a particular catalogue or upon the use of the items being catalogued. The need for judgement is indicated in these rules by words and phrases such as *if appropriate, important,* and *if necessary.* Such words and phrases indicate recognition of the fact that uniform legislation for all types and sizes of catalogue is neither possible nor desirable, and encourage the application of individual judgement based on specific local knowledge. This statement in no way contradicts the value of standardization. Apply such judgements consistently within a particular context and record the cataloguing agency's policy.[2]

Choosing among options and alternatives, extrapolating from known situations to new ones, all using rule-based judgment: These skills sit at the heart of every cataloger's job. Every cataloger exercising judgment hones these skills with each exercise thereof.

If the rules change from within because they acknowledge the inability to anticipate every situation, they also change from without because of the rapid changes in the world of resources being cataloged over the course of those decades. Think of just a few of the changes that had obvious and profound impacts on the world of cataloging: the evolution of sound recording from vinyl to compact disc to sound file, the evolution of video recording from reel-to-reel tape to videocassette to DVD to Blu-ray Disc, and the emergence of electronic resources from obscurity to ubiquity.

Extend these thoughts beyond the rules themselves and consider the changes to the Machine-Readable Cataloging (MARC) formats over the same period. Like AACR, MARC also had its origin in the 1960s and is haunted still by the ghosts of technologies past. The same developments that prompted new cataloging rules often required corresponding changes in MARC: new codes, new fields, new subfields, and new relationships among elements.

When first published in the 1960s, the bibliographic formats were simply "MARC formats." Later, when countless flavors of MARC proliferated around the globe, they were renamed "USMARC." Then as the millennium approached, they were again rechristened as "MARC 21" to remove the United States–centric designation and make international adaptation more palatable. Beneath the superficial title changes, though, the formats themselves were undergoing several transformations.

Most obvious was "Format Integration," defined as "the validation of USMARC data elements for all forms of material."[3] First discussed in 1978 and first proposed in 1983, Format Integration broke down the validation barriers among what had been up until then, separate bibliographic formats. Preparatory changes to MARC began to be defined in 1988 and were implemented in mid-1989. Format Integration itself was implemented in two phases, in January 1995, and in March 1996.

For all of its many shortcomings, MARC has proven itself to be incredibly resilient and adaptable to resources, situations, and purposes far beyond the imaginations even of those visionaries who created it. Format Integration and such innovations as the 856 field for Electronic Location and Access, and the 006 field that allows for the coding of such additional characteristics of a resource as seriality or electronic aspects, allowed MARC to account for many of the new types of resources wrought by the computer revolution.

Those conjoined twins of the AACR rules and the MARC data structure, both of which have persisted over more than four decades, have appeared to be stable. But those who use the standards on a daily basis have an acute awareness of how much AACR and MARC have continued to evolve. In other words, to an extent that non-catalogers are generally unaware, catalogers have dealt with change constantly. As it turns out, catalogers have proven themselves to be as resilient and adaptable as either AACR or MARC.

That resilience and adaptability will stand catalogers in good stead as we move from the world of AACR to the world of RDA, *Resource Description and Access*. Those qualities will come in just as handy as we also begin to evolve from MARC toward a post-MARC data structure, whatever it may turn out to be.

Because the development and proliferation of electronic resources over the past four decades both drove and reflected so many of these changes, it might be instructive to take a look back. When AACR1 was published in 1967, there was much more recognition than in any previous rules of a world beyond the printed book. AACR1 included rules for motion pictures and filmstrips (Chapter 12), phonorecords (Chapter 14), and pictures, designs, and other two-dimensional representations (Chapter 15).[4] There was no mention of computers, computer data, or computer software, and no apparent awareness that the world was soon to change.

By 1970, however, the American Library Association's Descriptive Cataloging Committee created a Subcommittee on Rules for Cataloging Machine-Readable Data Files. This subcommittee met regularly for the next five years beginning in 1971, during which time it became part of the Catalog Code Revision Committee (CCRC, the predecessor to the Committee on Cataloging: Description and Access, CC:DA), which was already looking toward something like AACR2. Its final report was issued in January 1976, reflecting a growing recognition that extending the rules to "non-book materials" was imperative.

A quick glance at what was going on mostly outside of libraries during this same period gives a hint of the source of this growing recognition. The first Random Access Memory (RAM) chip was created in 1970. The first microprocessor, the Intel 4004, and the first "floppy" disks appeared in 1971. Ethernet networking was introduced in 1973. During 1974 and 1975, the first computer "kits" for consumers, including the Mark-8 and Altair 8800, as well as the first "portable" computer, the IBM 5100, appeared.

That CCRC subcommittee identified several of the issues for computer files that continued to plague catalogers for years. They noted the frequent absence, inadequacy, or ambiguity of a chief source of information for many such resources. The question of what to call these things raised its gnarled head. They came up with the mellifluous phrase "Machine-readable data file." On occasion, the subcommittee was even prescient, recognizing the importance of content over carrier: "the physical form of a machine-readable data file can easily be changed without affecting bibliographic identification. Catalog records cannot be reactive to frequent changes and thus would frequently misrepresent the file."[5]

Two years later in 1978, the publication of AACR2 reflected the recommendations of the CCRC Subcommittee in the creation of its "Chapter 9: Machine-Readable Data Files." Because catalogers, in 1978, were dealing mainly with large data files that could change physical formats, often depending upon an institution's specific computer system, the original AACR2 Chapter 9 emphasized content over carrier in sometimes surprising ways. The chief source of information was the "internal user label," defined as "A machine-readable identifier containing alphabetic and/or numeric characters providing information about the file."[6] In cases where information was not available from the chief source, AACR2 recommended using documentation issued by the creator of the file, other published descriptions of the file, or other sources, including the container of the file and its labels. An underlying assumption seems to have been that the resource "in hand" was only one of many possible physical manifestations and that any external labels would tend not to be authoritative.

But perhaps the most explicit acknowledgement that something important was afoot was one that is rarely noticed. In the original AACR2 Part I, Chapters 1–8 and 10–12, the Area 5 is called the "Physical Description Area," whereas in Chapter 9, it was dubbed the "File Description Area." Although that would change by the time of the 1988 Revision of AACR2, it signaled an important step toward the notion of content over carrier.

So by 1978, there were cataloging rules for machine-readable data files, but it was not until the next year that work began in the MARC community to devise a MARC format for these resources. The first draft of this new MARC format was announced in LC's *Cataloging Service Bulletin* in the winter of 1980, and the final version was approved by MARBI (Machine-Readable Bibliographic Information committee of ALA) in October 1981. Early in 1982, OCLC began work on implementing the new format, a long and complicated process that came to fruition on October 1, 1984. It would be several years yet before the Library of Congress itself implemented the Machine-Readable Data Files format.

But if the rule makers and format designers thought they were making progress, the outside world never stopped moving during that same period. The Apple I was introduced on April 1, 1976. Through the course of 1977, the Apple II, the Commodore PET, and the Radio Shack TRS-80 all appeared. VisiCalc, the first computer spreadsheet program, was created in 1978 and introduced to the public in 1979. WordStar, the first successful word processing software, appeared in 1979. Then the biggie: on August 21, 1981, the IBM PC and its MS-DOS operating system were introduced.

By this point, it was clear that the computer revolution was in full swing. Both the machines themselves and the software that ran on them had become commonplace in libraries. Not so suddenly, by the early 1980s, the still-new AACR2 Chapter 9 of 1978 was looking about as useful as a standard for cataloging the proverbial buggy whip. There was, for instance, no guidance for describing the now-proliferating array of physical carriers such as reels, disks, cassettes, and cartridges; no provision for identifying such now-crucial information as the make and model of the computer or the operating system.

Before either LC or OCLC had a chance to implement the new Machine-Readable Data Files format, ALA's Committee on Cataloging: Description and Access (CC:DA) formed the Task Force on the Descriptive Cataloging of Microcomputer Software in 1983. That group's 1984 document, *Guidelines for Using AACR2 Chapter 9 for Cataloging Microcomputer Software*,[7] was intended to complement, rather than replace, the rules in the original Chapter 9, with an emphasis on the commercially available data and program files that libraries were gobbling up. Catalogers applied the guidelines for several years, during which time the Joint Steering Committee recommended the production of a preliminary draft of a revamped Chapter 9 in anticipation of the projected 1988 publication of a new revision of AACR2.

The 1987 "Draft Revision" of Chapter 9 changed the name to "Computer Files" and made other significant moves to align the rules with rapidly changing reality.[8] Perhaps most important was the change in the scope (AACR2 9.0A) to recognize the existence of both "direct access" and "remote access" files. This was 1987, and although the earliest versions of the Internet had been in existence since 1969, e-mail had been around in limited circles since 1971, and File Transfer Protocol (FTP) had been around since 1973, it would not be until the explosion of the World Wide Web in the early 1990s that what we now think of as "remotely accessed files" would begin to become as important a factor as they now are. These "remote" files were mostly files and data on a mainframe to which catalogers would not have direct, physical access. That was close enough, because the direct/remote distinction that would eventually become central to the cataloging of electronic resources was now in the rules.

Through the continuing computer revolution and the development of the Web, AARC2 and MARC kept leapfrogging each other in the attempt to keep up with changes. Catalogers were forever absorbing and adapting to the new rules and the new MARC elements, which was difficult enough. But catalogers truly proved their mettle each time they encountered something not yet accounted for in the rules or the format. The core notion of cataloger's judgment stands right there at the intersection of stated rule, structured format, and stubborn reality; and it is imagination that enables a skilled cataloger to determine a workable solution.

Catalogers have long been used to two constants. First, the world we are trying to describe keeps shifting under our feet. Second, our standards have never been able to keep up with the shifting. Both of those points seem especially apt when we're talking about such resources as remotely accessed documents and Web sites that themselves can change without warning.

When done conscientiously, cataloging has always been more art than science. We catalog real-world resources that may or may not conform to the theories that our rules try to codify. As I wrote in the introduction to my *Cataloger's Judgment*, "the world of stuff to catalog is so vast, so slippery, so surprising, that individual judgment will always enter into our decisions ... Catalogers are not the mindless drudges that many non-catalogers imagine, but instead are thoughtful judges concerning matters of description and access."[9] It is that judgment leavened with imagination that has carried catalogers through these decades of change. That same judgment and imagination will continue to stand them in good stead through the era of Resource Description and Access (RDA), any post-MARC data structure, and whatever future marvels the world sends them to catalog.

NOTES

Portions of this essay have been adapted from an address, "From ICPSR to Playaways: Evolving Standards for the Cataloging of Electronic Resources,"[10] delivered at the New England Technical Services Librarians Spring Conference, Worcester, Massachusetts, on April 4, 2008.

1. Joint Steering Committee for Revision of AACR, *Anglo-American Cataloguing Rules*, 2nd ed., 2002 Revision (Chicago: American Library Association, 2002), 2.

2. Ibid., 2–3.

3. Library of Congress, Network Development and MARC Standards Office, *Format Integration and its Effect on the USMARC Bibliographic Format* (Washington, DC: Library of Congress, 1995), 1.

4. *Anglo-American Cataloging Rules*, Prepared by the American Library Association, the Library of Congress, the Library Association, and the Canadian Library Association, North American text (Chicago: American Library Association, 1967).

5. American Library Association, Catalog Code Revision Committee, *Final Report of the Catalog Code Revision Committee Subcommittee on Rules for Cataloging Machine-Readable Data Files* (Chicago: American Library Association, 1976), 36.

6. *Anglo-American Cataloguing Rules*, 2nd ed. (Chicago: American Library Association, 1978), 203.

7. American Library Association, Task Force on the Descriptive Cataloging of Microcomputer Software, *Guidelines for Using AACR2 Chapter 9 for Cataloging Microcomputer Software* (Chicago: American Library Association, 1984).

8. *Anglo-American Cataloguing Rules*, 2nd ed., chap. 9, "Computer Files, Draft Revision" (Chicago: American Library Association, 1987).

9. Jay Weitz, *Cataloger's Judgment: Music Cataloging Questions and Answers from the Music OCLC Users Group Newsletter* (Westport, CT: Libraries Unlimited, 2004), xix–xx.

10. Jay Weitz, "From ICPSR to Playaways: Evolving Standards for the Cataloging of Electronic Resources" (address, spring conference of the New England Technical Services Librarians, Worcester, MA, April 4, 2008), http://www.nelib.org/netsl/pastprograms/2008/Weitz.ppt (accessed March 1, 2010).

12 CATALOGER SURVIVAL IN A SEA OF CHANGE AND A SURFEIT OF ACRONYMS

John F. Myers

What is a cataloger to do these days? Seemingly long gone are the days when one could get by on knowledge of the ISBD (International Standard Bibliographic Description), AACR2, and MARC (Machine-Readable Cataloging) alone, with a leavening of Cutter, Ranganathan, and Lubetzky. Complicating this simple past is a current welter of acronyms and initialisms to befuddle and confound the work-a-day cataloger: MODS, METS, SGML, XML, DACS, DCRM, CCO, FAST, IME ICC, DC, FRBR, FRAD, FRSAD, RDF, RDA,[1] and who knows what else. This cluster of acronyms is only symptomatic of a larger change in the world of cataloging as ever-increasing amounts of information and information resources are digitized, yielding greater amounts of metadata encoded in a dazzling array of schema, and a subsequent range of methods to manage it all.

I have no crystal ball that will tell me what the future cataloging world will look like. I am confident however, that as long as information resources are being created, there will be a need to describe, organize, and provide access to them. Until some very effective artificial intelligence is developed, there will be a need for human interaction to regularize and contextualize descriptions in order to foster access and organization. At its heart, what is the calling of our particular corner of librarianship? Is the mastery of arcane bodies of rules, standards, and encoding schema truly what draws us? Or is it some other higher purpose, to take the panoply of others' creative endeavors and add to it by making them more accessible? If, as I believe, it is the latter, then it becomes much easier to embrace an uncertain future in which our stalwart companions ISBD, AACR2, and MARC may no longer have a place.

We librarians design well when moved to redesign our work. We have long recognized the maxim that if one lacks the time to do a task properly, then neither will there be the time to fix it after it is done poorly. Historically, we have been well served by this impulse since we deal with large, complex, and long-term data systems, which until recently had record structures that were very challenging to change retrospectively. In other, more commercial fields of endeavor, data that are poorly conceived or maintained in poorly designed formats have a strong likelihood of rotating out as personnel or inventories evolve. A redesign or new release of the data system need only deal with a small residue to clean up during the transition. Libraries, however, do not enjoy the "luxury" of continuous inventory turnover and obsolescence. Instead, a significant amount of library data is preserved long term. This requires significant effort to maintain compatibility with prior systems and significant costs to handle large-scale data conversion. Over the past fifty years, to avoid the consequences of bad design, we have relied on Lubetzky's ideas as espoused in the Paris Principles, which then went on to inform the development of AACR and the ISBD family. We have also relied on the groundbreaking work of Henrietta Avram in the development of MARC to convert cataloging data recorded in card-based technology into an electronically conveyable format.

Above and beyond the obsolescence of the technology (linear-memory-access) on which Avram's work was founded, most of the products (i.e., cataloging records) generated from ISBD, AACR2, and MARC are predicated on the need for human parsing and interpretation of the descriptive metadata created for a resource. This situation is increasingly untenable, with respect to both the sheer volume of resources to be described and competition by other technologies and information providers. The calls are growing increasingly louder for machine-readable cataloging that is not just conveyable by machines, but also interpretable by machines. Hence, the multiplying slew of acronyms and initialisms that are encompassing the burgeoning set of standards and protocols being developed to achieve this end.

What is to be done in the face of this challenge? We need to realize that things are not as different as they may seem at first glance. Although the impact of digitization significantly affects the outward appearance of our standards, the essential form in many instances remains the same. An apt illustration is a comparison of Cutter's well-established Objects and Means,[2] which form the conceptual basis for both his *Rules for a Dictionary Catalog* and a century of cataloging codes, with the relative newcomer, Functional Requirements for Bibliographic Records (FRBR).[3] At first the two seem widely divergent, particularly given the significant difference in extent—Cutter's concise single page versus FRBR's 144 pages (including extensive tables and an index). As will be shown, however, the heartbeat of Cutter's principles lives on in FRBR.

First, some background. Cutter's Objects and Means are laid out in his Rules for a Dictionary Catalog as follows:[4]

OBJECTS

1. To enable a person to find a book of which either
   (A) The author is known

(B) The title is known
(C) The subject is known
2. To show what the library has
   (D) By a given author
   (E) On a given subject
   (F) In a given kind of literature
3. To assist in the choice of a book
   (G) As to its edition (bibliographically)
   (H) As to its character (literary or topical)

MEANS

1. Author-entry with the necessary references (for A and D)
2. Title-entry or title-reference (for B)
3. Subject-entry, cross-references, and classed subject-table (for C and E)
4. Form-entry* (for F)
5. Giving edition and imprint, with notes when necessary (for G)
6. Notes (for H)

   *Here the whole is designated by its most important member. The full name would be form-and-language entry. Kind-entry would not suggest the right idea. (Cutter's footnote)

The lengthier text of FRBR does not support so concise a quotation, but some of the key concepts to be drawn from it are:

1. User tasks of: "*Find* entities that correspond to the user's stated search criteria," "*Identify* an entity (i.e., to confirm [it] corresponds to the entity sought . . .)," "*Select* an entity that is appropriate to the user's requirements . . .," and "*Obtain* access to the entity described."[5]
2. Three entity groups, conveniently labeled Group 1, Group 2, and Group 3, respectively encompassing: "the products of intellectual endeavor,"[6] "those responsible for the intellectual or artistic content,"[7] and "the subjects of works."[8]
3. In the Group 1 entities, a further breakdown into four categories: Work, "distinct intellectual or artistic creation"; Expression, "the intellectual or artistic realization of a work"; Manifestation, "the physical embodiment of an expression of a work"; and Item, "a single exemplar of a manifestation."[9]

An easy contrast to make is what the cataloging records resulting from these two systems are intended to describe—books with Cutter versus bibliographic entities/resources with FRBR. This is, however, but a simple acknowledgement by FRBR's authors that the scope of the bibliographic universe has expanded greatly—commercial production of the tangible media prevalent through the twentieth century was just beginning in Cutter's day, while electronics and the digitization efforts of recent years were practically outside the scope of people's wildest dreams.

Once past this superficial difference, the parallels between the systems are stronger, first with the three verb phrases employed in Cutter's three objects: "find a book," "show what the library has," and "assist in the choice." These are but earlier renditions of three of the four FRBR user tasks: "find," "identify," and "select." The broader venue of users' information seeking behavior under consideration in FRBR, and the wider range of selection criteria, do make direct correspondence to Cutter's system somewhat challenging. While the words that describe user tasks in both conceptual systems are the same (or similar), their meanings are a little different: the FRBR task "find" is more analogous to Cutter's "show," while Cutter's "find" is more analogous to FRBR's "identify." The actions described by Cutter are still represented in FRBR, but have been modified for a larger bibliographic universe.

Another parallel can be drawn between the grammatical objects of Cutter's first object: author, title, and subject; which are directly analogous to FRBR's entity groups: "author" is equivalent to FRBR's Group 2 entities of the parties responsible for intellectual or artistic content; "title" to FRBR's Group 1 entities of the products of intellectual or artistic endeavor; and "subject" to FRBR's Group 3 entities of the subjects of works.

Even the breakdown of FRBR's Group 1 entities finds a rudimentary expression in Cutter across his objects. Part of Cutter's first object addresses title, analogous to the FRBR "work," or distinct intellectual/artistic creation; the second object partially concerns "a given kind of literature," which the footnote to the corresponding Cutter "Means" indicates as meaning the "form-and-language," and which is analogous to the FRBR "expression," or the intellectual/artistic realization of a work; and the third Cutter object addresses edition, analogous to the FRBR "manifestation," or physical embodiment of an expression of a work.

Of course, the facile equivalence of books with bibliographic resources in the previous analysis highlights the real challenge we face as we make the tripartite transition from: (1) dealing with books, moving to traditional tangible media, and then to the broad diversity of digital media; (2) using unitary standards that produced cards in a fixed format, moving to a suite of standards that separately address content, transfer, and display of data; and (3) working in an environment in which we deal with records on a one-by-one basis, and moving to one in which records are dealt with en masse. All three represent different facets of the challenge of moving from fairly concrete and empirical standards to standards addressing the abstract. This shift to the abstract has engendered an array of new, specialized vocabulary.

For instance, we can no longer assume a resource will be a book, expressed in a volume or volumes of written pages. Consequently, we have moved (or had to move) from the simple recording, in early cataloging codes, of the basic physical description of books with respect to their pagination or volumes, to the imminent scenario in RDA where we need to specify what is the medium of the content, what is the carrier of that content, and lastly, what is the extent of that content in terms appropriate to its carrier. We have moved from headings on a card, to access points in a database, and then, even more abstract, from "literal value strings" to "non-literal value strings."[10] For those bewildered, as I was, by those two phrases, "literal value strings" are the sequence of letters or numbers we can read that directly convey the thing meant, e.g., "Mark Twain" for Mark Twain, and "5" for 5; while "non-literal value strings" are surrogates to convey the thing meant, e.g., the Library of Congress Control Number (LCCN) "n79021164" for Mark Twain signifies the unique control number assigned to his Library of Congress name authority record, which represents this particular name authority heading.

What, then, is necessary to navigate these new complexities, beyond awareness that at their root, many new standards bear familiar underpinnings? It requires tapping into the fundamental ethos of our profession, and grasping a visualization of a future that transcends where we are today, yet adheres to the fundamental purpose of our endeavors. Despite the long and comfortable period in a cataloging environment defined by ISBD, AACR, and MARC, we must remember that these are only the means to an end. In the long run, it is not the ability to create the perfectly coded MARC record or the perfect application of ISBD punctuation that defines a cataloger. It is, rather, the ability to describe, organize, and provide access to information resources. Without standards, we would repeatedly need to develop practices from first principles. With them, we can easily and consistently refer to a given "rule," like AACR2 21.1B2 (general rule for entry of a work under a corporate body), without revisiting one hundred years' worth of thinking and practice concerning the nature of corporate responsibility for authorship. Standards foster the distribution of work by making the cataloging records resulting from their guidance have some common basis and mutual intelligibility. It is essential to retain a firm focus on the truth that standards of every shape are not our masters to intimidate us, but are instead our servants in the pursuit of our larger ideals. Only with such focus can we move forward with the confidence and flexibility needed to face the changing cataloging landscape.

NOTES

1. MODS, Metadata Object Description Schema; METS, Metadata Encoding and Transmission Standard; SGML, Standard Generalized Markup Language; XML, Extensible Markup Language; DACS, *Describing Archives: a Content Standard*; DCRM, *Descriptive Cataloging of Rare Materials* (in serials and books versions); CCO, *Cataloging Cultural Objects*; FAST, Faceted Application of Subject Terminology; IME ICC, IFLA Meetings of Experts on an International Cataloguing Code; DC, Dublin Core; FRBR, *Functional Requirements for Bibliographic Records*; FRAD, *Functional Requirements for Authority Data*; FRSAD, *Functional Requirements for Subject Authority Data*; RDF, Resource Description Framework; RDA, *Resource Description and Access*.

2. Charles A. Cutter, *Rules for a Dictionary Catalog*. 2nd ed. (Washington, DC: GPO, 1876), 8.

3. *Functional Requirements for Bibliographic Records: Final Report* (Munich: K. G. Saur, 1998).

4. Cutter, *Rules*, 8.

5. *Functional Requirements for Bibliographic Records*, 82.

6. Ibid., 12.

7. Ibid., 13.

8. Ibid., 16.

9. Ibid., 12.

10. Andy Powell et al., "DCMI Abstract Model. 2.2 The DCMI Description Set Model," Dublin Core Metadata Initiative, June 4, 2007 http://dublincore.org/documents/abstract-model/ (accessed May 12, 2010).

13   CHANGING MIND-SET, CHANGING SKILL SET: TRANSITIONING FROM CATALOGER TO METADATA LIBRARIAN

Christine Schwartz

INTRODUCTION

As I see it, there is a crisis in traditional library cataloging that continues to worsen with each passing year. Deprofessionalization, outsourcing, and the promises of the Internet and digitization have come together like a perfect storm. It's very hard to watch something that you've placed so much value on—the careful organization, subject analysis, and classification of print library materials—being devalued. Yet there's no denying that it is. A new digital culture, in many ways antithetical to the values of traditional cataloging, seems to have won the day. And we as a community have been slow to react. It's not clear yet whether cataloging as we know it will survive this digital turn, or become obsolete. There are voices on both sides of the debate (and in the middle) as to where cataloging will end up in the arsenal of the library profession. Those of us who are catalogers now are living through this confusing period of transition. One thing is for sure: we're not *sure* how print and digital library resources will be collected, preserved, and cataloged in the future. More and more, it seems that the digital is winning out over the printed book. We're told almost daily that we must compete with the Internet business giants such as Google and Amazon to deliver "information" to our users, and that their approach to metadata is to be preferred. As a result, in many libraries, working with traditional print library collections is being deemphasized in favor of developing digital collections, and staff and material resources are being shifted accordingly.

This essay is an attempt to describe some aspects of one cataloger's experience living through this period of transition. After eighteen years working as either a cataloger or head cataloger, I've now been a metadata librarian for two years.

While I was involved with metadata projects in some capacity in the past, the move to metadata librarian felt swift and drastic. I strictly work only with digital collections and no longer do any traditional AACR2/MARC (Machine-Readable Cataloging) cataloging. Also, my new job is more technical than some metadata librarians in that I've had to learn and work with XQuery, a programming language used to query and manipulate XML (Extensible Markup Language) data using a native XML database, the MarkLogic Server platform. I also work on metadata directly in an XML editor, not a user interface that neatly "hides" the XML. My work still rests on a solid foundation of traditional library cataloging, but has changed in significant ways. Most days, I feel like I'm doing a completely different job. My day-to-day tasks as a metadata librarian are very different from my work as a cataloger (although I can imagine that for other metadata librarians, this is not the case). Because we outsource the production end of digital image work and metadata creation, I oversee the process, designing the metadata prototype specifications and working on quality control after production.

METADATA MIND-SET

Actually, there's a part of me that's hesitant to write about metadata librarianship at all. This hesitancy rests on a couple of factors. First, I've had a long career as a cataloger, but a short tenure as a metadata librarian. So, I'm hardly the voice of authority. The second reason comes out of the nature of metadata librarianship itself and that is, it's not monolithic. This is not a cliché, but the reality of the work. While we are all doing similar things, metadata librarians approach metadata work and problems differently: different systems, tools, schemas and schema combinations, data models, workflows, types of digital objects, etc. This is one of the characteristics of metadata librarianship that can make it interesting. It's this lack of standardization, this ambiguity of how to apply "the rules," that may be a good starting place to begin looking at the differences between cataloging and metadata creation.

Jenn Riley, a metadata librarian who writes extensively and teaches in the field, comments about this diversity on her blog, Inquiring Librarian:

> I've found the metadata community in libraries to be a very open one. When I'm starting on a task that I haven't done before, I use what I can from my experience with similar tasks. But I also ask around for advice from others who do have that experience. **"Metadata" is a very big and diverse area of work. Even with the best abstract thinking, applying known principles to new environments, we all often need a boost for getting started from someone who has been through a given situation.**[1]
> [Emphasis added]

So the first step of going from cataloger to metadata librarian is really a change in mind-set, a paradigm shift away from standardization, toward a multiplicity of options. Accepting ambiguity sounds easy, but it's actually one of the hardest parts of the process. Traditional library cataloging standards and structures, while complex, are extensive and relatively clear. For those of us who have been cataloging a long time, we know what we're doing, and we know where to find the answers for something we haven't done before. We have a framework, an edifice that, for the most part, is stable and sure. One of the joys of library cataloging is working creatively within the limits of the rules and standards for bibliographic description, authority control, subject analysis, and classification. I often read comments from younger librarians in the library blogosphere complaining about the stringent cataloging rules. But for me, the value of the rules far outweighs their problems, because this edifice has allowed us to share our work. My respect for "the rules" comes from years of experience knowing that the users in the libraries where I've worked have benefited from not just my work, but the work of other catalogers who have contributed to bibliographic utilities. There is a sense that we, the cataloging community, are contributing to something greater than ourselves using shared bibliographic standards and structures. Contributing to the OCLC WorldCat database is a communal effort based on trust and OCLC policy. We strive for accuracy and consistency, and while by no means perfect, this sharing of work has been a great benefit to our library's users. So, it's a bit of a jolt to realize that while there are library metadata standards and schemes, there is much freedom in how they're applied to local digital projects. It's cataloger's judgment on steroids! And the metadata librarian is not the only voice in the choir when deciding how things will be done, since most digital projects are developed by teams.

Another voice from the library blogosphere, Irvin Flack writes: "I agree about the diverse [metadata] workflows. There are potentially as many types of metadata librarian as there are types and contexts of metadata, [i.e.] lots. I think that's one of the big differences between 'cataloguer' and 'metadata librarian' as job titles."[2] So, yes, while there are established metadata structures and standards, there is quite a bit of latitude in their application. A cataloger has to accept this freedom as part of the package.

How else does a cataloger's mind-set have to change? Another significant change is getting away from the idea of cataloging one item at a time. I first learned this from Diane Hillmann's "Metadata Standards and Applications" workshop, a professional development training course developed for the Library of Congress.[3] This concept stood out as being significant and has proved to be very true in my work as a metadata librarian. With traditional cataloging, we describe the physical items one at a time, and new items are integrated into the existing classified library collection. Classification is not just an address or location, but a system that intellectually and structurally makes sense out of large collections of library materials. With digital resources, I usually work on a project that encompasses batches of items all at once: a full-run collection of journals published by our institution or a complete archival collection going from microfilm to a digital version. A digital project is approached from a more holistic perspective. All my current work focused on several different digital projects. There are times when I'm working on an individual record, but since we outsource the production of metadata, this step is usually part of quality control at the end of the process.

METADATA SKILL SET

Let's turn now to changes in skill set and information technology (IT) competencies. This is probably the area of metadata librarianship that some catalogers are nervous about, and rightly so. As I already mentioned, it almost feels like we're being asked to do a new, more technical job. Some catalogers have already been pulled into systems work (especially those in smaller libraries where there isn't a staff position for systems librarian). In general, however, catalogers are traditionally users of the computer as a tool that gets the job done; we aren't necessarily involved in the more technical aspects of computing. While we're comfortable working with the structured data of the MARC format, we are not necessarily literate in the world of information technology. With metadata work, many of us are being asked to really stretch and learn new IT skills. I've focused on this issue in several posts on the blog, Cataloging Futures.[4] From these blog post comments, I've benefited from the insight of others, especially the technologists in our field, as to what type of IT skills need to be learned. Here's an overview including some IT competencies suggested from the Metadata Blog as well.[5]

- Metadata librarians should know XML.
- Relational database design: may not have to be an Oracle programmer, but should understand the structure, and be able to form queries.
- Be able to do data modeling.
- Have traditional cataloging skills as well as database, XML, XSLT (Extensible Stylesheet Language Transformations) skills.
- Maybe cannot do all of the computer programming, but should be able to read programs and know what they do. Basically, have the ability to speak the language.
- Learn a scripting language (Perl, Ruby, Python, etc.).
- Learn to move from the MARC environment to the non-MARC environment.
- Learn systems analysis/theory.
- Have a willingness to learn new technologies/standards and to experiment/play with them
- Learn to read code: XML, SQL (Structured Query Language), and CQL (Contextual Query Language).
- Learn about what makes the Web work.
- Talk to people who are making the Semantic Web work.
- Find a way to get your data onto the Semantic Web.
- Understand more about how computers work, what they can do, and what they can't do.
- Develop a fundamental understanding of computer systems and modern technology.

WHY CONSIDER LEARNING PROGRAMMING

So, computer programming came up on this list—a lot. There are a few reasons why a cataloger transitioning to metadata librarian should consider learning to program. One is the skill set reason. It is much easier to do quality control on metadata by using programming than by editing by hand. I've learned this the hard way through experience. When I started out, I was editing and creating METS (Metadata Encoding and Transmission Standard) documents by hand. The structural METS document is very detailed, complex, and incredibly tedious to edit. It did not take me long to figure out that this was an inefficient way to accomplish the task at hand. At the same time, my colleague was just starting to teach me XQuery, a programming language used to query and manipulate XML data. He told me that I would develop a toolkit of queries for my day-to-day metadata work. At first, this seemed like a daunting goal. I was a bit incredulous. Now two years later, I'm very comfortable using XQuery for my routine tasks to the point where I'm disappointed if I can't find a way to use programming to accomplish a task. There will always remain some work that requires human review and intervention, and this type of work is very similar to traditional library cataloging. For metadata librarians at large institutions, this may be the primary focus of their metadata work. For them, the change from cataloging to metadata creation is not so dramatic. But that's not my experience. However, even for these metadata librarians, there is another reason that they, too, should consider learning computer programming, and that is the simple fact that it helps you to communicate better with programmers (and programmers in the digital world are your best friends). For example, in 2008 and 2009, I worked on two software development projects for our digital library platform, the MarkLogic Server. In 2008, I was still struggling with learning XQuery. This year, however, I can now read the code for our digital library system, and this allowed me to better communicate and work with the programmers who developed the software architecture for our system. I will most likely get further training in system administration, and systems work may be a growing aspect of my job in the future.

A final reason to become familiar with computer programming brings us back to mind-set: understanding the concepts of programming helps change the way we think about library metadata. On his blog, Bibliographic Wilderness, Jonathan Rochkind introduced a concept coined by Jeannette Wing, called "computational thinking."[6] Basically, it's the idea that the thought processes of computer science, such concepts as "abstraction" and "automation," should become part of the skill set of the average person in the twenty-first century. Jonathan writes:

> And it's precisely this kind of perspective ("computational thinking") that I think the 21st century cataloger or metadata librarian absolutely needs, to be able to understand how what they do does and can fit into the digital landscape. I've thought before if it would be possible to design

some kind of curriculum in what I thought of as "computer science perspective" that wasn't in fact particularly technical and was not about teaching programming or computer science itself. I wonder if Wing is exploring that idea with "computational thinking," as she seems to think too that it's a way of thinking that's of utility for more than just computer scientists.[7]

Much like Diane Hillmann's writings, this blog post left an impression on me, reading it while I was still a head cataloger. I think we will be hearing more about this marriage of metadata librarianship and computer programming in the near future. For example, Dan Chudnov, a librarian and programmer at the Library of Congress, is starting to write a book to help librarians learn how to program.[8] This is definitely a developing aspect of our profession. Another example is the grassroots development and success of the Code4Lib community, a community that focuses on this intersect of librarianship and technology. Those who write in this community, their blogs and articles, have helped me grow as a metadata librarian probably much more quickly than if I had to struggle on my own. Characteristic of the change we're going through, I've never actually met most of my Code4Lib colleagues; rather, I've just been communicating with them via the Web.

CONCLUSION

So in the last two years of transitioning from cataloger to metadata librarian, where am I? Do I miss traditional cataloging and working with the printed materials? Yes, cataloging books is a creative and interesting process. (This is best described in a brief essay by Richard Murray, "The Whimsy of Cataloging."[9]) Do I enjoying being stretched to learn new things as a metadata librarian? Also, yes. For me, understanding metadata standards, XML technologies, and programming has replaced my previous careful study of the cataloging rules and MARC standards. In particular, I find a similar intellectual satisfaction in programming, working within a set of precise limits in a creative way, that I used to find with the more complex aspects of cataloging. My hope for our profession is that there will be room for both traditional cataloging and metadata creation. My prediction for the future, however, is that traditional cataloging will gradually be replaced by the type of work that metadata librarians are doing now. We as a profession are sometimes overly concerned with the technical. How to solve the technical problems and changes in cataloging is a different question from whether or not we need library cataloging at all. On the second question, I'm completely sanguine that library cataloging has a future. I hope that we will continue to create interesting, intelligent "road maps" for our users that will be of valuable and lasting use for their study and research, and that serendipitous discovery will move from the stacks to the Web. The work of the metadata librarian rests on the shoulders of the catalogers who have gone before them.

Let's respect and retain what is valuable from traditional cataloging, but gear up for the changes expected of us.

NOTES

1. Jenn Riley, "On Metadata 'Experts,' " Inquiring Librarian, April 4, 2006, http://inquiringlibrarian.blogspot.com/2006/04/on-metadata-experts.html (accessed January 14, 2010).

2. Irene Flack, August 28, 2008, comment on Christine Schwartz, "A Negative Take on the Future of Cataloging," Cataloging Futures, August 19, 2008, http://www.catalogingfutures.com/catalogingfutures/2008/08/a-negative-take-on-the-future-of-cataloging.html (accessed January 15, 2010).

3. Library of Congress, Catalogers Learning Workshop, "Metadata Standards & Applications," http://www.loc.gov/catworkshop/courses/metadatastandards/index.html (accessed January 14, 2010).

4. Christine Schwartz, "More Resources on Upgrading Catalogers' Skills," Cataloging Futures, June 9, 2007, http://www.catalogingfutures.com/catalogingfutures/2007/06/more_on_upgradi.html (accessed January 15, 2010).

5. Kristin Martin, "NRMIG Meeting at ALA Annual, Sunday June 28, 2008, 8–10 AM," Metadata Blog, http://blogs.ala.org/nrmig.php?title=nrmig_meeting_at_ala_annual_sunday_june_&more=1&c=1&tb=1&pb=1 (accessed January 14, 2010).

6. Jeannette M. Wing, "Computational Thinking," Communications of the ACM 49, no. 3 (March 2006): 33–35, http://www.cs.cmu.edu/afs/cs/usr/wing/www/publications/Wing06.pdf (accessed January 14, 2010).

7. Jonathan Rochkind, "Computational Thinking," Bibliographic Wilderness, June 18, 2007, http://bibwild.wordpress.com/2007/06/18/ computational-thinking (accessed January 14, 2010).

8. Dan Chudnov, "What Questions Do You Have about Learning Programming?" One Big Library, November 1, 2009, http://onebiglibrary.net/story/what-questions-do-you-have-about-learning-programming (accessed January 14, 2010).

9. Richard A. Murray, "The Whimsy of Cataloging," LIScareer.com, Career Strategies for Librarians, http://www.liscareer.com/murray_cataloging.htm (accessed May 10, 2010).

14 REALITIES OF STANDARDS IN THE TWENTY-FIRST CENTURY

James Weinheimer

In a podcast of a panel debate, "There's No Catalog Like No Catalog,"[1] hosted by LITA (Library and Information Technology Association) at the ALA Annual 2008, you can hear a description of the library catalog. One of the panelists said that the library catalog is the greatest repository of the most "anal-retentive, obsessive-compulsive" activity that he had ever seen. While I won't take issue with this assertion, what was interesting was the response from the audience: embarrassed laughter. I conclude from this that there is some sort of general agreement that anal-retentiveness in such a task is fundamentally a bad thing. This kind of attitude is understandable since terms like anal-retentiveness bring to mind such images as a baby sucking its thumb; and anyone unfortunate enough to be labeled anal-retentive is emotionally in the same early stage of development. This is in contrast to the fully developed adult who has a wider and ultimately better understanding of reality, and who—of course—can focus on more important and far more interesting topics.

I genuinely sympathize with this viewpoint, but I also find it rather strange. Blind adherence to standards is not such a bad thing in all cases. For example, I hope that when I am flying on an airplane, the airplane mechanics working on my plane are rather obsessive-compulsive about their work and they do not simply say, "Well, this isn't quite right, but, it is *good enough*." Or if someone is working on the roof of my house, I hope the carpenter doesn't say, "Well, it's too much trouble to see how these pieces are supposed to fit together. I'll just use this nail I have handy."

I suspect there are several people out there who would agree on this point, and they would join me in hoping (and expecting) that the professionals whom we rely upon would put out some extra effort to check and follow the standard ways of doing their work. If that means they are being anal-retentive or obsessive-compulsive, then so much the better. This is one of the problems I have always had with using terms such as "anal-retentive" toward at least some people and professions. While it may or may not be true, the mere act of disputing such a term almost immediately labels you as ridiculous; while at the same time, we expect others to rely upon, and even more importantly, to *follow standards rigorously* so that our society can function safely, without the wings of airplanes falling off in mid-flight or the roofs of our homes caving in while we are having our morning cup of coffee.

Some may reply that obsessive-compulsiveness is not bad in those instances that are critically important, but for other areas of our economy and society, there should be a more relaxed attitude. While medicine and law would be examples of the former, we can assume that bibliography and cataloging would be examples of the latter, since errors in bibliography and cataloging do not threaten anyone's life or fortune. But that is not entirely true, either. Legal and health professionals rely on research found through bibliographies and catalogs, and as a result, they rely on those who make the bibliographies and catalogs. Errors in information retrieval for a physician or a lawyer may result in health risks to their patients or loss in court. There has been a regular succession of articles that discuss the problems of citation errors in scholarly publications, with results that range from citation analyses incorrectly performed, to suspicions that the authors never read the articles they cited in the first place.[2] Of course, none of this is news to reference librarians, who immediately assume there is a problem with the citation the moment they experience any trouble finding something.

But why do catalogers have these standards? Do they serve any real purpose other than to give some rather dubious employment to a part of our society? True, some may get caught up in the overwhelming work of the moment; and they do things just because "the rule says so." Does that make it bad? In fact, it turns out that the reason we have these standards—believe it or not—is to save our libraries, and our users, time and money. How, someone may ask, could this possibly be? Look at all of these crazy rules. Look at all the exceptions. Why do we have these things?

I shall only discuss that part of cataloging dealing with bibliographic description in this essay. I don't think you will find too many people who maintain that author access or subject access is simply unnecessary, although it may be very poorly implemented in our catalogs. In the eyes of many people, however, bibliographic description is akin to performing an autopsy on a corpse. These people are perhaps thinking, or voicing, some of these questions and statements:

- Who needs this level of boring detail?
- It just can't be that hard—it's the catalogers who are making it hard.
- Anyone who looks at the rules can see that there are far too many of them.
- They are horribly boring to read and cover too many inane possibilities.
- It is much better to let people decide these things for themselves and this is where both time and money can be saved.

- It takes a lot of training just to learn how to use the rules; it takes even more time to use them, and time is what we don't have.
- Nobody is going to die if a book on art or philosophy is cataloged a little bit wrong.
- Who cares?

On the last question, I shall answer: *you* care. But to explain this further, I must resort to citing specific examples. I can come up with thousands of examples, but I shall discuss only one. This is the kind of example that makes people sigh and causes their eyes to roll back in their heads: counting the number of pages in a book. The rules for counting the number of pages in a book go on and on. In the newest ISBD (International Standard Bibliographic Description) standard, rules for counting pages go from p. 182 to 191, in its online PDF version.[3] What difference does it make? Who cares?

I shall make a confession that may come as a surprise: as a cataloger, I don't care, either. I couldn't care less how many pages a book has. Whether it has 12 pages or 120, or is 25 volumes, is of absolutely no interest to me. Yet, I do care about making my job easier and more efficient. Part of my job as a cataloger is to determine if an item I am working on is a copy of an item already in the collection. So let's think about this: while a single book has only so many pages, one thing I have discovered is that there are many, many different ways to count those pages. Let's take some examples that come readily to hand. Here is the paging information for three books of Mark Twain, taken from the catalog of the University of Michigan Library.

The abbreviations in the following examples are defined in ODLIS (Online Dictionary for Library and Information Science)[4] as follows.

1. p. L. or L. means pages of leaves and leaf, respectively. A folded single sheet has two pages, one on each side of the sheet, but often only one side is printed and numbered. This is the "leaf."
2. p. means page, which is one side of a leaf. A folded single sheet of paper has two pages, recto (right side) and verso (left side), and both pages generally are printed and numbered.
3. pl. signifies plate, which is generally an illustration printed on one side of thicker or glossier paper, with the reverse side of the page remaining blank, or with a legend describing the illustration.
4. port., front., and illus. are abbreviations for illustrations: portrait, frontispiece, and illustration(s). Frontispiece is an unnumbered illustration that comes before the title page or first page.

EXAMPLE 1: 4 p. L., 3-264 p. front. (port.) 2 pl.

This is the pagination and illustration data found in the physical description field (MARC 300 field) of the MARC cataloging record for a 1935 edition of Mark Twain's *Christian Science* work, in Michigan's online catalog, as transcribed by the cataloger from the physical work itself. The MARC record is available at http://mirlyn.lib.umich.edu/Record/000439243/Details#tabs.

Compare this transcription of the pagination and illustration of the work to the Hathi Trust Digital Library full text, original scanned version, available via a "Full text" link in Michigan's online catalog at http://mirlyn.lib.umich.edu/Record/000439243, or directly available at http://hdl.handle.net/2027/mdp .39015064368478.

EXAMPLE 2: 6 p. L., [17]-274, [1] p. incl. front., illus.

This is the pagination and illustration data found in the physical description field (MARC 300 field) of the MARC cataloging record for an 1881 edition of Mark Twain's *The Adventures of Tom Sawyer*, in Michigan's online catalog, as transcribed by the cataloger from the physical work itself. The MARC record is available at http://mirlyn.lib.umich.edu/Record/000200694/Details#tabs

Compare this transcription of the pagination and illustration of the work to the Hathi Trust Digital Library full text, original scanned version, available via a "Full text" link in Michigan's online catalog at http://mirlyn.lib.umich.edu/Record/000200694, or directly available at http://hdl.handle.net/2027/mdp .39015062680924

EXAMPLE 3: iv p., 2 L., 522, [1] p. front. (port.) illus., 7 pl.

This is the pagination and illustration data found in the physical description field (MARC 300 field) of the MARC cataloging record for a 1906 edition of Mark Twain's *The $30,000 Bequest and Other Stories*, in Michigan's online catalog, as transcribed by the cataloger from the physical work itself. The MARC record is available at http://mirlyn.lib.umich.edu/Record/000664372/Details#tabs.

Compare this transcription of the pagination and illustration of the work to the Hathi Trust Digital Library full text, original scanned version, available via a "Full text" link in Michigan's online catalog at: http://mirlyn.lib.umich.edu/Record/000664372, or directly available at: http://hdl.handle.net/2027/mdp.39015047754505.

The paging examples given here show earlier practices that were highly complex, describing leaves, frontispieces, portraits, and other aspects of the book. These practices have been simplified dramatically over the years. For instance, in former times, the "L." could be capitalized as here, or it may have been in lower case; "port." may become "por." or even "por. of gr." for a group portrait.[5] Whereas before, people would note down, or transcribe, blank pages, the beginnings and ends of page sequences, and so on, today we simply cite the final page of each sequence of paging. Not everyone in the world follows ISBD and AACR2, however. Other bibliographic agencies have quite different practices and may take this complexity and add them together in various ways. Because there is no single standard to record pagination over time and in all countries, the number of *pages* in the examples could be interpreted in many ways.

In Example 1, paging might be *limited only to the pages with page numbers on them*: 4 p.L. + (264–3 unnumbered pages), which could be interpreted and recorded as *265 p.* Example 2 paging might be read as: 6 p.L. + (274–17 unnumbered pages), or *263 p.* Example 3 would follow the same pattern: 4 p. + 522 p., for *526 p.*

In the modern era, leaves are not included in the page count as they are simple leaves, not pages. They are usually recorded separately in modern-era pagination as found in the third example: "2 L." or they may be ignored altogether. Similarly, plates, "pl." in Examples 1 and 3, are recorded in a separate pagination count for plates in the modern era, and are not included in the page count.

Other agencies may add in all the blank pages, and even the end papers; some ignore everything except the main paging. Some count plates, some ignore plates. Others leave that up to the cataloger.

This very small example should make it clear that the information about the number of pages is very closely connected to *how it is done*. As a cataloger, I do not care at all how it is done. While I have my own opinions on the *best way* to do it, what is far more important is that everybody does it in the *same way*. It wouldn't bother me one bit if somebody made a list of all the ways of counting the pages, printed them out, hung them on a wall, and then handed a dart to a monkey and let it decide with a toss. I honestly do not care, but if everybody can do whatever they want, then "256 p." ceases to mean anything at all. As a cataloger, I simply want to know if I am looking at the same item or not, without having to get up and walk into the stacks to get the book; or, now that we catalog into cooperative databases, I don't want to have to bother people at other libraries, where there may be a possible copy of my book, to ask them to check the number of pages for me. I say if the paging ceases to mean anything, why continue recording it? As a cataloger, I'll confess that I really don't care.

But now I shall change my "hat" and cease being a cataloger. Suddenly, I am a library book selector. Do I care about the paging? Yes, because if I am considering buying a book, I need to know if it already exists in the collection. If I waste my funds on mounds of duplicates, that won't make my users or my supervisors very happy. If I am forced to march into the stacks every time I need to know the real number of pages in a book, that is a huge waste of my time, and I will complain.

I'll change hats again: now I am a library patron. Do I care about the paging of Mark Twain's work? Yes, that is, if I am interested in studying Mark Twain and it is vital to me to know the number of pages that each item has. I need to know that one version of *Huckleberry Finn* has 275 pages while another has 283 pages, since this probably indicates a textual variant. In fact, if I am studying the printing history of *Huckleberry Finn*, I may prefer the older methods of paging cited in the examples above, or perhaps I would prefer something with far more detail than that. This is important information to some scholars, and it turns out that they will actually incur the expense of traveling from one library to another just to see a variant. If they can get the resource they need through interlibrary loan, this also has considerable costs. So, does this user who is considering making a trip to another collection to view a particular copy of a book care about the paging? Does the interlibrary loan librarian, who is responsible for a budget and staff time, care? Absolutely, and consequently, if there are problems, the user and interlibrary loan librarian will both complain.

Now for the final hat: I am the library manager who tries to balance the desires of the users with the resources at hand. I know that there is a frightening amount of material waiting for cataloging, which is growing every day, and it is absolutely vital to keep these materials moving so that they will be on the shelves where people can use them. Therefore, I am interested in my catalogers making records as quickly as possible. Doing incredibly detailed paging is time consuming, and tradeoffs have to be made. It was mentioned earlier that the catalogers will do what they are told to do to manage the collection, so if tomorrow the managers said to stop adding the paging to records, there would be some howling, but they would do it since they are professionals. The real screams would come from the selectors, the users, and the interlibrary loan librarians because the catalog records would no longer serve their needs. So, the current ISBD rules offer a compromise among all parties concerned.

Does the library manager care about the paging? No, but the manager doesn't want to hear a lot of complaints from everybody and must try to keep the business of the library moving smoothly.

To sum up, the information in a record is certainly important, but just as important are the rules (standards) that determine what that information means. That is why each part of a catalog record is governed by rules and standards: to guarantee that it means something, and means the same something to everyone. This goes for "256 p." as much as "2008," "Twain, Mark, 1835–1910," or "World War, 1914–1918." We can't just put in whatever we want, that is, not if we want the records to mean the same thing to everyone. Maybe the result is not roofs caving in or wings falling off of airplanes, but there will be gross levels of inefficiency, and everyone, including our users, will be increasingly skeptical of the information they see in the catalog.

STANDARDS AND THE WORLD WIDE WEB

The paging variation examples provide a basic idea of the importance of standards, but when we discuss standards in terms of today, matters are somewhat different. The changes stem primarily from an unavoidable fact: the number of materials available to our users has increased exponentially, and even when we limit these to the so-called "worthwhile" materials (i.e., items that always would be selected for a library's collection, no matter the format), the numbers are still enormous and absolutely overwhelming for our current library methods.

This situation is not entirely unprecedented and has happened before during the nineteenth and early twentieth centuries when the creation of books became automated and their numbers grew rapidly. The library community responded by sharing the catalog records they created. This took quite a bit of work: not only was a standard-sized card necessary for sharing, but more importantly, the information itself needed to be standardized. In practice, this meant that smaller libraries followed the methods and processes (i.e., the standards) of the "big boys," meaning the national libraries, e.g., Library of Congress, British Library, Bibliothèque nationale de France, and so on. One of the most wrenching changes in librarianship today is the realization that these institutions are the big boys no longer. Today, the big boys are huge, powerful nonlibrary corporations such as Google, Yahoo, and Facebook, with corporate values completely at odds with those of traditional library values. These are the organizations that are creating the tools that our modern information society is currently using, and will use in the future. It is almost impossible to imagine that libraries could create separate tools that could compete meaningfully in such an environment.

This means that libraries are in the process of losing control of the tools their patrons use for information access; in fact, libraries have already lost control of many of them. The only place where librarians can still exert control is within their own catalogs, but fewer and fewer people use them. Even if libraries agreed to work with entities such as Google, that leaves all the power in Google's hands, as when Google decided that they would no longer work with the OAI-PMH (Open Archives Initiative Protocol for Metadata Harvesting) format in favor of site maps.[6] If OAI-PMH is too much, where does that leave MARC21? I believe the answer is all too clear.

On a more positive note, Google, Yahoo, and the others mostly do not create the data (or metadata), and anything they *do* make will be created automatically. What they actually do is take the metadata created by others and rework it in different ways. As a result, these industries rely on our work.

It's not so simple, though. This can have strange results, and although there have been concerns expressed over the quality of the Google Books metadata,[7] what is even more enlightening is to see exactly where Google has placed the traditional library information. For example, following a link[8] and reviewing the resulting screen displays in Google Books for *Rome: An Oxford Archaeological Guide* (by Amanda Claridge and others, published in 1998 by Oxford University Press) results in sixteen types of data displayed in the course of five screens. The data are:

1. Book Overview
2. User Ratings
3. Preview the Book
4. Search in this Book
5. Get this book (includes link to WorldCat)
6. Reviews
7. Related Books
8. Common Terms and Phrases
9. References from Web Pages
10. Selected Pages
11. Maps
12. References to this Book
13. Popular Passages
14. Contents

15. Other Editions
16. More Book Information

What do we see in the actual screen displays? The following five figures show how Google Books displays set out this information. Figure 14.1 represents the first screen displayed in Google Books for our title, *Rome: An Oxford Archaeological Guide*. Included in this screen are: Book Overview, User Ratings, Preview the Book, Search in this Book, Get this book (includes link to WorldCat), Reviews, Related Books, and Other Editions.

Figure 14.2 displays the second screen displayed in Google Books for *Rome*. Included in this screen are: a continuation of Related Books, and, Common Terms and Phrases, displayed as a tag cloud.

Figure 14.1
Rome: An Oxford Archaeological Guide, Google Books display screenshot one. (Screenshot courtesy Google Books.)

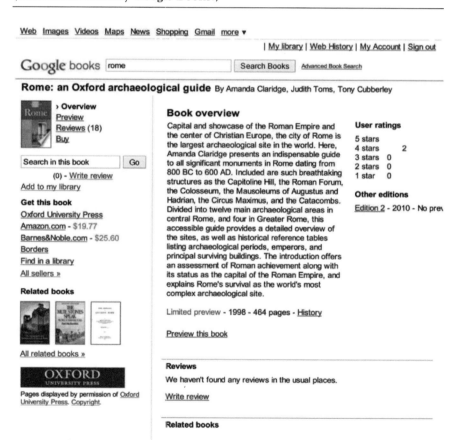

Figure 14.2
Rome: An Oxford Archaeological Guide, Google Books display screenshot two. (Screenshot courtesy Google Books.)

The topography and monuments of ancient Rome
by Samuel Ball Platner
Snippet view - 1911

The Mute Stones Speak: The Story of Archaeology in Italy
by Paul MacKendrick
No preview available - 1984

The remains of ancient Rome
by John Henry Middleton
Snippet view - 1892

All related books »

Common terms and phrases

altar ancient Antoninus Pius Appia apse arcades arch architectural Augustus Aurelius Basilica Basilica Julia Baths Baths of Caracalla brick bronze building built C1 BC C2 BC Caelian Caesar Capitoline Capitoline hill Caracalla catacombs cella church Circus Circus Maximus colonnade columns Comune concrete Constantine Corinthian corner dating decorated Domitian early C2 east emperor entrance Esquiline excavations exhedra facade floor Forum Forum of Caesar fragments frieze front Gate Greek Hadrian hall hill imperial inscription late C1 marble Marcus Marcus Aurelius Mausoleum Maxentius Maximus METRES monuments mosaic Museum Nero Numidian yellow original outer painted palace Palatine Palazzo panels Phrygian purple Piazza podium porch porphyry Porta Porticus precinct probably Quirinal hill rebuilt reconstructed Roman Roman Forum Rome Rome's roof sculpture Septimius Severus Severus shafts side staircase statue stone surviving Temple Tiber tomb Trajan travertine tufa Vatican Museums vaults Vespasian Villa wall

The third screenshot for Google Books *Rome*, Figure 14.3, shows References from Web Pages, Selected Pages, and Maps.

Figure 14.4 displays the fourth screen displayed in Google Books for *Rome*. Included in this screen are: Continuation of Maps from Figure 14.3, References to this Book, and Popular Passages.

Figure 14.5, the last screenshot for *Rome*, shows Contents, Other Editions, and More Book Information.

Figure 14.3

Rome: An Oxford Archaeological Guide, Google Books display screenshot three. (Screenshot courtesy Google Books.)

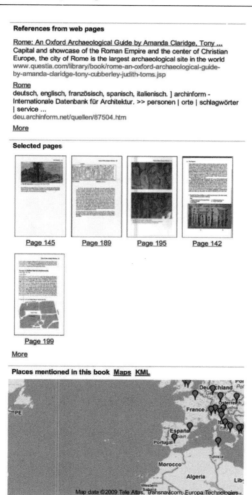

Figure 14.4
Rome: An Oxford Archaeological Guide, Google Books display screenshot four. (Screenshot courtesy Google Books.)

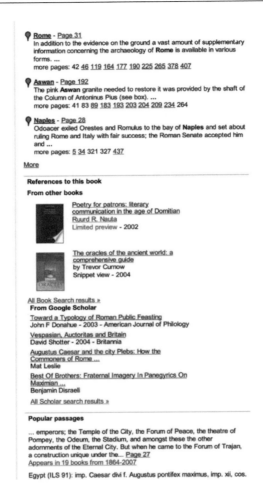

What we have seen in these five screen displays, other than a great number of links to different Google products and other agencies where the searcher can spend money, are all different types of metadata, from social to corporate to tag clouds and more. It turns out that Google has taken the metadata from libraries and placed it in the area *More book information,* at the very bottom of the page in Figure 14.5; in fact, Google has mashed it together with BISAC (Book Industry Study Group) and perhaps other metadata as well.[9]

Figure 14.5
Rome: An Oxford Archaeological Guide, Google Books display screenshot five.
(Screenshot courtesy Google Books.)

xi, trib. pot. xiv, Aegupto in potestatem populi Romani redacta Soli donum
dedit. Page 192
Appears in 8 books from 1880-1998

More

Contents

More

Other editions

Rome
Amanda Claridge
No preview
available - 2010

More book information

Title	Rome: an Oxford archaeological guide
	Oxford archaeological guides
Authors	Amanda Claridge, Judith Toms, Tony Cubberley
Edition	illustrated
Publisher	Oxford University Press, 1998
ISBN	0192880039, 9780192880031
Length	464 pages
Subjects	Excavations (Archaeology)
	Excavations (Archaeology) - Italy - Rome - Guidebooks
	History / Ancient / Rome
	History / Europe / Italy
	Rome
	Rome (Italy)
	Rome (Italy) - Antiquities - Guidebooks
	Rome Region (Italy)
	Rome Region (Italy) - Antiquities - Guidebooks
	Social Science / Archaeology
	Travel / Europe / Italy
	Travel / Museums, Tours, Points of Interest
	Travel / Reference

About Google Books Beta - Help - Privacy Policy - Blog - Mobile - HTML mode - Information for Publishers -
Provide Feedback - Google Home

©2009 Google

A quick comparison, in Figure 14.6, of the Google record with the WorldCat record shows a number of differences that would be very important to a librarian, from differences in titles, to extent and publication information.

The records in Figure 14.6 seem to show that the only information in the Google record taken from the WorldCat record are the author and subject headings, and perhaps the series, since there are changes in all of the other fields.

Figure 14.6
Comparison of Google Books and WorldCat bibliographic records. (Google Record Screenshot courtesy Google Books. WorldCat® record, from OCLC's WorldCat® database, is used with OCLC's permission; WorldCat® is a registered trademark of OCLC Online Computer Library Center, Inc.)

WorldCat Record

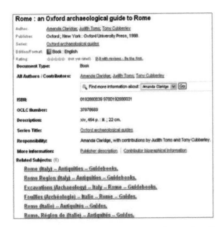

Differences in WorldCat and Google Records

Title
- o Different titles
- o Google record: No space before colon
- o Google record: No statement of responsibility. Authors are listed, similar to WorldCat record

Extent
- o Google record: No place of publication
- o Google record: Incomplete paging, no dimensions

Edition
- o "Illustrated" is not a true edition statement

Google Record

Note:

Reformatted LC Subject Headings mashed-up with BISAC Subjects

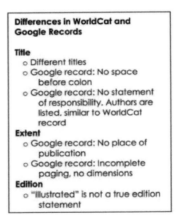

Any Web designer will tell you that the least important part of any Web page is at the bottom, since very few people get that far. This shows quite clearly what Google Books, one of the most powerful information organizations in the world, thinks of our library metadata: it has been placed on the last screen display of five screens, in the last part of the display, as shown in Figure 14.5. Therefore, if people choose not to use separate library catalogs, there is a real possibility that library metadata could end up ignored completely. Of course, another possibility remains, which is to make our metadata more useful and accessible to everyone in general, so that organizations such as Google will be encouraged to bring it further up to the top, perhaps at least above "Popular Passages," as seen in Figure 14.4. This set of screen displays demonstrates the problem of competing metadata very clearly, and how little power libraries have.

What can we do? There is an opportunity today in that all metadata creators are facing practically the same issues and the same challenges of overwhelming numbers of materials and shrinking resources. It is possible today that in the face of a shared threat, people may become more willing to cooperate, although all must admit this will involve tremendous changes for everyone, including libraries, just as it happened in the late nineteenth and early twentieth centuries. It has become almost commonplace today to say that cataloging must be shared, but what does that actually mean? It means that if we are to maintain standards, these standards must be shared as well. Yet, if we are going to cooperate and share, the very first task is to understand what the bibliographic concepts are, and what practices others use.

Different communities have different standards. For example, the Food and Agriculture Organization (FAO) of the UN needs a special way to search by *project*. AACR2 treats these as regular corporate bodies, but that is not nearly specific enough for FAO's needs. There are many other similar examples of different, but very similar needs. Since we have seen that entities such as Google will just mash everything together, we must assume that all this metadata, each following the standards of its respective bibliographic agency, will be mashed together. The result could be sheer chaos, such as in the saying, "Too many cooks spoil the broth." Or something more positive could happen. I submit that with some changes in our thinking, everyone could benefit, and the final result could lead to vastly greater efficiencies for all.

Many, if not most, of the agencies that create bibliographic information will not be libraries, but will be publishing agencies, international organizations, think tanks, entertainment industries, open archives, scholars, teachers, and who knows what others. The task of library cataloging *cannot* be: "we will tell you the way to do this." Instead, it must be somewhat different: if you make and use your metadata in one of these specified ways (e.g., standards), this will enable your records to work together with other records in the most efficient and coherent ways for the general public, resulting in a much better chance of someone finding your materials.

How can this begin? I have recently created the Cooperative Cataloging Rules Wiki[10] as a tentative first step in this direction. The wiki contains the publicly available updates to rules currently followed by libraries in the Anglo-American library community, i.e., the Library of Congress Rule Interpretations. It also links into the online ISBD, plus other links to various other aids for cataloging materials. The Cooperative Cataloging Rules Wiki is a place for the different metadata communities to begin a discussion of bibliographic concepts, their importance, and how to work together. It is hoped that some kind of agreement will be reached, but it is very early in this initiative and no one knows how it will turn out.

Going all the way back to the beginning: where does this leave standards? What role do libraries have today? How do standards work when they are all mashed together, each following different practices and for different purposes? Are standards useless today?

Perhaps in some areas, standards will be of much less use. Applying the rules of general descriptive cataloging to integrating resources (i.e., items that are updated regularly) may prove to be of little benefit. In these cases, the pagination examples above may not have relevance to an online resource that changes daily or weekly. But perhaps new methods will be found, and determining the extent of these types of resource will become important. The same could go for other areas of the bibliographic description. As materials are digitized and made available for computer manipulation, word counts, file compares, and automatic updates from the item itself (e.g., the title of a Web page may change and the update could be automatic) are methods that may take the place of many of our traditional processes, and the final result could actually become more accurate. Standards in other areas may acquire greater importance, especially in the areas of access. For example, as people begin to see problems with the vagaries of keyword access, they may begin to appreciate the control allowed through our name and subject authority work.

PUBLIC AWARENESS

Still, the public needs to be made aware of other methods that may work much better than the Google searches they have become accustomed to using. The library community needs to publicize some popular examples of genuine power searching. I cannot think of anything better than to look at James Burke's episodes 4 and 5 of *The Day the Universe Changed*.[11] Mr. Burke discusses some of the problems of medieval information retrieval, with a discussion of the problems facing the monks who wanted to know what was contained in a manuscript book with the title "Sermones Bonaventurae." (The answer is: Who knows?) This was solved by making a catalog.

Burke then demonstrates the power of indexing, as he uses an index to learn the relationships between "how to survey" and "how to aim cannons." He follows the index from "Surveying" to "Range finders" to "Photography" to "Ballistics," showing that a person can learn much more by using an index than not, and concluding that by using an index, "1 + 1 = 3."

By comparing these types of search methods and tools with Google results, librarians today could demonstrate that certain useful searching possibilities that were available at one time, such as browsing through an index, are not replicated in the newer computer-generated search algorithm and search result ranking tools. This just might lead some inquisitive persons to wonder what else they may be missing.

CONCLUSION

It seems to me that when it comes to metadata, libraries cannot provide more, faster, or cheaper metadata in comparison to automatic production because computers can provide such information in quantities and at speeds that humans cannot hope to challenge. Library cataloging can provide one thing, and one thing alone, that automatic means cannot, at least not yet: and that is quality. Quality means that some kinds of standards are followed, and that someone using a product that follows those standards, whatever that product happens to be—traveling safely in an airplane, or eating chicken that is free of disease, or drinking water that is clean—can safely rely on it.

Standards in the modern information universe are evolving and may mean something quite different from before; this is only being worked out right now. One thing is clear, however: libraries have very little power to compel other metadata creators to follow their rules, and they have lost control over the primary means that their patrons find, identify, and interact with information. Since this situation is unlikely to improve, this means cooperation and change for all concerned, but it seems vital that solutions are found.

If it is decided that standards are useless and therefore should be ignored, then perhaps libraries themselves will be seen as useless and should be ignored. Each library cataloging task (for that matter, *all* library tasks) is based on reliable (not standard, as was shown in the University of Michigan examples—you can have many ways of doing the same thing, as happens in library catalogs now, but results can *still* be reliable) description and access that is used to enable the patron to identify, find, and bring together, in one search, "all" of the books by a specific author (within certain, known parameters)—for example, the author Leo Tolstoy. This reliable description and access (in this case, standard authority control, which brings all works by an author together in one search) makes it clear that a more or less random selection of an author's writings based on how the form of his or her name appears in the text is not "good enough." Another standard, necessary in reliable access and description, is the transcription rule for the date of publication. A resource must have a defined and reliable date of publication, not one that has been chosen at random from five possible dates.

These traditional library tasks of description and access may be accomplished using completely differently methods than those we use today; we may find new efficiencies, or we may be able to rely on other metadata providers to provide certain information; e.g., publishers could provide the publication information, while authors could provide the equivalent of the statement of responsibility. Who knows what will happen? Yet, only with this type of reliable description can a selector confidently add something new to the collection; only with this type of reliable access can a reference librarian answer questions such as, "Do you have a catalog of the holdings of the Budapest Museum of Fine Arts?" Without these tools, there is no reliable access, and librarians are just as helpless as anyone else.

We can do better than that.

NOTES

1. "There's No Catalog Like No Catalog" podcast, hosted by LITA's Internet Resources and Services Interest Group, 2008 American Library Association annual conference, http://litablog.org/2008/07/05/ultimate-debate-2008 (accessed March 2, 2010).

2. Malcolm Wright and J. Scott Armstrong, "The Ombudsman: Verification of Citations: Fawlty Towers of Knowledge?" *Interfaces* 38, no. 2 (March–April 2008): 125–32, http://interfaces.journal.informs.org/cgi/reprint/38/2/125 (accessed May 13, 2010). The authors cite multiple reports for the sciences, going anywhere from 12 percent to 67 percent error rates. Another version of the paper is available as MPRA Paper No. 4149, http://mpra.ub.uni-muenchen.de/4149/1/MPRA_paper_4149.pdf (accessed May 13, 2010). Citation errors in medicine are detailed in: J. E. Fenton, et al., "The Accuracy of Citation and Quotation in Otolaryngology/Head and Neck Surgery Journals," *Clinical Otolaryngology and Allied Sciences* 25, no. 1 (February 2000): 40–44, in Academic Search Premier, EBSCOhost (accessed August 7, 2008). Ethical problems of legal research are discussed in Carol M. Bast and Susan W. Harrell, "Ethical Obligations: Performing Adequate Legal Research and Legal Writing," *Nova Law Review* 29 (Fall 2004): 49–74, in LexisNexis Academic (accessed August 7, 2008).

3. International Federation of Library Associations and Institutions, *International Standard Bibliographic Description (ISBD)*. Preliminary consolidated ed. (Munchen: K. G. Saur, 2007), section 5.1.3–5.1.4, http://www.ifla.org/VII/s13/pubs/ISBD_consolidated_2007.pdf (accessed March 1, 2010).

4. Joan M. Reitz, ODLIS—Online Dictionary for Library and Information Science, http://lu.com/odlis/index.cfm (accessed May 13, 2010).

5. See the abbreviation sections of different cataloging rules. For example, the abbreviations used in *Rules for a Dictionary Catalog* of Charles Cutter, are quite interesting for a modern cataloger. Charles A. Cutter, *Rules for a Dictionary Catalog*, 4th ed., rewritten (Washington, DC: GPO, 1904). "Appendix III: Abbreviations." http://www.archive.org/details/rulesforadictio04cuttgoog (accessed May 13, 2010).

6. John Mueller, "Retiring Support for OAI-PMH in Sitemaps," Google Webmaster Central Blog, April 23, 2008, http://googlewebmastercentral.blogspot.com/2008/04/retiring-support-for-oai-pmh-in.html (accessed November 8, 2009).

7. Geoff Nunberg, "Google Books: A Metadata Train Wreck," Language Log, August 29, 2009, http://languagelog.ldc.upenn.edu/nll/?p=1701 (accessed March 1, 2010). See also the associated comments from Jon Orwant, September 1, 2009, http://languagelog.ldc.upenn.edu/nll/?p=1701#comment-41758 (accessed March 1, 2010).

8. Amanda Claridge, et al. *Rome: An Archaeological Guide* (Oxford: Oxford University Press, 1998). See "Book Overview," "Reviews," "Related Books," and more on Google Books, http://books.google.com/books?id=RX_MPqbjOp0C (accessed November 5, 2009).

9. Eric Hellman, "Google Exposes Book Metadata Privates at ALA Forum," Go to Hellman blog, January 18, 2010, http://go-to-hellman.blogspot.com/2010/01/google -exposes-book-metadata-privates.html (accessed March 3, 2010). Google recently mentioned that they are getting metadata from over 100 sources.

10. The Cooperative Cataloging Rules Wiki, http://sites.google.com/site/ opencatalogingrules (accessed March 14, 2010).

11. James Burke, Richard Reisz, John Lynch, and Carl Davis, *The Day the Universe Changed* (New York: Distributed by Ambrose Video Publishing, 2009). DVD video.

IV

CATALOGING AND METADATA LIBRARIANS: RESEARCH, EDUCATION, TRAINING, AND RECRUITMENT

The Brick Wall: Attracting People to a Career in Cataloging
Janet Swan Hill

Blogs and Their Place in the Continuing Education of Catalogers
Jennifer Marie Eustis

Cataloging/Metadata and Library Science Education Programs for Catalogers and Metadata Specialists: Challenges for the Twenty-first Century
Sylvia D. Hall-Ellis

Chronological Bibliography of Selected Works Related to Cataloging and Libraries through 1800; and, Selected Bibliography of Library and Cataloging History
Elaine R. Sanchez

15 THE BRICK WALL: ATTRACTING PEOPLE TO A CAREER IN CATALOGING

Janet Swan Hill

INTRODUCTION

In the early 1980s, as head of a cataloging department in a major research library, I began to notice a drastic reduction in the number of catalogers applying for cataloging vacancies. Where once we had attracted applicant pools of a hundred or more, we began to see pools of fifteen or twenty. After several years of watching the numbers dwindle, I became an activist in the cause of education for cataloging. I discussed the trend in a paper in *American Libraries*,[1] and formed a task force in the American Library Association (ALA) whose report identified factors that might contribute to the problem.[2] In succeeding years, I pursued various avenues to bring attention to the issue,[3] and before long, other voices were heard.[4] It became generally recognized that there was a shortage of qualified catalogers in the field, and catalogers joined children's librarians on the list of endangered species.

Unfortunately, despite recognition of the problem, despite identification of factors that contribute to the difficulty of attracting people to cataloging, and despite suggestion of possible remedies, little improvement has been seen. This may not indicate that the suggestions were flawed, because it is difficult to tell how energetically they have been pursued. Instead, it may simply illustrate that it does little good to identify a problem, to decide how it came about, or even to suggest solutions if we don't implement them. Not just a few of us, not just employers, not just educators, but all of us.

As we move farther into the twenty-first century, activities associated with the organization of information have become more diverse. People who might once have applied a single set of rules to information resources to build a library catalog now apply many standards to multiple formats of resources to build multifarious discovery tools. "Catalogers" have become "metadata specialists."

"Bibliographic control" has become "Information Organization (IO)." The underlying nature of the work, however, remains essentially the same, as do the problems and their possible solutions. For the sake of simplicity, therefore, the terms "cataloging" and "cataloger" will be used in this paper to encompass all that cataloging has become.

WHY IS IT HARD TO GET PEOPLE INTO CATALOGING?

Problem: We Are Invisible and Unknown

What we do is invisible to most library users. The people we encountered in libraries when we were children were manning reference and circulation desks. Accordingly, when people are deciding what to do with their lives, they *may* think of becoming a librarian, but they think of direct public service, and don't even know that such a thing as cataloging exists. People with classificatory bents, or "puzzle people" who might enjoy cataloging don't realize that such work can be found in librarianship.

Problem: Librarianship Attracts from the Wrong Disciplines

Historically, librarianship has drawn people from fields such as English, history, and sociology—fields that may not be the richest sources of people who would enjoy cataloging. Many other disciplines, such as biology, mathematics, music, and computer science, could be good incubators of potential catalogers, but not only are students in those disciplines unaware of a possible affinity for cataloging, their instructional faculty who might provide career guidance are probably also unaware of it.

Problem: Career Guidance Is Off Target

Career guidance tools may have too narrow a profile of what kinds of personalities, penchants, and skills are appropriate for librarianship, so that many people who might have been well suited to cataloging are steered in other directions. I have recently been assured that career preference tests have improved since I was told to become a forest ranger, but I still recall discovering that several other people, including the head of technical services at Northwestern, the previous head of cataloging, the authorities librarian, and another cataloger had all been given "forest ranger" as a career choice. When I posted this observation to the electronic discussion list AUTOCAT in 2007, many others responded that they had received the same advice.[5]

Problem: Women Have More Careers Open to Them

Librarianship used to be one of the few professions, along with teaching and nursing that women pursued in large numbers. The feminist movement of the

1960s and 1970s put an end to that. Where librarianship had once been one of the few "respectable" careers that women with an analytical bent might pursue, the opening up of other fields decreased the draw of librarianship, and women who might have become catalogers instead became lawyers, doctors, and economists.

Problem: In LIS Programs, the Cataloging Curriculum Is Limited and Not Required

Library and information science (LIS) programs tend not to have rich offerings in cataloging and related topics. Although every accredited program offers some kind of cataloging-related course, only a minority require students to take it, and the first (sometimes the only) cataloging-related course offered is often not a cataloging class at all, but instead a course called something like "Introduction to the Organization of Information," sometimes derisively known as "Cataloging Appreciation."[6]

While the cataloging curriculum has shrunk over time, what there is to know about cataloging has exploded. As a consequence, many students, whether they take one cataloging course or several, realize when they finish that they still know very little about cataloging. The breadth and complexity of the specialty is so intimidating that they don't pursue it as a career. Further, when the curriculum is nearly devoid of substantial cataloging content, prospective librarians discern the unspoken message that this carries and shy away from cataloging.

Problem: In LIS Programs, Classwork Includes Little Exposure to Actual Cataloging

As has been noted, in many LIS programs, the first cataloging-related course is a general introduction that tries to cover the history and theory of information organization, and systems for providing it. There is so much territory to cover in limited class hours that there is little time to talk about cataloging per se, and no time to practice it.

People who know that they are interested in cataloging, perhaps through having cataloged at a paraprofessional level, may be self-directed to take more than one cataloging course, but chances are that those without such a background won't develop a thirst for cataloging based on their Introduction to Organization course. In preparation for this paper, I asked AUTOCAT members how they had become catalogers, and received hundreds of responses full of opinions and personal stories. Something that was mentioned time and again by current catalogers was that until they had had some practical exposure to cataloging, either through paraprofessional experience, a class, or an internship, they had no idea how satisfying it could be.

Problem: In LIS Programs, Cataloging Faculty Are Scarce, and Others May Convey an Inaccurate Message about Cataloging

Several other respondents to my AUTOCAT query mentioned being pointed away from cataloging by their LIS advisers or by other faculty who conveyed some version of the message that, "Cataloging is dull, clerical, and about to be obsolete."

That many library school faculty should be misinformed about cataloging is not surprising, as only a small portion of full-time LIS faculty are specialists in cataloging. Since it is full-time faculty who determine the direction of the academic program and do the advising, having so few cataloging specialists is bad for cataloging. If cataloging isn't your specialty, you may understandably have misperceptions about the work, its nature, its future, and what types of people become catalogers. If you are in the supermajority on your faculty, your opportunity to encounter information or opinions that might disabuse you of your beliefs is limited.

Problem: The Impact of Automation Is Overestimated

Galloping automation is responsible for many people believing that catalogers will soon be obsolete. As a profession, we ought to have learned that our vision of the future, and our anticipation of the impact of automation, is often wide of the mark. But, believe we do, and, project the future onto the present we do. Many people who believe that automation will make cataloging obsolete make decisions and take action as if the imagined future had already come to pass. These people, whether they are LIS faculty, other library school students, or other librarians, have an influence on guiding those who might be excellent catalogers into other paths.

Problem: The Jobs Sound Old-fashioned

Finally, the language we use to describe our jobs is not terribly groovy. Terms like bibliographic control, authority control, subject analysis, and even catalog sound obscure, rigid, and old-fashioned. The fact that these terms remain relevant in the Internet age doesn't matter if they sound stodgy. Jobs that are described with these words can sound boring, obsolete, or forbidding.

ARE THERE SOLUTIONS?

In this section, I will consider each of the problems identified above, and suggest possible remedies. Some items will be touched on only briefly, not because they are less important, but because solutions may be difficult, indirect, undesirable in one case, or they may have a minimal or only long-term payoff.

Solutions for: We Are Invisible and Unknown

How can we address invisibility and counter the view that librarianship equals reference? In our wildest dreams, perhaps someone could write a screenplay for a movie like *Major League*, and make Rene Russo a cataloger, or turn Noah Wyle as *The Librarian* into a cataloger, but keep the adventure. We could have TV mysteries solved not by psychics or pathologists, but by a cataloger whose detailed knowledge of how information is organized is key. More achievable might be some catchy YouTube videos,[7] or a story arc in the online library comic strip, *Unshelved*.[8] Less frivolous would be devising strategies to draw social taggers into our net.

Solutions for: Librarianship Attracts from the Wrong Disciplines

Librarianship as a field does minimal proactive recruiting. We tend to wait until people cross our threshold as they apply to a library school or work as student assistants or paraprofessionals. LIS programs send recruiting materials to undergraduate schools, but this passive strategy relies mainly on people happening across the material on their own.

We need to get to people while they are undergraduates beginning to wonder whether they really want to be mathematicians or Latin teachers. We need to get to people in graduate school who are pondering whether they want to finish that PhD, or if there's anything else they might do with their background in taxonomy or Italian. Getting to students means getting to their professors. If an academic department offers sessions on careers, we should contribute to them.

Perhaps we need a kit for academic librarians to use in approaching teaching faculty. It might include a suggested letter to department chairs; talking points to use when speaking to faculty; a customizable poster that asks, "What else can you do with your major in [discipline]?" and includes a snappy description of cataloging. The kit might also include hints for mounting an exhibit in the library or putting up a display at a career fair.

These suggestions call on academic librarians who have the most plausible entry to academic departments, but similar tactics could be aimed at high school students and carried out by school or public librarians. All such campaigns involve motivating and equipping catalogers for outreach. The support of bodies such as the Association for Library Collections and Technical Services (ALCTS) and the Committee on Education, Training, and Recruitment for Cataloging (CETRC) could be critical. The formation of a pool of recruiters, modeled along the lines of ALA's Committee on Accreditation Site Visitors Pool, could help assure continuity.

Faculty at LIS programs can perform outreach at their own institutions. They might obtain grants targeted at educating catalogers, or propose scholarships or other incentives for people to pursue a specialization in cataloging. They might develop joint programs with other departments and the university's library to coordinate student fellowships or internships in the library.

Solutions for: Career Guidance Is Off Target

We might approach providers of career preference tests with the goal of assuring that cataloging and related activities are adequately represented in their questions and formulae, and that the kind of people who might enjoy cataloging aren't all being steered to being lawyers, forest rangers, accountants, or police. This effort would need to be backed up with the credibility and support of an association such as ALA, since it is unlikely that test providers would respond to a single individual with a pet theory.

Solutions for: Women Have More Careers Open to Them

The fact that women have more careers open to them than in the past is not something to be corrected, but our plans need to recognize that librarianship cannot rely on smart women to choose librarianship by default, but must instead be attracted to the field because of its interest, worth, and rewards.

Solutions for: In LIS Programs, the Cataloging Curriculum Is Limited and Not Required

I understand why the cataloging curriculum has diminished over time, and why it is difficult to add courses or offer them more frequently. LIS programs have my sympathy. But understanding and sympathy are not enough. We need improvement.

We can't just ask LIS programs to offer more cataloging courses and expect quick results, but it should be possible for practitioners and educators to work together to develop a set of basic competencies that it is reasonable to expect cataloging coursework to convey.[9] In the same way, operating either as individuals or through professional organizations, we can also urge those schools that do not require cataloging to do so. We can pay close attention when the ALA accreditation standards are being revised, and work to make them a little less vague, and to assure that bibliographic control is adequately represented in even broad umbrella statements.

Solutions for: In LIS Programs, Classwork Generally Includes Little Exposure to Actual Cataloging

We can urge LIS programs to assure that all students are exposed to actual cataloging practice in every cataloging course, including "Introduction to Information Organization." Cataloging is an activity that is difficult to imagine. Time and time again, people have said that they never dreamed they would like cataloging until they tried it. If cataloging is invisible and essentially unimaginable, it is irresponsible of LIS programs not to give every prospective librarian a taste of it. The burden of providing that taste, however, shouldn't fall entirely on LIS faculty. Practitioners can appear at library schools as guest lecturers to talk about cataloging in an upbeat way. We can appear in webcasts. We can participate in discussions in online cataloging classes, or act as online mentors.

We can offer internships. Hosting an intern is labor intensive, but interns can contribute to the work of a department, and by providing an interesting work experience, we might attract someone to cataloging, or at least provide a positive perspective on cataloging to someone who doesn't become a cataloger after all. It was once possible for libraries located far from any library school to disclaim responsibility for providing internships, but with the increase in online courses, being located near a library school is no longer necessary. A host library just needs to be near a student.

Perhaps CETRC could maintain a clearinghouse to help prospective interns locate willing hosts. Perhaps it could prepare a tip sheet for finding appropriate work for an intern and for structuring internships that would be useful both to interns and the host.

Another way that prospective librarians get experience in cataloging is through work as a paraprofessional, a student assistant, or a volunteer. If someone working in our library shows an aptitude for cataloging, we need to encourage them to consider a library degree and a career in cataloging. Librarians should be able to guide potential catalogers to the ALA Committee on Accreditation Web pages for the list of accredited programs and to content on the ALCTS Web pages that might be of help to someone considering cataloging.[10] Further, if there is something that we think ALCTS ought to provide, such as catchy, effective, and up-to-date recruiting materials, or an up-to-date summary of cataloging coursework offered by each of the accredited programs, we need to suggest it, and be willing to work with others to produce such documents.

Solutions for: In LIS Programs, Cataloging Faculty Are Scarce, and Others May Convey an Inaccurate Message about Cataloging

The exact number of full-time faculty teaching cataloging at ALA-accredited LIS programs is fugitive, as faculty retire, move to administration, or change focus, but it is certain that the number is extremely low, as most LIS programs use practitioner adjuncts or faculty with other interests to carry all or part of their cataloging curriculum.[11] Granted, it is hard to put catalogers on the faculty if there aren't catalogers with PhDs willing to accept teaching salaries and the obligations of tenure, and graduating more PhDs in cataloging is difficult when there are few faculty qualified to educate and advise candidates who wish to pursue it. Nevertheless, we can and should urge schools to be proactive in seeking and encouraging more candidates with an interest in our subdiscipline.

In the meantime, LIS programs might solicit the help of practitioners to formulate a reasonable cataloging curriculum, and if they do rely heavily on adjuncts to handle that curriculum, to seek ways for adjuncts to have a real voice in the faculty.

Combating long-held mistaken beliefs is difficult. LIS faculty with a specialty in bibliographic control need to help their colleagues understand that the cataloging of old is no more; that catalogers of today are not who they remember; that having a basic introduction to cataloging is essential for every librarian; that the concepts remain valid, and an understanding of how information is derived and structured is critical to anyone seeking to serve users; that while cataloging is evolving, it is not going away; and that when they say something dismissive about cataloging or advise students not to pursue it, they are doing a disservice to students, the program, and the profession.

Solutions for: The Impact of Automation Is Overestimated

We need a better understanding of the actual impact of automation on cataloging and related activities, not just as it enables greater efficiencies in the workflow, but also its impact on discovery and its ability to substitute for or augment processes that have hitherto required human judgment. We need to have realistic thoughts about the future, and we need to be able to convey the message clearly, without defensiveness, and without sounding in denial, to library school faculty, to students, and to our colleagues, so that they are not easily seduced by a delicious-sounding, though distant or inaccurate vision of the future.

Solutions for: The Jobs Sound Old-fashioned

Cataloging jobs should be described in an engaging way, and existing jobs should be examined to see if they can be reenvisioned and redefined to be more enticing. Recruiting materials should describe jobs in ways that make cataloging sound important, satisfying, and intriguing. If jobs entail participation in management, liaison with other departments, Web page design, customization of discovery tools, or experimentation with new technology, we need to mention it in distinctly non-stodgy language.

The current generation of prospective librarians wants interesting, modern jobs, and they tend to want to be in charge now. Some might be satisfied to sit at a desk and fondle books and turn out bibliographic records by the bundle, but most want something more. Jobs need to be structured and described accordingly.

CONCLUSION

If problems with recruiting catalogers can be regarded as a brick wall, we have some choices:

- We can leave them standing, and accept the boundaries.
- We can butt our heads against them.
- We can dismantle them brick by brick, and reuse the bricks to build a path.

The last option would be my choice. I encourage all who read this to identify ways in which you might take action, because the wall won't be torn down by understanding how to do it. It will only be torn down by people who take sledge-hammers and chisels, and go to work.

NOTES

This paper is derived and updated from one originally presented at an American Library Association preconference sponsored by the Committee on Education, Training, and Recruitment of Catalogers (CETRC) of the Cataloging and Classification Section (CCS) of the Association for Library Collections and Technical Services (ALCTS).

1. Janet Swan Hill, "Wanted, Good Catalogers," *American Libraries* 16 (November 1985): 728–30. Paper derived from a presentation made to the RTSD/CCS Heads of Cataloging Discussion Group. The discussion that followed made it clear that my experience was far from isolated.

2. Resources and Technical Services Division. Cataloging and Classification Section. Task Force on Education and Recruitment for Cataloging, "CCS Task Force on Education and Recruitment for Cataloging Report, June, 1986," *RTSD Newsletter* 11, no. 7 (1986): 71–78. The Task Force evolved into the current ALCTS/CCS/CETRC.

3. Including: Janet Swan Hill, "Stalking the Elusive Cataloger," *American Libraries* 20 (May 1989): 458–60; Hill, "Recruitment for Catalogers," in *Libraries for the New Millennium* (Chicago: ALA OLPR, 1988), 26–36; formation, with Sheila Intner, of the Technical Services Interest Group in the Association for Library and Information Science Education (ALISE); a Simmons College Symposium on Recruiting, Educating, and Training Cataloging Librarians which yielded Sheila S. Intner and Janet Swan Hill, eds., *Recruiting, Educating, and Training Cataloging Librarians: Solving the Problems* (Westport, CT: Greenwood Press, 1989), and Intner and Hill, eds., *Cataloging: The Professional Development Cycle* (Westport, CT: Greenwood Press, 1991); and Hill and Intner, "Preparing for a Cataloging Career: From Cataloging to Knowledge Management," commissioned for American Library Association Congress on Professional Education, May 1, 1999, http://www.ala.org/ala/educationcareers/education/1stcongressonpro/1stcongresspreparing.cfm (accessed November 2, 2009).

4. Among notable early papers to pick up on the trend were: Roxanne Sellberg, "The Teaching of Cataloging in U.S. Library Schools," *Library Resources & Technical Services* 32, no. 1 (January 1988): 30–42; and Daren Callahan and Judy MacLeod, "Recruiting and Retention Revisited: A Study of Entry Level Catalogers," *Technical Services Quarterly* 11, no. 4 (Spring 1994): 27–43.

5. AUTOCAT is an electronic discussion list devoted to cataloging-related topics. For more information, see http://www.cwu.edu/~dcc/Autocat-ToC-2007.html (accessed November 2, 2009). The list has a membership of more than four thousand subscribers from more than forty countries.

6. Sylvia Hall-Ellis, in a message posted to AUTOCAT, July 27, 2007, in the thread titled "MLS in cataloging," Hall-Ellis noted that "as of the end of the 2006–07 academic year (May–June 2007), there are currently eight ALA-accredited library programs that require students earning the MLIS to take a cataloging course. These schools are Clarion, Hawaii, Denver, North Carolina–Greensboro, Southern Mississippi, SUNY Buffalo, Toronto, Wisconsin–Madison. The initial accreditation of Valdosta brings another school to this elite group. While some schools consider an organization of information course to be cataloging, my research suggests that the texts provide more appropriate insight into the content and learning objectives. Consequently, organization of

information courses don't quality as 'legitimate' cataloging in my book";Daniel N. Joudrey, "A New Look at US Graduate Courses in Bibliographic Control," in *Education for Cataloging and the Organization of Information: Pitfalls and the Pendulum*, ed. Janet Swan Hill (New York: Haworth Press, 2002), 59–101. Joudrey's paper is the most thorough recent examination of LIS curricula. Although some things will have changed since its publication, changes are likely relatively small.

7. There are some videos on YouTube about cataloging, but most are instructional, intended for current catalogers. One light-hearted rap video, entitled "Catalog Books," (http://www.youtube.com/watch?v=LrbdW9OjXnc, accessed November 2, 2009), includes no information about cataloging per se. Another set of three videos presented by James Ascher, entitled "The Battle against Information Ataxy," is intended to provide nonlibrarians with an idea of the purpose and process of cataloging: Part 1, http://www.youtube.com/watch?v=x4oKs16OlaM; Part 2, http://www.youtube.com/watch?v=VTBS_fFxHpc; Part 3, http://www.youtube.com/watch?v=rm8hkORStBs (all accessed November 2, 2009).

8. *Unshelved*, http://www.unshelved.com (accessed November 2, 2009). The strip follows the day-to-day experiences of a public services librarian in a public library.

9. In 2009, ALA adopted the "ALA's Core Competences of Librarianship," http://www.ala.org/ala/educationcareers/careers/corecomp/corecompetences/index.cfm (accessed May 12, 2010), but the section covering the "Organization of Recorded Knowledge and Information" is highly general. In 1995, ALCTS produced "ALCTS Educational Policy Statement," http://www.ala.org/ala/mgrps/divs/alcts/about/governance/policies/cepolicy.cfm (accessed November 2, 2009), whose appendix includes suggested competencies for intellectual access and information organization. The ALCTS Cataloging and Classification Section (CCS) has subsequently produced a more detailed statement of "Core Competencies for Cataloging," which the author received from ALCTS headquarters, but which is not, as of May 12, 2010, available on the ALCTS Web site.

10. "Directory of ALA-Accredited Master's Programs in Library and Information Studies," http://www.ala.org/ala/educationcareers/education/accreditedprograms/directory/index.cfm (accessed November 2, 2009); ALCTS home page, http://www.ala.org/ala/mgrps/divs/alcts/alcts.cfm (accessed November 2, 2009).

11. Sylvia Hall-Ellis tracks how the cataloging curriculum is covered at ALA-accredited LIS programs. As of August 2009, she could identify only eleven full-time tenure-stream faculty in ALA-accredited programs whose primary specialty is bibliographic control. Of those, several are near retirement or moving into administrative positions. Other programs cover cataloging with adjunct practitioners, with regular faculty whose specialty is in other areas of librarianship, or with permanent non-tenure-stream faculty. (Private correspondence with Hall-Ellis, August 2009); Shawne Miksa, in a message posted to AUTOCAT, July 26, 2007, as part of the thread "Martha Yee's comments on LIS education," commented on the low number of cataloging faculty, and observed, "It would nice to have more reliable numbers on exactly how many courses are taught, the syllabi, assignments, and reading lists, as well as actual numbers of students who enrolled and finished the course and what the enrollment cap was originally set at for the course, how often the course was offered, the number of students on a waiting list to get into a full course, etc."

16 BLOGS AND THEIR PLACE IN THE CONTINUING EDUCATION OF CATALOGERS

Jennifer Marie Eustis

The cataloging profession is rapidly evolving. These changes require catalogers not only to be aware of new trends, but also to understand how these new trends affect their jobs. This is a difficult task because catalogers need to have a comprehensive yet flexible set of skills and a broad knowledge base. Most catalogers would agree that courses in cataloging did not fully prepare them for these changes, or for the range of proficiencies and knowledge asked of them. Such skills and knowledge tend to be cultivated in the workplace. As a result, many catalogers receive some on-the-job training.[1] More to the point, most, if not all, require and want to continue their cataloging education. Common solutions are workshops, conferences, webinars, or online courses. However, another way to do this exists, and has been mainly overlooked until recently: that is, blogs and blogging. In this essay, I will discuss how blogs can help catalogers learn about their profession, new ideas, and technologies, and can allow them to participate in a professional and supportive social network. Accordingly, blogs can help catalogers keep their skill set up to date, flexible, and wide ranging.

Library programs typically offer at least one cataloging course that introduces students to the basics of organizing information. Of course, over a period of fourteen or so weeks, it is difficult to broach the subject of organizing information and cataloging. The result is that much of the history of cataloging and how information has been organized are left out of syllabi. In addition, the full spectrum of current and national standards and rules are not fully treated. Even advanced courses in cataloging and information organization are limited by time constraints and the sheer wealth of information about the topic. Inevitably, finer details as well as how cataloging fits into such things as integrated library systems get lost. These time constraints are similar, if not worse, for workshops, online courses, or webinars, which often last only a couple of hours or, at most, a month.

Another problem that cataloging programs face is that catalogers are asked to complete a variety of tasks that demand a wide range of skills. The literature, as well as training documents such as the one provided by ALCTS (Association for Library Collections and Technical Services),[2] illustrates that catalogers must know copy, complex, and original cataloging (descriptive and subject); authority work; current and national standards (AACR2); and encoding of content designation (MARC21). Catalogers should be aware of such programs as NACO (Name Authority Cooperative) and PCC (Program for Cooperative Cataloging). They should be familiar with at least one integrated library system and several print and online cataloging tools such as the main types of classification schedules, OCLC Connexion, Cataloger's Desktop from LC (Library of Congress), and the LC Subject Cataloging Manual, to name only a few. Furthermore, they should be familiar with current and emergent metadata sets, encoding schemas, and content standards associated with metadata sets. A cursory knowledge of XML (Extensible Markup Language) is, in some cases, being asked of catalogers, and of metadata librarians in particular. Catalogers require knowledge of their ILS (Integrated Library System) system, including maintenance, record loads, and other administrative database tasks. Furthermore, catalogers must know and understand the purposes of cataloging rules in order to know when to bend them, and when to adhere to them. Then, there are more general tasks such as supervising full-time employees and/or work study students or interns, committee work, budgets, reference, vendor relations, and licensing. These tasks demand a wide range of skills that require the cataloger to smoothly wear different hats such as business manager, computer technician, project manager, or linguist. This is perhaps why many catalogers find the courses they took in library school insufficient for the task of training them for a career in cataloging.[3] The continuing need for these skills is most likely why many in the profession are constantly drawn to continue their education. The fact of the matter is that "library school faculty members teaching the sequence of cataloging courses face a daunting challenge."[4] Therefore, continuing education is a necessary task among the many others for catalogers.

Like many of its counterparts in the array of continuing education opportunities, blogs offer a chance to gather new information about cataloging. In the recent edition of *American Libraries*, Mary Ellen Quinn refers to blogs as "the brash new kid on the block."[5] Despite this, she sees the way in which blogs can help catalogers further their education. Quinn reasons that evocative blogs are driven by good and informative content. Content-driven blogs thus fall under the rubric of continuing education tools. Furthermore, a good blog is unlike its counterparts. "[B]logs bring immediacy, interactivity, and informality to our ongoing conversation about what it means to be a library."[6]

Are blogs really brash? Is it the case that the content found in blogs is irritatingly unsubstantial and self-promotional? Of course, such a gross generality is not true. Like many things, a critical eye is, however, needed to evaluate the blog and its content, because blogs are created and maintained typically by one individual. As such, the content is not subject to a time-honored editorial process like peer-reviewed journals, or, to a certain extent, to moderated electronic mailing lists. With an absent and independent editorial process, there is the possibility that posts could be written in haste. Posts could also be published without any references, leaving conclusions unconfirmed. There exists, as well, the chance that bloggers could create posts with impunity and without having taken into account the consequences that could result from the content of the post. This leaves the door open to unsubstantiated hearsay, unhelpful opinions, or harmful finger-pointing. On the one hand, bloggers should adopt some form of editorial process. On the other, readers should also critically review blogs, including a blogger's disclaimers, and then make a decision to continue reading the blog or not. It is also a fact that without an independent moderator(s), as most electronic mailing lists have, obstructive comments and spam can make any blog inappropriate and even a risk for viruses. Because of these shortcomings, blogs can seem, and some are indeed, brash.

While all of this is true, it does not paint the whole picture. Blogs have an independent and different party to moderate them. This was clearly illustrated in M. E. Quinn's article on blogs. As blogs are a different form of publication than moderated electronic mailing lists and peer-reviewed journals, the way in which blogs are reviewed diverges. Blogs are assessed by the public sphere of people who read them. It is hoped that a negative, obstructive, or unsubstantiated blog will be dismissed by the community. With lists such as the top 100 blogs, aggregated blogs like Planet Cataloging, or articles like those of Quinn, people will be attracted to blogs that have been reviewed over a long period of time and by many people in and out of the cataloging profession.

Though public opinion can be uncertain, cataloging blogs are written for a specific audience. As a result, the blogs might be controversial at times. Yet, their public nature forces them to respond to the needs and wants of their audience through persuasive arguments and content that is relevant and timely for the cataloging profession. Cataloging blogs are continually being reviewed by seasoned catalogers and new professionals, as well as by those who have an interest in cataloging. This moderation is done by carrying on a conversation through blog comments, consulting reviews of blogs, and critically reading blogs on cataloging. These interactive assessments create an environment of constant public scrutiny regarding the quality of cataloging blogs.

Even with this type of review by the community, it still remains essential to critically review any blog, especially when using blogs as a continuing education tool. In reading a blog or combination of blogs that help with one's work, the content found can lead to amazing learning opportunities. The blog or a combination of blogs that publish probing, sound, and instructive content are not brash new kids. Catalogers can use them to become informed and participate in discussions of how the cataloging profession is changing.[7] Jeff Utecht is correct to highlight that blogs act as "conversations" and, as such, they promote reflective and critical thinking about topics in cataloging and its future.

Blogs help the cataloger learn of new cataloger tools and resources. A number of cataloging and/or technical services departments, such as the Library of Congress's Web sites for libraries or Yale's music cataloging Web site, have long had a presence on the Web. These departments have detailed their policies, provided links to cataloging tools, and sometimes provided helpful cataloging examples. A problem, though, is that these Web sites are static. New ones are occasionally created, while some older ones are no longer updated. Blogs are information-sharing tools that can help advertise these Web sites to the community, and, thanks to the archival nature of blogs, the reader is aware of when a Web site was reviewed. With this information, the reader has more information available to critically evaluate a Web site as well as the blog. Recently, blogs have started to post cataloging tools and resources, which are very useful posts. A good example is the blog by William Denton, the FRBR Blog, which is a valuable resource about FRBR and RDA. By posting new cataloging tools and resources on blogs, it is easy to determine if the information is new or has been updated thanks to the fact that blogs create date- and time-stamped content. With the coming changes of RDA, for example, and more frequent technical updates related to RDA, blog posts act as significant tools in gathering current information.

Blogs help catalogers learn about new directions and possible futures of the profession. It can be difficult to keep abreast of changes that the cataloging profession is currently undergoing. Library programs and continuing education venues such as online courses, webinars, or workshops face time constraints that limit the amount of information that can be presented. These venues also impart material that has been researched and thus has the possibility of being slightly out of date. There is also the fact that many of the skills and much of the knowledge required for cataloging is wide ranging, varied, and adaptable. This breadth cannot be covered in one course but must be cultivated over a period of time, optimally with the help of seasoned catalogers. As an answer to the rising amount of cataloging and metadata information to disseminate, blogs offer a significant advantage. Thanks to the immediate way in which blogs can be published, information can be quickly and almost immediately shared with the cataloging community. This is particularly useful when posts advertise upcoming events. Another practical aspect of blogs is that they can document the current mood of the cataloging community. In a manner of speaking, blogs not only act as a tool to procure current information, but they also provide a means to analyze the developments within the field, as well as what people think about current cataloging issues. Thanks to the ability to post comments, bloggers and their readers can have a conversation about their profession—where it is now, and where it is headed.

Most importantly, blogs allow people to communicate with other professionals and hence be part of a professional network. If there is a task that a cataloger is asked to complete, most probably there is a blog that has a posting about it. The reader has the ability to learn from the posts, and can interact with the blog through comments. This allows the opportunity for a conversation between blogger and reader. Because of the informal nature of blogs, the reader and blogger can learn from each other in an interactive social community of professionals. How is this different from webinars, online courses, or electronic mail lists? Unlike webinars or online courses, blog posts are ongoing. These posts provide current information and attempt to describe certain aspects of the profession to others. Depending on the interest of the community, a post can take on a life of its own. Not only will there be comments on the blog where it was originally posted, but soon other blogs will begin discussing the post, and adding to it. In this way, the topic will enter into a discussion on several different levels: between the blogger and other bloggers, between the blogger and people from the community, and even between the blogger and electronic mailing lists. Thanks to the interactive nature of blogs, information that might be communicated through one venue can be reported on in another. This is seen frequently when bloggers link topics that arise in blogs, electronic mail lists, conferences, workshops, or webinars. As a result, blogs are capable of bringing together information that was, until the blog appeared, broadcast separately through different and isolated information silos. This helps catalogers, in particular, learn how many of their tasks are related to the larger picture of cataloging. In addition, this allows catalogers to take advantage of the wealth of information and knowledge that the community has regarding cataloging and librarianship. Instead of just asking about "240 (uniform title field) versus 700 subfield t," (author/title added entry field), through blogs, it is possible to link that topic with how the OPAC will display the record, or how it would be recorded according to RDA. Blogs can be an invaluable source of learning, especially for catalogers who work with metadata where the focus is beyond MARC21 and AACR2.

There is another aspect to blogs that increases their usefulness as a continuing educational tool. That is *becoming* a blogger. Many use an RSS feed reader to read blogs. Thanks to Google Reader or Bloglines, readers can not only read blogs, they can also organize them, share them with friends, and delete them on the spot. As most would agree, it is easy to dismiss blog posts, especially if the blog is extremely active and time is short. Bloggers know that reading about a topic is different from writing about it; and writing about a topic requires some knowledge of that topic. The better the blog, the better the content. Good content takes work, research, and editing before it is posted. Therefore, the blogger has to learn how to research and be comfortable with a topic before reporting on it. If the blogger is presenting an opinion piece, then the writer must adopt some sort of review process in order to present a post that is thought-out, clear, and informative and that contributes to the cataloging community. This is a learning exercise. The blogger has to learn, or have the innate ability to learn, how to write clearly and present a topic in such a way that it is of interest to others. To do this, the blogger must keep up with blog postings and comments on the Web in various forums. Good blog-writing requires that the blogger learn how to communicate more effectively, not just through the medium of postings, but also through comments and reactions to his or her blog.

Writing a blog also requires the writer to become more involved in the cataloging profession and related communities. Sometimes it is about scouring the Web for information. Other times, it is about going to conferences or speaking to colleagues. Writing a blog is also learning how to juggle reporting and commentary in the public sphere in a manner that is respectful and ethical, and that encourages discussions within the community. This is perhaps why libraries have created blogs for their institutions—through their blogs, they can more easily reach their users.

Whether or not one writes or just reads blogs, it is undeniable that blogs have a place within the continuing education of catalogers. Catalogers belong to a profession that is rapidly changing. The skill sets of a cataloger tend to be diverse and flexible, so in this sense, catalogers must be generalists, rather than having only a limited set of specialized knowledge. However, perhaps most importantly, catalogers must know how to acquire more specialized knowledge when necessary, and know how to apply it. This is because it is not just the latest and most fashionable information that catalogers need to process; catalogers must be able to examine all available past, present, and even predicted future information trends, in order to analyze, organize, describe, and provide access through very practical cataloging for their institutions, their users, and the world of users. Blogs are one way to seek out not just specialized knowledge, but also information about cataloging and other related fields. What's more, blogs offer the chance to join ongoing conversations about the profession: where it can, should, or should not go. Blogs are not just tools for continuing cataloging education; they are a means to become involved in the profession, providing opportunities for both blog readers and writers alike to reflect on their profession and enhance their critical thinking skills. Consequently, a well-written, content-driven blog is timely and invaluable help for catalogers to keep their skill set up to date, flexible, and wide ranging for the work ahead of them.

NOTES

1. Rebecca L. Mugridge, "Experiences of Newly-Graduated Cataloging Librarians," *Cataloging & Classification Quarterly* 45, no. 3: 61–79.

2. Association for Library Collections & Technical Services, "Training Catalogers in the Electronic Era: Essential Elements of a Training Program for Entry-Level Professional Catalogers," http://www.ala.org/ala/mgrps/divs/alcts/resources/org/cat/traincatalogers.cfm (accessed May 7, 2010).

3. Nicole E. Engard, "Library School Requirement Survey Results," message posted to the Author's Blog, What I Learned Today . . ., September 18, 2007, http://www.web2learning.net/archives/1212 (accessed May 7, 2010).

4. Sylvia D. Hall-Ellis, "Cataloger Competencies . . . What do Employers Require?" *Cataloging & Classification Quarterly* 46, no. 3: 305–30. Abstract available online at: http://www.informaworld.com/smpp/content~db=all?content=10.1080/01639370802034565 (accessed September 1, 2010).

5. Mary Ellen Quinn, "Learning with Blogs," *American Libraries* 40, no. 8/9 (August–September 2009): 59–61.

6. Ibid., 59.

7. Jeff Utecht, "Blogs Aren't the Enemy: How Blogs Enhance Learning," *Technology & and Learning* 27, no. 9 (April 2007): 32–34.

8. Liping Deng and Allen H. K. Yuen, "Blogs in Higher Education: Implementation and Issues, *Tech Trends* 53, no. 3 (May–June 2009): 95–98.

FURTHER READING ABOUT BLOGS, BLOGGING, AND CATALOGING EDUCATION

Benson, Amy, and Robert Favini. "Evolving Web, Evolving Librarian." *Library Hi Tech News* 27, no. 7 (2006): 18–21.

Boyd, Danah. "A Blogger's Blog: Exploring the Definition of a Medium." *Reconstruction* 6, no. 4 (2006), http://reconstruction.eserver.org/064/boyd.shtml (accessed May 7, 2010).

Coombs, Karen A., and Jason Griffey. *Library Blogging.* Columbus, OH: Linworth Pub., 2008.

Davis, Jane M. "A Survey of Cataloging Education: Are Library Schools Listening?" *Cataloging & Classification Quarterly* 46, no. 2 (2008): 182–200. Abstract available online at http:dx.doi.org/10.1080/01639370802177604 (accessed June 15, 2010).

Hart, Kim. "Portrait of a Blogger: Under 30 and Sociable." *Washington Post*, July 20, 2006, D05, http://www.washingtonpost.com/wp-dyn/content/article/2006/07/19/AR2006071901900.html (accessed May 10, 2010).

Lenhart, Amanda, and Susannah Fox. "Bloggers: A Portrait of the Internet's New Storytellers." *Pew Internet & American Life Report*, July 19, 2006, http://www.pewinternet.org/Reports/2006/Bloggers.aspx (accessed May 10, 2010).

Moeller, Paul, and Nathan Rupp. "TalkLeft, Boing Boing, and Scrappleface: The Phenomenon of Weblogs and Their Impact on Library Technical Services." *Library Resources & and Technical Services* 49, no. 1 (2005): 7–13.

"State of the Blogosphere 2008." Technorati blog, http://technorati.com/blogging/state-of-the-blogosphere/who-are-the-bloggers (accessed May 10, 2010).

Tarulli, Laurel. "What Makes a Good Cataloguer?" Cataloguing Librarian blog, September 24, 2009, http://laureltarulli.wordpress.com/2009/09/24/what-makes-a-good-cataloguer (accessed May 10, 2010).

17 CATALOGING/METADATA AND LIBRARY SCIENCE EDUCATION PROGRAMS FOR CATALOGERS AND METADATA SPECIALISTS: CHALLENGES FOR THE TWENTY-FIRST CENTURY

Sylvia D. Hall-Ellis

Technical services librarians, library educators, and employers share interest in the recruitment and education of traditional catalogers and metadata specialists.[1] Each constituency has studied and articulated its thoughts and perspectives regarding the preparation for library school students and paraprofessionals who seek positions as professional catalogers or metadata specialists. Recent library school graduates,[2] managers and supervisors,[3] and practitioners[4] conduct studies about cataloging, bibliographic description, and associated work, disseminating their observations and recommendations through conference presentations and in library literature. The importance of experiential learning to bridge the gap between classroom instruction and the library or information setting workplace has remained a topic of interest and concern to LIS educators for many decades.

HISTORICAL OVERVIEW OF LIS EDUCATION

Librarianship has a long and proud tradition, perpetuating itself for generations through a form of apprenticeship wherein each librarian trained his or her successors in the philosophical and practical arts of the discipline.[5] Prior to 1850, there was little concern or need for specially trained librarians. Although most colleges had a library, librarians were junior faculty members who were assigned the duty of maintaining the library in addition to a full teaching assignment.[6] Not until the passage of legislation establishing free public libraries were full-time library personnel needed. What training existed was purely a function of obtaining paid employment in a library and learning on the job.

From 1850 to 1900, higher education can be characterized by the rise and proliferation of universities: the evolution of the American college, the creation of the land-grant colleges, the rise of electivism, and the birth of the research university.[7] Each of these developments increased the need for supplemental and research collections in academic libraries, and exacerbated the need for trained library personnel. Increasingly complex library institutions needed trained librarians to organize and administer the collections.

There was no expressed need for formal library instruction or training. The popular conception of the librarian was as a scholar, devoted to the collection and care of books. Novices looked to established practitioners in the field for advice on how to be a librarian. They read available printed material on library economy, modeled themselves on successful librarians, and sought employment in a well-run library for on-the-job training.

The dramatic growth of public libraries and universities created a demand for trained library personnel. Melvil Dewey recognized the need for efficient ways of training library workers and suggested that a formal apprenticeship system might be superior to the practice of on-the-job training. He proposed the establishment of a library school that would emphasize "a systematic apprenticeship in library science."[8] Although Dewey established the first library school at Columbia College in 1887, the institution did not accept the ideas of technical education and exerted pressure to prevent admitting the more technical aspects of professional studies. Although Columbia was a men's college, when the first formal library class of twenty was enrolled in 1887, the majority of students were women. Thus, the school's affiliation with Columbia was accidental, based on Dewey's presence, not because library training was seen to be of collegiate character.

Library and information science (LIS) educators and practitioners have historically attempted to achieve a balance between theory and practice. Practica, internships, and hands-on work experience in LIS education trace their roots to the apprenticeships that Dewey required students to complete.[9] Several early library training schools were attached to developing technical institutes that over time supplanted the apprenticeship-based system of training workers for selected vocations. Classes included lectures by noted practitioners. As late as 1917, other agencies turned out two to three times as many librarians as the library schools.[10] The Pratt Institute (1890), the Drexel Institution (1891), Chicago's Armour Institution (1893), the Carnegie Institution (1901), and Simmons (1902) initiated library training programs based on Dewey's model.[11] Prior to 1920, library schools made no pretense of providing professional education, but intended to prepare the lower echelons of library workers.

A deliberate shift away from this zealous commitment to train library workers through apprenticeships in public libraries followed the publication of Charles C. Williamson's 1923 landmark report, *Training for Library Service*. Williamson criticized library education for its reliance on learning that took place in the workplace and called for a move to a more theory-based curriculum with instruction in formal classroom settings.[12] When the University of Chicago opened its graduate library program in 1926, LIS educators were members of the higher education establishment, and theory became an integral part of the curriculum.[13] Formal library schools provided entry into librarianship, other types of training claimed to accomplish the same end, and all used the same type of instruction.[14]

Alarmed at the trend, Dewey warned that library schools of doubtful value did not follow standards; he suggested that schools that maintained high standards form a separate organization. By 1923, there was general consensus among ALA and major library employers that library education should take place within the context of a graduate school in a university. Librarianship was emerging as a professional field of study, and the American Library Association (ALA) was organizing, gaining credibility, and beginning to develop standards for accrediting master's degree programs in library and information studies programs. ALA identified four curricular areas of critical importance: technical services, bibliography, foundations, and library services.[15]

HISTORICAL OVERVIEW OF EDUCATION FOR CATALOGERS AND METADATA SPECIALISTS

The early training for catalogers ranged from on-the-job learning to formal technical training in the library school.[16] Library employees and aspiring workers received on-the-job training and informal apprenticeship programs that enabled an individual to learn by rotating through the various departments of the library. Apprenticeships included classroom lectures and assignments to supplement actual work. Larger public libraries conducted training classes. State library commissions and other groups conducted summer schools to provide intensive training. Formal library schools were founded. It was not until the later years of this period that the library school method of preparing librarians began to supplant the others. By 1919, the curriculum at the Los Angeles Library Training School included four basic competencies: technical (cataloging, accession, and classification); bibliographic (book selection and reference); administrative; and, historical (knowledge of books and libraries).[17]

The basic competencies of library education remained relatively unchanged for six decades. During the 1980s, an economic downturn, coupled with lowering rates of enrollment in universities, resulted in the closure of seventeen library schools, including the original master's program at the University of Denver, which had awarded the first ALA-accredited fifth-year degree in 1947.[18] The shock of these closures shook the library and information studies programs and caused LIS educators to take a hard look at how library professionals were being prepared.

Intner and Hill's *Recruiting, Educating, and Training Cataloging Librarians: Solving the Problems* presented a compilation of practitioners' perspectives on the education of novice catalogers.[19] Hill's updated volume of perspectives and concerns about cataloging education, *Pitfall and the Pendulum: Reconsidering Education for Cataloging and the Organization of Information*, offered insights into changes for the twenty-first century.[20]

Chaffin and Smith provided a brief overview of the need for the community of catalogers to take a new and serious look at their critical role in the education of new hires.[21] Turvey and Letarte[22] noted a gap between what practitioners consider important knowledge for a new library school graduate and the learning outcomes of their academic programs, confirming the importance of the partnerships among the community of catalogers and library educators. Rapp[23] reported personal characteristics of successful catalog librarians, including tolerance for ambiguity in a changing workplace; Intner[24] confirmed the customary ability to organize information and information materials; and, Hill[25] identified the ability to exercise judgment, make decisions, solve problems, manage time and resources, possess computer skills, show a commitment to public service, supervise staff, communicate in languages other than English, and utilize good communication skills. DeZelar-Tiedman[26] concluded that technical services librarians must possess an array of skills and competencies, including (but not limited to) knowledge of the cataloging system, the design of the Online Public Access Catalog (OPAC) interface, and contact with acquisitions, while Vellucci[27] emphasized the importance of keeping catalog librarians in contact with the databases that they created and the users who search them.

Based on an overview of LIS education in 2000, graduate library programs included "core" course requirements required of all students and specializations focused on specialized interests. Nine of the ALA-accredited programs required all students to take an introductory cataloging course; forty-eight rely on organization-of-information courses and a limited number of cataloging courses that are electives. If the textbook doesn't have the word cataloging in it, or descriptive, or metadata, it is probably organization of information. Twenty-nine schools employ part-time adjunct and part-time practitioners to teach the courses, if they are taught at all. Most LIS programs offer one course; the average is two courses.

Despite the reduction in the presence of cataloging courses as a requirement in LIS programs, Saye maintained that the library catalog's role in promoting information retrieval is paramount. The decrease in required cataloging courses has occurred at a time when the proliferation of formats has increased. While Saye lamented the end of a cataloging "golden age," he emphasized the discipline's importance to furthering information retrieval and new metadata standards.[28]

In her report to the Association for Library Collections and Technical Services (ALCTS) describing a plan to train metadata and cataloging educators, Hsieh-Yee suggested that the scope of cataloging education will need to be broader.[29] Hsieh-Yee[30] and Glaviano[31] developed and discussed courses focused on metadata and the cataloging of electronic resources, extending the work of Connaway,[32] MacLeod and Callahan,[33] and Evans[34] on the skills, responsibilities, and qualities that employers expect new hires to possess.

CURRENT STATE OF EDUCATION FOR CATALOGERS AND METADATA SPECIALISTS: COMPETENCIES AND CURRICULUM

Observations and comments from the community of catalogers remind practitioners and LIS educators alike of the importance that thoughtful, research-based sequences of courses, coupled with hands-on experiences, prepare students for careers in bibliographic access and description. The "typical" library school graduate hired into an entry-level cataloging position experiences the challenges of enhancing and creating bibliographic data in multiple formats and languages. In the digital era, preparation for a career as a cataloger requires mastery of cataloging and metadata competencies, and knowledge of non-English languages, digital publishing, and Web authoring conventions. Earning an ALA-accredited library degree requires an investment of time, money, and effort.

Fifty-seven public and private colleges and universities in North America award the ALA-accredited graduate degree to approximately 15,000 students each year. The students fulfill a number of requirements in order to earn the degree in thirty-six semester hours or fifty-eight quarter hours. Their core course requirement ranges from two courses to a very prescriptive core of eight courses.[35] LIS programs recognize the "ALA Core Competences of Librarianship" that defines the core competencies of the newly graduated generalist librarian.[36] Regardless of the location, course of study, and instructional delivery system, the question remains: Do employers require what professors teach?

Employers and students expect graduate library education for catalogers to include the mastery of technical skills supported through the incorporation of computer-dependent technologies into the teaching and learning environment. Consequently, in order to meet these expectations, basic and advanced cataloging courses need to include metadata and classification schemes, bibliographic utilities, electronic resources, Internet tools, integrated library systems, interoperability technologies, human-computer interactions, networking, and telecommunications.

The conclusions of field-based studies reinforce the importance of continued collaboration between employers and LIS educators to close the gap between the classroom and workplace. MacLeod and Callahan[37] surveyed employers who reported that cataloging courses were inadequate preparation for entry-level catalogers. Hall-Ellis[38] studied employers' expectations and reported that cataloging courses alone do not prepare promising students for successful careers as catalogers. Hill[39] identified essential nonlibrary skills, including—but not limited to—basic computer competencies, familiarity with software for library and technical services to meet local library needs, and well-developed written and oral communication skills. The conclusions of these studies suggest that the curricular coverage in a limited number of cataloging courses does not meet employers' expectations.

The goal of LIS education is to prepare students to be information professionals. LIS educators are engaged in the student cycle of recruitment, admissions, matriculation, graduation, and placement. The mission, vision, and goals of home institutions and LIS programs, coupled with accreditation requirements, theoretical knowledge, professional competencies, and technical skills need to be incorporated into every course for each student in response to the ALA Committee on Accreditation (COA) learning outcomes, which are both programmatic as a unit and for each individual course.[40]

Since 1993, when the Cooperative Cataloging Council (CCC) suggested that the preparation of new catalog librarians include a list of overall skills to meet students' and prospective employers' expectations, library school faculty have faced significant challenges to develop and teach a comprehensive curriculum.[41] In recognition of the dynamic changes in public and private information environments, ALCTS issued an educational policy statement in June 1995.[42] Their theoretical framework of knowledge and skills for new library school graduates included intellectual access and information organization; preserving access; identifying, selecting, and acquiring information resources; management skills; and research analysis and interpretation skills. The ALA Executive Board created the Task Force on Core Competencies in 1999 in response to recommendations from the Steering Committee of the First Congress on Professional Education. Their draft statement included forty-five competencies in seven areas: organization of knowledge resources, information and knowledge, connecting people to ideas, facilitating learning, management, technology competencies, and research.[43]

The ALA Task Force on Core Competencies' report from the Third Congress on Professional Education delineated expectations for paraprofessionals working in technical services[44] and considered provocative questions raised by Hill during the First Congress on Professional Education regarding education for the first professional degree.[45] These discussions are supplemented by the proposed response to the LC Action Plan for Bibliographic Control of Web Resources submitted to the ALCTS/ALISE Task Force[46] and documents from the ALCTS Education Action Summit.[47]

Attempting to respond to changes in the library workplace and information environment, while watching the convergence of technologies, LIS educators encounter institutional mandates, dwindling financial resources, the external accrediting body (COA), the alumni, and employers. They communicate regularly with employers who hire students and graduates. Teaching students how to describe resources using standard metadata schema includes changes in rules and conventions, interfacing with online public access catalogs (OPACs) and database systems, and an array of formats. It is very challenging to walk a student through that kind of curriculum, and yet employers want new entry-level folks to have a comprehensive background in descriptive cataloging, subject access, classifying, programming language scripting, along with skills in managing, training, and supervising.

The list of employers' expectations grows and grows. There is a growing concern among students that they will graduate and that there will be no jobs. The reluctance of libraries to hire in difficult economic environments impacts students and library employees negatively. In 2006, Calhoun stated that the catalog "represents a shrinking proportion of the universe of scholarly information."[48] When catalogers retire, employers may replace them with significant difficulties in finding, recruiting, and hiring suitable candidates. No specific research studies have identified the number of new graduates seeking positions and the impending retirements within the community of catalogers. In 2002, Wilder surveyed technical services units in ARL (Association of Research Libraries) institutions and discovered that 16 percent of professional catalogers were nearing retirement age as compared to 10 percent among librarians.[49] He reported that 32 percent of the catalogers were over the age of 55, almost twice that of the comparable reference population, and concluded that it is "possible that fully one-third of the 2000 ARL cataloging population will retire by 2010."[50]

Libraries are disbanding technical services departments and outsourcing. Professional cataloging positions are being collapsed into paraprofessional jobs. Therefore, new graduates must have key understandings and skills that exceed those of their paraprofessional counterparts. Differentiating the knowledge of professionals from paraprofessionals is critical so that both employers *and* library users can tell the difference between the two different levels of library employees.

Internships, practica, mentorships, and service learning provide invaluable learning experience for students. These experiences are critical for initial professional job placement, particularly in cataloging and metadata positions. If a student has no practicum experience and no hands-on work experience in a library, he or she is not likely to secure a professional job. A growing number of new graduates learn cataloging on the job, which is difficult if the only cataloger has retired, taking away decades of tacit knowledge and experience. In order to make sure that talented students who really want to join the community of catalogers have a cataloging knowledge base from which to learn, there must be a stable, reliable, recognized entry point.

Cataloging faculty members understand their importance as supportive partners to public service, archives, and special collections. LIS educators teach cataloging in an environment with competing graduate degrees; cataloging continues to be a moving target. The potential adoption and implementation of RDA and its training challenges loom in the future as we approach 2010. Several studies identified gaps between what employers expect students to be taught in preparation for careers in cataloging and metadata services, and what LIS educators teach.

In 1995, MacLeod and Callahan surveyed library educators at ALA-accredited schools and heads of cataloging at ARL libraries. Although 98 percent of the LIS educators stated a need to consider the needs of the community of catalogers when developing cataloging courses, 58 percent of the library managers indicated that educators did not address their concerns. The researchers discovered some agreement among practitioners and educators regarding the importance of introductory cataloging principles versus the practical elements of cataloging, supporting the idea that entry-level catalogers need theoretical knowledge in addition to practical experience.[51]

In 1997, Vellucci reviewed cataloging courses taught by fifty-two ALA-accredited schools. She analyzed the types of cataloging courses offered and stratified them into two categories: introductory and advanced.[52] In 90 percent of the LIS programs, each student was required to take a course that introduced students to broad principles or a different course focused on topics like information transfer theory, natural language processing, organization of records, and information retrieval theory. An additional 73 percent of the LIS programs offered advanced cataloging courses: comprehensive cataloging, subject analysis, classification theory, descriptive cataloging, and nonprint cataloging.[53] Although she identified an increase in the number of introductory courses, Vellucci noted a broadening of subject matter. Rather than focusing solely on cataloging rules, a significant number of the introductory courses gave a broad view of cataloging and information organization. As technology evolves and catalogers needed additional technical skills, Vellucci warned "that diluting the existing cataloging and classification curriculum by adding new subject areas within existing courses is not the answer."[54]

Joudrey reviewed courses taught by forty-eight ALA-accredited schools in the 2000–2001 and 2005–2006 academic years.[55] In his initial study, he categorized courses by focus and separated introductory courses that concentrated on the organization of information from those in cataloging and classification principles. He found that 60 percent of the LIS programs offered introductory courses in information organization, and 89 percent offered beginning courses in cataloging. Joudrey reported a 46.2 percent increase in the number of programs that required information organization courses, a decrease of 19.2 percent in the number of required introductory cataloging courses, fewer advanced cataloging courses, a course in nonprint cataloging at 25 percent of the schools, and a dramatic increase in the offering of indexing and abstracting courses.[56] He concluded that although required courses, introductory courses, and courses in specialized cataloging topics were increasing, the number of traditional cataloging courses was declining.

In his recent study, Joudrey reported that the fifty-six ALA-accredited graduate LIS programs offered 267 cataloging and organization-of-information (OI) courses, 225 of which were actually taught.[57] He concluded that students could take cataloging and OI courses because LIS schools routinely offer them. Among the 56 LIS programs, 54 required an OI course, which was fulfilled with a beginning cataloging course at 40 percent of the schools. These data suggest that a majority of LIS programs believe students are better served by an OI course. While in 2000, fewer than 50 percent of ALA-accredited LIS programs required an organization course; by 2005, 66 percent of the schools required an organization course. In 2000, basic cataloging was required by 36 percent of LIS schools; in 2005, the course the number had decreased to 29 percent.[58]

Based on the Vellucci, Hsieh-Yee, and Joudrey studies, the likelihood of OI, cataloging, metadata, and specialty courses in description, classification, authority control, indexing, and thesaurus construction will increase. Students who seek careers as catalog librarians and metadata specialists will have opportunities to pursue extensive studies of the Anglo-American Cataloguing Rules (AACR2), the Resource Description and Access rules (RDA), the Library of Congress Rule Interpretations (LCRI), and the Subject Cataloging Manuals (SCM). These students find their way to specializations in cataloging and metadata schema when they discover their affinity for cataloging through a well-taught OI course. Interested, capable students are excited by the cerebral qualities of the topic and take advanced cataloging courses.

Hill outlines the education and skills that catalogers require in order to "function in a world in which the organization of information includes not just the creation of the same kind of cataloging data we have been supplying for decades, but now also includes the creation, application, integration, and harvesting of various kinds of metadata."[59]

No longer is cataloging the department in which the shy, inarticulate, problem student seeks a career. The brightest, inquisitive, focused student must be deliberately identified, recruited, and mentored in careers as the catalog librarian and metadata specialist of the future.

CATALOGING AND METADATA PEDAGOGY: MENTAL MODELS

Organizing data, information, and knowledge is a hallmark of the work that catalog librarians and metadata specialists perform. Therefore, they become keenly aware of schemas around their professional endeavors and personal interests. Because they are self-aware of schemas, they can maximize their use, understand them, and explain the world around them. Using their personal constructs or schemas empowers them to define, organize, and provide access to global, multilingual resources for a diverse user community.

A schema is a mental structure (or model) used to organize and simplify personal knowledge of the world. Schemas can be interrelated (akin to a personal Semantic Web) in a hierarchical arrangement in which an individual classifies past experiences and anticipates the future regarding objects, people, events, and the like. Self-sustaining schemas provide familiar frameworks to understand and interpret the world.

Teaching the theoretical knowledge, core competencies, and technical skills of cataloging and metadata lends itself to the use of a mental model strategy.[60] A mental model is an explanation of the thought process for how something works in the real world. Attributed to Scottish philosopher and psychologist Kenneth James Williams Craik, the term represents how the mind constructs models of reality and uses them to predict similar future events.[61]

The importance of understanding cognitive thought processes and human-computer interaction prompted information professionals to consider and adopt mental models. Usability and design professionals frequently use the term "mental model" loosely. Although an exact English-language definition of mental models is difficult to identify, cognitive scientists, information professionals, system engineers, and researchers discussed and used the concept as a foundation for advances in human-computer interaction and usability studies. Preeminent cognitive scientist Donald Norman used the term "user-centered design" to describe design based on the needs of the user.[62] Noted usability computer consultant Steve Krug recommended that computer screens and Web sites should not make the user think unnecessarily. Consequently, mental models can provide a framework for understanding how users will find, search, and use Web sites and online catalogs.[63]

Mental models share four key characteristics: the inclusion of what a person thinks is true, not necessarily what is actually true; a similarity in structure to the thing or concept they represent; the potential to allow a person to predict the results of future actions; and simplicity and enough information to allow accurate predictions. In addition, mental models consist of several components: an image (if the mental model represents a physical object), a script (if the mental model represents a process), a set of related mental models, a controlled vocabulary, and a set of assumptions.[64]

The mental models strategy is ideal for helping students in library and information settings to develop and refine problem solving and decision-making skills.[65] The instructor can use a variety of mental models to help students become acquainted with problem-solving techniques. Decision-making and problem-solving models include (but are not limited to) a random search, a systemic random search, hill climbing, means-ends analysis, working backward, a split-half method, simplification, using actual data, graphs and diagrams, analogy, and contradiction. Guiding students through a variety of mental models allows them to practice the techniques and strategies that will enable them to be effective practitioners and managers in twenty-first-century information settings.

The use of mental models is particularly appropriate when teaching cataloging and classification. The application of standard rules, cataloging conventions, and local practices allows students to practice the selection of cataloging rules and experience the vagaries of enhancing or constructing a metadata record that describes a printed, online, or digital asset. Students engage in active selection, use, and monitoring of mental models to manage cognitive overload and to apply them to their real-life roles under circumstances of challenge, support, and safety. Their motivation comes from an intrinsic desire to solve problems and make decisions that have positive consequences. Serving as a facilitator, the instructor should encourage and support students as they recognize that they are preparing for professional work, using authentic resources and real problems in a safe and sheltered learning environment.

The most important task for the instructor is to work as a facilitator who is familiar with problem-solving and decision-making techniques using a variety of mental models. It is the instructor who selects the key learning objectives for the course and creates the environment in which the students interact with them. The facilitator's role is to set the scene, provide materials, use cases or examples, intervene or step back (as appropriate), deliver introductory discussions, observe, manage the time, debrief the participants, and provide verbal and written feedback.

Using mental models to teach cataloging and classification requires the instructor to ensure that students have access to the resources they will use in the workplace. These resources include the Anglo-American Cataloging Rules in paper or through Cataloger's Desktop, the Library of Congress Rule Interpretations, MARC 21 formats and documentation, classification schedules (e.g., Library of Congress Classification, Dewey Decimal Classification, the National Library of Medicine Classification), the Library of Congress Subject Headings, OCLC, and an integrated library system. Students work in a learning environment that most closely simulates the workplace when they have actual books, DVDs, CDs, photographs, Web sites, and representative library resources in hand that reflect the array of formats and languages found in the collections of libraries and information centers.

The strengths of mental models rest in their potential to provide sufficient complexity and challenges to engage participants in lively, thought-provoking exercises and discussions. Students can search for legitimate answers to real-world problems. Mental models provide opportunities for students to practice and become familiar with tools and resources, engage them with a variety of problem-solving strategies, and create the next-best thing to workplace experience. On the other hand, the use of mental models requires the instructor to invest in significant preparation, master the actual tools and resources, and select appropriate library materials for use in class. The instructor must be prepared to handle high levels of student frustration, technology failures, and a myriad of questions that require complex responses. In order to use mental models successfully, the instructor needs to possess a high level of analytical ability, patience, persistence, and a supportive attitude toward impatient learners who seek easy answers. Teaching with mental models for a positive learning experience may require usually unfamiliar and difficult facilitation skills, and flexibility to walk students through unfamiliar processes with a great number of possibilities and vagaries.[66]

Mental models are applicable when learning the steps involved in problem solving is critical (such as cataloging or classification). A script of the series of steps expressed verbally, as a flowchart, or in a decision tree can be used. The art of documenting a mental model is choosing the right representation. Selecting the right model shows students how users think, and relates the model to learning how to perform descriptive cataloging, classifying, and subject analysis. Each mental model has a set of key definitions and variants. Librarians are adept at creating controlled vocabularies; therefore, mental models designed to support the teaching of cataloging and classification courses contain a small, controlled vocabulary. Because definitions are essential in order to build a foundation for cataloging and metadata work tasks, learning definitions and subtle variations in meaning for terms is critical.

The assessment of skill development in using mental models for decision making and problem solving involves not only determining the answers, but evaluating the process that the participant uses to arrive at them.[67] To the extent possible, the assessment should reflect workplace review and evaluation. For example, the assessment for a cataloging and classification assignment should include a careful analysis of the item to be described and classified, a consideration and selection of the rules and local cataloging practices, the placement of data elements within the appropriate schema, and reasons for each of the decisions.

The assessment is proof that the student can use the mental model and achieve results that are equivalent to those expected in the workplace. Although assessment for the mental models strategy frequently results in a product, feedback and a conversation with the student provides an opportunity for the instructor to understand the learner's thinking process and decision-making strategies.

THE DREYFUS MODEL OF SKILL ACQUISITION

This section on the Dreyfus Model of Skill Acquisitions sets the stage for comprehension of the learning continuum from novice to expert, which is necessary for understanding the next section of this essay that addresses the actual teaching of cataloging and metadata to aspiring catalogers and metadata librarians and covers library tasks, job descriptions, and learning levels in detail.

A professor of philosophy for over fifty years at MIT and the University of California, Berkeley, Hubert Dreyfus is an outspoken critic of the claims of the cognitivists and the artificial intelligence community. Drawing on the philosophies of Heidegger, Wittgenstein, and Merleau-Ponty, he argues that "attempts to treat intelligence as rational or at least analytic had never worked" and that "perception could not be explained by the application of rules to basic features."[68] Therefore, Dreyfus suggests that all cognitive activities are not fundamentally problem solving in nature. Although he admits that human beings solve problems when confronted by puzzles or unfamiliar situations, Dreyfus states that:

> They typically go on to generalize their results too far, accepting as essentially true, without supporting this claim by any arguments or empirical evidence, that all intelligent behavior is of the problem-solving form. But there is not a shred of evidence that [problem solving] is "necessary," that we cannot be intelligent without solving problems.[69]

In an attempt to understand the artificial intelligence community and its goal of replacing human beings in manufacturing plants, Dreyfus and his brother, Stuart, maintained that equating the rules of production systems with skill and expertise does "fundamental violence to the real nature of human intelligence and expertise."[70] Based on that contention, they focused their studies on unstructured problems rather than structured areas of decision making in which the "goal and relevant information are clear, effects of decisions are known and verifiable solutions can be reasoned out."[71] Unstructured problems have an unlimited number of possibly relevant facts and features; elements interrelate and determine other events.

Together, the two brothers developed a model of skill acquisition based on their studies of airplane pilots, chess players, automobile drivers, and adult learners of a second language. First developed and proposed in 1980, the Dreyfus Model of Skill Acquisition postulates that when individuals acquire a skill through external instruction, they normally pass through five stages: Novice, Advanced-Beginner, Competent, Proficient, and Expert.[72] Progression through the five stages is viewed as a gradual transition from rigid adherence to rules to an intuitive mode of reasoning that relies heavily on deep tacit understanding, with similarities to Schön's theory of "knowing-in-action." Anthony has summarized the model in Table 17.1.[73]

In the novice stage, the beginner learns objective facts and features relevant to the skill and acquires rules for determining actions based on these facts and figures. Although the novice stage in their model appears similar to the first stage in the information processing model, Dreyfus and Dreyfus stress that the facts, features, and rules learned by the novice are context-free: "they are so clearly and objectively defined for the novice that they can be recognized without reference to the overall situation in which they occur."[74] They equate the novice stage with their definition of information processing: the "manipulation of unambiguously defined context-free elements by precise rules," e.g., recognizing the letter E because it has horizontal and vertical lines in a prescribed relationship.

Learners move beyond the exclusive use of information processing in the advanced-beginner stage as a result of their experience with real situations. Because they begin to perceive similarities with prior situations and events, learners begin to recognize situational (meaningful) features and elements in addition to the context-free facts and rules. Competence is developed only when learners begin to recognize the relative importance of both situational and context-free features and utilize the most salient ones to simplify and improve their performances. They organize and develop plans to efficiently and effectively achieve goals. The competent stage of the Dreyfus model is essentially what cognitive psychologists refer to as problem solving.

The fundamental difference between the Dreyfus model and the information-processing model of skill acquisition is seen in the proficient and expert stages. These final two stages of the Dreyfus model are when know-how, "the understanding that effortlessly occurs upon seeing similarities with previous experiences," is acquired.[75] Therefore, an important assumption of the Dreyfus model is that with experience and mastery, skill is transformed. Rules and procedures do not simply move to the unconscious level; there is a discontinuity between the competent, proficient, and expert levels. In fact, as experts pay

Table 17.1
Dreyfus Model of Stages of Skill Acquisition

Skill Level	Performance Characteristics	How Context Is Assessed	Decision Making
Novice	• Rigid adherence to context-free rules or plans (information processing) • Little situational perception • No discretionary judgment	Analytically	Rational
Advanced-Beginner	• Begins recognizing situational aspects (aspects are global characteristics of situations recognizable only after some prior experience) • All attributes and aspects are treated separately and given equal importance		
Competent	• Begins recognizing salience, meaning of aspects • Deliberate choice of plans • Emotional involvement as well as detached (disembodied) rule following (equated with problem solving)		
Proficient	• Sees situations holistically rather than in terms of aspects • Intuitive behavior replaces reasoned responses, yet still incorporates detached decision making • Sees what is most important in a situation • Perceives deviations from the normal pattern • Uses maxims for guidance, meanings of which vary according to the situation	Holistically	Intuitive/ Rational (transitional)
Expert	• No longer relies on rules, guidelines or maxims • Intuitive grasp of situations based on deep tacit understanding • Analytic approaches used only in novel situations or when problems occur • Vision of what is possible		Intuitive (arational)

attention to rules and guidelines that they used as beginners, their performance actually deteriorates. The implication is that formal structural and process models that are integral to systemization and building expert systems cannot fully describe higher levels of expert performance.

Situated learning was first proposed by Jean Lave and Etienne Wenger as a model of learning in a community of practice. At its simplest, situated learning is learning that takes place in the same context in which it is applied. Lave and Wenger argue that learning should not be viewed as simply the transmission of abstract and out of context, but a social process in which knowledge is co-constructed; they suggest that such learning is situated in a specific context and embedded within a particular social and physical environment.[76] They asserted that situated learning is not an educational form, but "legitimate peripheral participation."[77] However, since their writing, others have advocated different pedagogies that include situated activity, such as:

- Workshops, kitchens, greenhouses, and gardens used as classrooms
- Stand-up role playing in the real world setting
- Field trips (including archaeological digs and participant-observer studies in an alien culture)
- On-the-job training (including apprenticeship and cooperative education)
- Sports practice, music practice, and art with the same equipment or instruments
- Service learning

Many of the original examples from Lave and Wenger concerned adult learners. Situated learning still has a particular resonance for adult education. For example, Hansman shows how adult learners discover, shape, and make explicit their own knowledge through situated learning within a community of practice.[78]

APPLICATION OF THE DREYFUS MODEL FOR CATALOG LIBRARIANS AND METADATA SPECIALISTS: THEORETICAL, APPLIED, ON-THE-JOB, AND LIFELONG LEARNING

The tripartite education of library school students who seek careers as catalogers begins in library school. Preparation for a career as a catalog librarian or a metadata specialist includes the mastery of technical competencies supported through the incorporation of computer-dependent technologies into the teaching and learning environments. The breadth and scope of material that must be included in order to prepare a student for a career in bibliographic control, cataloging, or technical services is far-reaching and complex. Consequently, basic and advanced cataloging courses include metadata and classification schemes, bibliographic utilities, electronic resources, Internet-resident tools,

integrated library systems, interoperability technologies, human-computer interactions, and networking. Course instruction and hands-on exercises need to
include the construction and enhancement of descriptive cataloging data; selection and completion of classification numbers in several schemas; importance,
identification, and construction of authority records; and the use of bibliographic
utilities. According to Hall-Ellis, the domains within cataloging, metadata, and
bibliographic description include theoretical knowledge of the cataloging tools
and of descriptive cataloging; authority control, classification schemes, and subject analysis competencies; familiarity with collaborative initiatives; and, multilingual proficiencies.[79]

In order to prepare students for employment in the practitioner community,
full-time faculty members and their part-time colleagues must be aware of factors
that have an impact on the theoretical knowledge, professional competencies,
and technical skills required of novice catalog librarians and metadata specialists. The importance of experience as a defining feature of adult learning is
expressed in the aphorism that "experience is the adult learner's living textbook."[80] Therefore, adult education can be considered "a continuing process of
evaluating experiences."[81]

As a library school student, the novice cataloger or metadata specialist learns
three processes that make up the tasks referred to collectively as cataloging. Students learn to describe the information package of a work (descriptive cataloging), determine where the work fits into a given hierarchy (classifying), and
discern the concepts addressed in a work through subject analysis (subject cataloging).

The process mental model is appropriate for teaching students how to prepare, review, and enhance a bibliographic record describing a library resource.
The descriptive cataloging process can be divided into twelve sequential steps.
If the instructor clearly explains each of the steps, the required items, and the
anticipated outcomes, students can build their process mental model for cataloging. With guided practice and experience, students can learn how to prepare bibliographic descriptions independently, whether based on a master record in a
bibliographic utility or from scratch.

As broadly noted previously, cataloging or metadata description is routinely
referred to as the process of describing an information package, choosing name
and title access points, conducting subject analysis, assigning subject headings,
and constructing a classification number. As a global framework for the description of information packages evolves and the implementation of RDA
approaches, catalogers and metadata specialists are beginning to refer to an
information package as the manifestation of a work, focusing on the physical
object as distinct from its intellectual content. The cataloging of information
packages is performed to support four activities: to identify items in a collection,
to organize items within the collection, to provide access to each item, and to
perform inventory of the collection. At the end of the cataloging process,
whether theoretical or applied, the final result is a surrogate bibliographic record
that describes the information package.

The preparation of surrogate records for individual information packages ensures bibliographic control for the collection and empowers the cataloger or metadata specialist to identify the existence of all types of available information packages, determine the editions (e.g., hardcover, paperback, e-book, etc.), assemble them into collections and subcollections, construct data elements for access resources, provide the means of locating items (i.e., copies), and produce lists (e.g., bibliographies or finding aids) according to standard citation rules.

Learning these processes moves the student from novice to advanced-beginner within the Dreyfus Model of Skill Acquisition framework. The three accepted stages of professional education for catalog librarians and metadata specialists include formal graduate coursework, on-the-job training, and continuing education experiences throughout a career. Employers and students articulate expectations that graduate library education includes the mastery of theoretical knowledge, core cataloging competencies, and technical skills supported through the incorporation of computer-dependent technologies into the teaching and learning environment. Conversations among the practitioner community and researchers indicate that work remains to be done by everyone concerned about the recruitment, education, and careers of new LIS graduates, and to confirm the importance of partnerships between the community of catalogers and library educators to educate, mentor, and support novice catalog librarians and metadata specialists.

Novice catalog librarians and metadata specialists earn an MLIS and leave graduate school ready to launch their careers. LIS faculty members recognize librarianship as a way of knowing in its own right, and seek ways to find developmental and advancement opportunities for their students. They understand that the learning experiences in the classroom serve as a stepping stone to post-MLIS education and training through the information professional's career. Successful graduates leave library school with an appreciation for librarianship as a discipline that is based on collective and cumulative research and education. They are vitally connected to practice, socially organized into the profession, and embedded with knowledge and ethics.

Yet, members of the practitioner community and LIS educators are unaware of the fact that this model for professional education is central to our collective efforts. LIS graduate education provides a theoretical foundation, complemented by an array of core competencies and technical skills designed to last an entire career. As with professional education in law, medicine, accountancy, and social work, LIS education serves as the basic foundation for a successful, multi-decade career.

A fundamental characteristic of the information age is the emphasis on continual learning, transformation, and personal development. Librarians and information professionals who embrace lifelong learning in their personal lives and careers will seek, hold, and thrive in such an environment.[82] In the twenty-first century, cataloging and metadata description focus on the transcription, indexing, and use of descriptive data. Many new types of metadata—rights, technical, structural, administrative, evaluative, preservation, and linking metadata—are needed for the array of information objects in which libraries now have an interest. Traditional cataloging practices have given way to library information systems, and the future of libraries requires transformation. In a transformed library, librarians stop putting the majority of resources into preserving and maintaining current library collections; serve the mission of the higher education institution rather than a specific job description; develop robust information partnerships; and, manage a broad range of information objects in traditional and nontraditional formats, including many that previously were outside of the library's purview, such as learning objects, data sets, and institutional data. Flexibility, personal development, and lifelong learning are basic substructures of the transformed library and librarian.[83]

Human resources (HR) officers generally prepare position descriptions in consultation with library managers. While the goal of HR personnel is to craft a position description so that a person who fills the organizational needs may be hired, they work within the constraints of previous descriptions and legally acceptable language. Writing job descriptions does not lend itself to the recognition of nuanced levels of skills development, to transformation of knowledge, or to the relationship between tacit understanding and ability. Rather, the focus is on the cognitive abilities and explicit skills needed to do the work. Therefore, position descriptions use verbs reflecting levels of skill tied to educational preparation, years of experience, and salary. The resulting job descriptions do not easily fit into a model like the Dreyfus. Table 17.2 shows their skill development.

Table 17.2
Dreyfus Model of Explicit Skill Acquisition Applied to Catalogers and Metadata Specialists

Skill Level	Performance Characteristics	Skills: Catalogers and Metadata Specialists
Novice	• Rigid adherence to context-free rules or plans (information processing) • Little situational perception • No discretionary judgment	• Perform copy cataloging of monographic materials using OCLC and ILS • Knowledge of MARC 21, AACR2, DACS, LCC, DDC, LCSH, and authority records.[84] • Familiar with integrated library systems
Advanced-Beginner	• Begins recognizing situational aspects (aspects are global characteristics of situations recognizable only after some prior experience) • All attributes and aspects are treated separately and given equal importance	• Perform complex copy cataloging of monographic materials using OCLC and ILS • Use MARC 21, AACR2, DACS, LCC, DDC, LCSH, and authority records • Knowledge of integrated library systems

(continued)

Table 17.2. (*continued*)

Skill Level	Performance Characteristics	Skills: Catalogers and Metadata Specialists
Competent	• Begins recognizing salience, meaning of aspects • Deliberate choice of plans • Emotional involvement as well as detached (disembodied) rule following (equated with problem solving)	• Perform original cataloging of print, online, and electronic materials using OCLC and ILS • Skill with MARC 21, AACR2, DACS, LCC, DDC, LCSH, and authority records • Experience with integrated library systems
Proficient	• Sees situations holistically rather than in terms of aspects • Intuitive behavior replaces reasoned responses, yet still incorporates detached decision making • Sees what is most important in a situation • Perceives deviations from the normal pattern • Uses maxims for guidance, meanings of which vary according to the situation	• Train and review copy and original cataloging for print, online, and electronic materials using OCLC and ILS • Train and supervise staff in use of MARC 21, AACR2, DACS, LCC, DDC, LCSH, and authority records • Manage and supervise staff operating integrated library systems
Expert	• No longer relies on rules, guidelines or maxims • Intuitive grasp of situations based on deep tacit understanding • Analytic approaches used only in novel situations or when problems occur • Vision of what is possible	• Extensive knowledge of technical rules and standards for library cataloging, including MARC 21, AACR2, DACS, LCC, DDC, LCSH, and authority records, metadata, and structure and coding of both local and national cataloging systems

A formal review and examination of position descriptions provides insight into the correlation among theoretical knowledge, core competencies, and technical skills. When analyzing position descriptions, the information provides a reflection and interpretation of the profession and identifies good practice. Employers' expectations, emerging areas of specialization, and shifting task emphasis expose changes in the workplace and knowledge gaps among current employees and new hires.

Training throughout a professional career is not routine or repetitive. Professional development opportunities focus on specific forums for personal growth in support of organizational change. Coupled with on-the-job training and years of experience, professional development experiences move the individual through the next stages of the Dreyfus model. The re-crafting of position descriptions in response to the fluid workplace, and flattening organizational models, reflects skills and competencies rather than the same old tasks. In these ever-changing times, the Dreyfus model has applicability; as a profession, librarians just haven't used it enough.

OBSERVATIONS

As potential knowledge workers in a profession driven by technological change, LIS students require graduate education that equips them with the theoretical framework, core competencies, and technical skills for a fluid work environment and ongoing professional development.[85] Graduate LIS students are physically mature and fill adult niches in society. They continue to pursue formal education, consistent with Malcolm Knowles's assertion that education "should no longer be seen as a process of transmitting what is known, but as a lifelong process of continuing inquiry."[86] These students continue their formal education and perceive themselves as self-directing with a deep psychological need to be seen in the same way by others when they deliberately embark on the most important learning of all: "learning how to learn" and attempting to master the skills of self-directed inquiry. Because they are adult learners, they follow the process of self-evaluation, measuring gains in competence, re-diagnosing competence levels, and entering into a new cycle of learning. The success of adult learners is affected by the degree to which their learning is experience-based and problem-centered and how well they can integrate the learning process into improving personal abilities to cope with life problems.[87]

Grounded Theory and Position Descriptions

Grounded theory is a research methodology where theoretical construct emerges from the richness of the data. This essay used the grounded theory methodology to analyze the library school course offerings and position descriptions data.[88] The objective of grounded theory studies is to explain social processes and develop theoretical frameworks by involving constant comparative coding procedures, connecting categories, and emerging theory.[89] Adapting Glaser's grounded theory of emerging design allows for theory to emerge from the data, not from preset categories, and focuses on connecting categories through constant comparative coding procedures, and on the theory as it emerges after each round, without reference to a diagram or picture. Because of this possibility for theory to emerge from data, four emergent theories on learning and cataloging education, based on the data set of position descriptions, follow for further consideration and review.

Independently created position descriptions, when collected and analyzed, constitute such a rich data set for grounded theory analysis. These data, when considered alongside the Dreyfus model, reveal natural stratification with regard to education, years of experience, and salary. The data further reveal trends, which may lead to the development of hypotheses and guiding principles, which in turn (with further study) may emerge as theoretical underpinnings of our profession.

Workplace experience and participation in professional development activities results in skill level increases. The acquisition of increased skills that build on one another can be termed as scaffolded learning, and the Dreyfus model is an example of scaffolded learning and increasing skill development throughout the career. Position descriptions, although written independently by library personnel without the intent of consideration as a group, are snapshots along the continuum of skill development, providing a critical mass of data whose richness allows grounded theory to emerge. A review of position descriptions against the Dreyfus Model of Skill Acquisition framework results in the four following emergent theories.

Emergent Theory #1: Expanding Cataloging Curriculum

Emergent theory #1 suggests that graduate library education needs to be expanded from the coursework originally designed for the traditional cataloger, in order to meet the needs of aspiring catalog librarians and metadata specialists. Courses that focus on the bibliographic description, subject analysis, and classification of print and nonbook materials are no longer sufficient. Learning outcomes and a competency-based education movement with well-defined behavioral objectives, and the context of the ALA standards for accreditation, provide an institutional process for further development and modification of course offerings.

A careful examination of technical services units reveals that work in cataloging, resource description, and bibliographic control is far more complex than most formal theories predict because of high levels of judgment, knowledge, and ethical behavior. Major aspects of the work cannot be captured in formal descriptions of processes and techniques. The transformation of courses is essential in order to prepare students for careers as catalog librarians and metadata specialists. Describing resources in contemporary library collections requires a familiarity with many types of materials. Cataloging instructors should consider teaching formats in the order that aligns with employers' preferences: electronic resources, continuing resources, projected graphics, monographs, sound recordings, cartographic materials, scores, realia, and special collections. The traditional order should be abandoned. Examples of transformed learning objectives for a basic cataloging course appear in Table 17.3.

Emergent Theory #2: LIS Need to Prepare Library School Students for Lifelong Learning: Novice to Expert

Emergent theory #2 indicates the need to prepare students for career trajectory through the Dreyfus model. LIS educators focus on the preparation of students for the first professional position. The combination of formal courses,

Table 17.3
Transformation of Basic Cataloging Course

Traditional Learning Objectives	Transformed Learning Objectives
Identify and compare theories and systems dealing with the organization and description of materials in multiple formats for access and retrieval;	Define, assess, create, and evaluate systems for managing information and descriptive content for print, electronic, online, digital objects, and cultural heritage assets;
Appropriately use subject (classification and verbal access) cataloging tools to demonstrate competency in the bibliographic description of print, nonprint, and electronic materials;	Analyze, synthesize, describe, index, and communicate information and knowledge for intellectual works in a variety of languages and formats;
Explain trends and research in the field of cataloging and explain their impacts on the organization and retrieval of information; and,	Apply standards, tools, and systems relevant to specific information service activities to organize information; and,
Develop a philosophy of bibliographic control and technical services.	Evaluate information problems, develop solutions, and articulate the relationship of information organization to information access, drawing from a wide range of information technology tools and practices.

hands-on labs, projects (service learning and community engagement), internships, and practica provide the library school experience and socialization into the profession. However, LIS education also serves as the springboard to move individuals from novice to advanced-beginner in the Dreyfus model.

Emergent Theory #3: Library Employers as Mentors and Teachers for Professional Growth

Emergent theory #3 reveals that employers are responsible to create and maintain learning environments for all staff. These activities are resource dependent, requiring significant investments of time, money, and personnel. It is the responsibility of library managers and supervisors to move employees from advanced-beginner to competent. Moving employees along the Dreyfus model continuum benefits both the library as a learning organization and the individual. Employees who are skilled in mentoring and coaching require time to move their colleagues from competent to proficient and expert.

Emergent Theory #4: Libraries as Learning Organizations

Emergent theory #4 suggests that the Dreyfus model has applicability for libraries as learning organizations. Mentoring and coaching new hires and providing opportunities for professional development empower new hires and less experienced staff members to prepare for movement up organizational career ladders. They need guidance and mentoring in order to prepare for advancement. In order to maximize human capital, managers and administrators need to determine skill development levels among staff so that they can identify skill "gaps." By hosting or sponsoring staff development and training sessions, managers and supervisors can identify and solicit individual interests to use when selecting and supporting individuals moving from one level to the next. They can fill "gaps" internally, create new career ladders, identify emerging stars, and enhance evidence of values for staff contributions.

CONCLUSION

The training and education of catalog librarians did not change significantly for many years, consisting of theoretical knowledge about librarianship, emulation of technical skills, cataloging competencies, and supervision. As libraries expand their societal roles and transform into learning commons and community information centers, the search for information is more complex, forcing changes and expansion of the LIS graduate education model.

Learning takes place in the context in which it is applied, thus becoming a social process through which knowledge is co-constructed by instructors and learners alike,[90] and during the process the learner may be professionally socialized. In her adaptation of the Dreyfus model for nursing education, Benner explains that her book's purpose "is to present the limits of formal rules and call attention to the discretionary judgment used in actual clinical situations."[91]

> Once the situation is described, the actions taken can be understood as orderly, reasonable behavior that responds to the demands of a given situation rather than rigid principles and rules. More descriptive rules could be generated to allow for multiple exceptions, but the expert would still function flexibly in other new situations requiring new exceptions.[92]

Graduate library school education, professional experience, and the continued building of technical skills and competencies, prepare catalog librarians and metadata specialists for career advancement and leadership positions. Leadership within the practitioner community is a logical progression up the career ladder and movement through the Dreyfus model's continuum. Employers across all types of libraries agree that cataloging, metadata, and bibliographic control unit managers need to possess an accredited library degree, to have worked at least three years in a library or information center environment, to have developed sophisticated written and verbal communication skills, to understand integrated library system operations, to work well independently and collaboratively, and to remain current with technological and bibliographic changes.

The Dreyfus Model of Skills Acquisition incorporates five developmental stages that individuals pass through when acquiring skills through external instruction, the assumption being that the progression from novice to expert follows the gradual personal transition from strict adherence to rules to a more intuitive mode of reasoning that draws on tacit knowledge and understanding. The Dreyfus model provides a useful lens for viewing the development or maturation of professionally educated librarians, as the transition from *advanced-beginner* to *competent* signals the threshold for entry-level professional practice.

Providing a comprehensive graduate education for catalog librarians and metadata specialists of the future is vitally important. These students need a solid introduction to courses that allow them to explore cataloging standards and tools in depth. They need an introductory course and electives that help them to develop judgment and to extrapolate core competencies and technical skills beyond the traditional library to new materials, projects, and environments that they will encounter upon graduation. Research studies over the last two decades suggest that aspiring catalog librarian and metadata specialists cannot rely solely on cataloging courses to prepare them for successful careers. The evidence indicates that work remains to be done by everyone concerned to develop a framework of professional advancement throughout a career for catalog librarians and metadata specialists.

NOTES

1. Taemin Park, "The Integration of Electronic Resources into Cataloging Instruction in the LIS Curriculum," *Serials Librarian* 41, no. 3/4 (2002): 57–72; Daniel N. Joudrey, "A New Look at US Graduate Courses in Bibliographic Control," *Cataloging & Classification Quarterly* 34, no. 1/2 (2002): 57–99; Sherry L. Vellucci, "Cataloging across the Curriculum: A Syndetic Structure for Teaching Cataloging," *Cataloging & Classification Quarterly* 24, no. 1/2 (1997): 35–59; Doris H. Clack, "Education for Cataloging: A Symposium Paper," *Cataloging & Classification Quarterly* 16, no. 3 (1993): 27–37; Desretta V. McAllister-Harper, "An Analysis of Courses in Cataloging and Classification and Related Areas Offered in Sixteen Graduate Library Schools and Their Relationship to Present and Future Trends in Cataloging and Classification and to Cognitive Needs of Professional Academic Catalogers," *Cataloging & Classification Quarterly* 16, no. 3 (1993): 99–123; Arlene G. Taylor, "A Quarter Century of Cataloging Education," in *Technical Services Management, 1965–1990: A Quarter Century of Change and a Look at the Future, Festschrift for Kathryn Luther Henderson*, ed. Linda C. Smith and Ruth C. Carter (New York: Haworth Press, 1996), 300–303; Lynn S. Connaway, "A Model Curriculum for Cataloging Education: The Library and Information Services Program at the University of Denver," *Technical Services Quarterly* 15, no. 1/2 (1997): 27–41; Michael Gorman, "How Cataloging and Classification Should Be Taught," *American Libraries* 23 (1992): 694–97; Joan M. Leysen and Jeanne M. K. Boydston, "Supply and Demand for Catalogers: Present and Future," *Library Resources & Technical Services* 49, no. 4 (2005): 260; Paul L.

Anthony and Jill A. Garbs, "A Scarce Resource? A Study of Academic Cataloger Recruitment, 2000–2002," *Cataloging & Classification Quarterly* 41, no. 1 (2005): 45–62; Daniel N. Joudrey, "Another Look at Graduate Education for Cataloging and the Organization of Information," *Cataloging & Classification Quarterly* 46, no. 2 (2008): 137–81; Jane M. Davis, "A Survey of Cataloging Education: Are Library Schools Listening?" *Cataloging & Classification Quarterly* 46, no. 2 (2008): 182–200.

2. Beatrice Kovacs and Nancy Dayton, "If I Knew Then What I Know Now: UNCG LIS Graduates' Perspectives on Cataloging Education," *Cataloging & Classification Quarterly* 34, no. 1/2 (2002): 145–63.

3. Debra W. Hill, "Requisite Skills of Entry-Level Catalogers: A Supervisor's Perspective," *Cataloging & Classification Quarterly* 23, no. 3/4 (1997): 75–83.

4. Anaclare E. Evans, "The Education of Catalogers: The View of the Practitioner/Educator," *Cataloging & Classification Quarterly* 16, no. 3 (1993): 50–51; Judy MacLeod and Daren Callahan, "Educators and Practitioners Reply: An Assessment of Cataloging Education," *Library Resources & Technical Services* 39, no. 2 (1995): 154.

5. Marcia Kehl, "Library Education," unpublished Capstone, University of Denver, 2001.

6. Elmer D. Johnson, *History of Libraries in the Western World* (Metuchen, NJ: Scarecrow Press, 1970).

7. William Bruce Leslie, "Age of the College," in *History of Higher Education*, 2nd ed., ed. Lester F. Goodchild and Harold S. Wechsler (Needham Heights, MA: Simon & Schuster Custom Publishing, 1997): 333–46.

8. C. Edward Carroll, "History of Library Education," in *Administrative. Aspects of Education for Librarianship: A Symposium*, ed. Mary B. Cassata and Herman L. Totten (Metuchen, NJ: Scarecrow Press, 1975), 6.

9. Henry Watson Kent, *What I Am Pleased to Call My Education*, ed. Lois Leighton Comings (New York: The Grolier Club, 1949): 15–17.

10. Carroll, "History of Library Education," 7.

11. Ibid.

12. Charles C. Williamson, *Training for Library Service: A Report Prepared for the Carnegie Corporation of New York* (New York: The Carnegie Corporation, 1921).

13. Mary E. Clack, "The Role of Training in the Reorganization of Cataloging Services," *Library Acquisitions: Practice & Theory* 19, no. 4 (Winter 1995): 439–44.

14. Carroll, "History of Library Education."

15. Wayne A. Wiegand, "Socialization of Library and Information Science Students: Reflections on a Century of Formal Education for Librarianship," *Library Trends* 34, no. 3 (1986): 383–99.

16. Lloyd J. Houser and Alvin M. Schrader, *The Search for a Scientific Profession: Library Science Education in the U.S. and Canada* (Metuchen, NJ: Scarecrow Press, 1978).

17. Wiegand, "Socialization of Library and Information Science Students."

18. Kehl, "Accredited Library and Information Studies Master's Programs from 1925 through present," http://www.ala.org/ala/educationcareers/education/accreditedprograms/directory/1925present/index.cfm (accessed November 30, 2009).

19. Sheila S. Intner and Janet Swan Hill, eds., *Recruiting, Educating, and Training Cataloging Librarians: Solving the Problems* (Westport, CT: Greenwood Press, 1989).

20. Janet Swan Hill, ed., "Pitfall and the Pendulum: Reconsidering Education for Cataloging and the Organization of Information," special issue of *Cataloging & Classification Quarterly* 34, no. 1–3 (2002).

21. Nancy Chaffin and Patricia Smith, "Education and Training for Technical Services: A Brief Look," *Colorado Libraries* 29, no. 2 (Summer 2003): 38–39.

22. Michelle R. Turvey and Karen M. Letarte, "Cataloging or Knowledge Management: Perspectives of Library Educators on Cataloging Education for Entry-Level Academic Librarians," *Cataloging & Classification Quarterly* 34, no. 1/2 (2002): 165–87.

23. Joan Rapp, "Personnel Selection for Cataloging," *Library Resources & Technical Services* 34, no. 1 (January 1990): 97.

24. Sheila S. Intner, "We Keep Saying Libraries Need Catalogers, But Outsourcing Says It Isn't So," *Technicalities* 17, no. 5 (May 1997): 2.

25. Hill, "Requisite Skills of Entry-Level Catalogers: A Supervisor's Perspective."

26. Christine DeZelar-Tiedman, "A Perfect Fit: Tailoring Library Positions to Match Individual Skills," *Journal of Library Administration* 29, no. 2 (June 1999): 29–39.

27. Sherry L. Vellucci, "Future Catalogers: Essential Colleagues or Anachronisms?" *College & Research Libraries News* (July–August 1996): 443.

28. Jerry D. Saye, "Where Are We and How Did We Get Here? Or the Changing Place of Cataloging in the Library and Information Science Curriculum: Course and Consequences," *Cataloging & Classification Quarterly* 34, no. 1/2 (January 2003): 121–44.

29. Ingrid Hsieh-Yee, "Cataloging and Metadata Education: A Proposal for Preparing Cataloging Professionals of the 21st Century: A Response to Action Item 5.1 of the 'Bibliographic Control of Web Resources: a Library of Congress Action Plan': Final Report (Dec. 2002), Web version (April 2003)," submitted to the ALCTS/SLISE Task Force, http://www.loc.gov/catdir/bibcontrol/CatalogingandMetadataEducation.pdf (accessed November 30, 2009).

30. Ingrid Hsieh-Yee, "Organizing Internet Resources: Teaching Cataloging Standards and Beyond," *OCLC Systems & Services* 16, no. 3 (2000): 130–40.

31. Cliff Glaviano, "Teaching an Information Organization Course with Nordic DC Metadata Creator," *OCLC Systems & Services* 16, no. 1 (2000): 33–40.

32. Lynn S. Connaway, "Educating Catalogers to Meet the Diverse Users in a Technological Environment," *Colorado Libraries* 25, no. 3 (1999): 49; Connaway, "A Model Curriculum for Cataloging Education: the Library and Information Services Program at the University of Denver," *Technical Services Quarterly*, 15, no. 1/2 (September 1997): 27–41.

33. Judy MacLeod and Daren Callahan, "Educators and Practitioners Reply: An Assessment of Cataloging Education," *Library Resources & Technical Services*, 39, no. 2 (April 1995): 153–65.

34. Anaclare F. Evans, "The Education of Catalogers: The View of the Practitioner/Educator," *Cataloging & Classification Quarterly*, 16, no. 3 (October 1993): 49–57.

35. Sylvia D. Hall-Ellis, "Cataloging Education: A New Emphasis for the LIS Curriculum," Presentation delivered to the ALCTS/CETRC Pre-conference, "What They Don't Teach in Library School: Competencies, Education, and Employer Expectations for a Career in Cataloging," 132nd Annual Conference, American Library Association, Washington, D.C., June 22, 2007, http://www.loc.gov/aba/professional (accessed November 30, 2009).

36. "ALA Core Competencies of Librarianship," http://www.lama.ala.org/lamawiki/images/e/eb/Info_doc_-_ALA_Core_Competences_June_6.pdf (accessed November 30, 2009).

37. MacLeod and Callahan, "Educators and Practitioners Reply: An Assessment of Cataloging Education."

38. Sylvia D. Hall-Ellis, "Descriptive Impressions of Entry-Level Cataloger Positions as Reflected in *American Libraries, AutoCAT,* and the *Colorado State Library Jobline,* 2000–2003," *Cataloging & Classification Quarterly* 40, no. 2 (2005): 33–72; Hall-Ellis, "Descriptive Cataloging Proficiencies among Beginning Students: A Comparison Among Traditional and Virtual Class Students," *Journal of Library & Information Services in Distance Education* 2, no. 2 (2005): 13–44; Hall-Ellis, "Descriptive Impressions of Managerial & Supervisory Cataloger Positions as Reflected in *American Libraries, AutoCAT,* and the *Colorado State Library Jobline,* 2000-2004: A Content Analysis of Education, Competencies, and Experience," *Cataloging & Classification Quarterly* 42, no. 1 (2006): 55–88; Hall-Ellis, "Cataloging Electronic Resources & Metadata: Employers' Expectations as Reflected in *American Libraries* and *AutoCAT,* 2000–2005," *Journal of Education for Library and Information Science* 47, no. 1 (2006): 38–51; Hall-Ellis, "Cataloger Competencies . . . What Do Employers Require?" *Cataloging & Classification Quarterly* 46, no. 3 (2008): 305–30.

39. Hill, "Requisite Skills of Entry-Level Catalogers: A Supervisor's Perspective."

40. "Standards for Accreditation of Master's Programs in Library and Information Studies," http://www.ala.org/ala/educationcareers/education/accreditedprograms/standards/standards_2008.pdf (accessed November 30, 2009).

41. Cooperative Cataloging Council Task Force Group V—Cataloging Training Task Force, "Final Report," October 28, 1993.

42. Association for Library Collections & Technical Services, "ALCTS Educational Policy Statement," approved by the ALCTS Board of Directors, June 27, 1995, http://www.ala.org/ala/mgrps/divs/alcts/about/governance/policies/cepolicy.cfm (accessed November 30, 2009).

43. Task Force on Core Competencies "Draft Statement," Congress on Professional Education: Focus on Education for the First Professional Degree, http://ala.org/ala/educationcareers/education/1stcongressonpro/1stcongresstf.cfm (accessed May 17, 2010).

44. Sheila S. Intner, "Persistent Issues in Cataloging Education: Considering the Past and Looking Toward the Future," *Cataloging & Classification Quarterly* 34, no. 1/2 (2002): 16.

45. Janet Swan Hill, "Some Perceived Weaknesses in the Current System of Accreditation," Congress on Professional Education: Focus on Education for the First Professional Degree, http://www.ala.org/ala/educationcareers/education/1stcongressonpro/1stcongresspanelpresentationjanet.cfm (accessed November 30, 2009).

46. Hsieh-Yee, "Cataloging and Metadata Education: A Proposal for Preparing Cataloging Professionals of the 21st Century."

47. Association for Library Collections and Technical Services, "Midwinter '06 Reports," *ALCTS Newsletter Online* 17, no. 1 (February 2006), http://www.ala.org/ala/mgrps/divs/alcts/resources/ano/v17/n1/index.cfm (accessed November 30, 2009).

48. Karen Calhoun, "The Changing Nature of the Catalog and Its Integration with Other Discovery Tools, Final Report March 17, 2006," prepared for the Library of Congress, 5, http://www.loc.gov/catdir/calhoun-report-final.pdf (accessed May 17, 2010).

49. Stanley J. Wilder, "Demographic Trends Affecting Professional Technical Services Staffing in ARL Libraries," in *Education for Cataloging and the Organization of Information: Pitfalls and the Pendulum,* ed. Janet Swan Hill (Binghamton, NY: Haworth Information Press, 2002), 53–57.

50. Ibid., 55.

51. MacLeod and Callahan, "Educators and Practitioners Reply: An Assessment of Cataloging Education," 156.

52. Vellucci, "Cataloging Across the Curriculum: A Syndetic Structure for Teaching Cataloging."

53. Ibid.

54. Ibid., 56.

55. Joudrey, "A New Look at US Graduate Courses in Bibliographic Control," *Cataloging & Classification Quarterly* 34, no. 1/2: 59–101; Joudrey, "Another Look at Graduate Education for Cataloging and the Organization of Information."

56. Joudrey, "A New Look at US Graduate Courses in Bibliographic Control."

57. Joudrey, "Another Look at Graduate Education for Cataloging and the Organization of Information," 172.

58. Ibid., 174.

59. Janet Swan Hill, "Analog People for Digital Dreams: Staffing and Educational Considerations for Cataloging and Metadata Professionals," *Library Resources & Technical Services* 49, no. 1 (2005): 14–18.

60. Deborah S. Grealy and Sylvia D. Hall-Ellis, *From Research to Practice: The Scholarship of Teaching and Learning in LIS Education* (Westport, CT: Libraries Unlimited, 2009).

61. Kenneth James Williams Craik, *The Nature of Explanation* (Cambridge: Cambridge University Press, 1943).

62. Donald A. Norman, *The Design of Everyday Things* (New York: Doubleday, 1990).

63. Steve Krug, *Don't Make Me Think! A Common-Sense Approach to Web Usability* (Berkeley, CA: New Riders Pub., 2006); "Meet the Masterminds: Common Sense Web Design with Steve Krug," Management Consulting News, http://www.management consultingnews.com/interviews/krug_interview.php (accessed November 30, 2009).

64. Scott McDaniel, "What's Your Idea of a Mental Model?" Boxes and Arrows, February 10, 2003, http://www.boxesandarrows.com/view/whats_your_idea_of_a_mental_-model_ (accessed May 17, 2010).

65. James R. Davis and Adelaide B. Davis, *Effective Training Strategies: A Comprehensive Guide to Maximizing Learning in Organizations* (San Francisco: Berrett-Koehler Pub., 1998), 225.

66. Grealy and Hall-Ellis, *From Research to Practice.*

67. Davis and Davis. *Effective Training Strategies,* 457.

68. Herbert L. Dreyfus and Stuart E. Dreyfus with Tom Athanasiou, *Mind over Machine: The Power of Human Intuition and Expertise in the Era of the Computer* (New York: Free Press, 1986), 4.

69. Ibid., 27.

70. Ibid., xii.

71. Ibid., 20.

72. Stuart E. Dreyfus and Hubert L. Dreyfus, "A Five-Stage Model of the Mental Activities Involved in Directed Skill Acquisition," Storming Media, http://www.stormingmedia.us/15/1554/A155480.html (accessed November 23, 2009).

73. Denise Anthony, "Beyond Description: An Exploration of Experienced Archivists' Knowledge and Searching Skills," PhD diss., University of Michigan, 2006.

74. Dreyfus and Dreyfus, *Mind over Machine,* 21.

75. Ibid., 31.

76. Jean Lave, "Situated Learning," http://tip.psychology.org/lave.html (accessed November 23, 2009).

77. Jean Lave and Etienne Wenger, *Situated Learning: Legitimate Peripheral Participation* (New York: Cambridge University Press, 1991).

78. Catherine A. Hansman, "Context-Based Adult Learning," *New Directions for Adult and Continuing Education* 89 (Spring 2001): 43–51.

79. Hall-Ellis, "Cataloger Competencies . . . What Do Employers Require?"

80. Eduard Lindeman, *The Meaning of Adult Education* (New York: New Republic, 1926), 7.

81. Ibid., 85.

82. Sylvia D. Hall-Ellis, Deborah S. Grealy, and Denise Anthony, "Library Apprenticeship and the Dreyfus Model of Skills Acquisition," in *Library Residency Programs*, Megan Z. Perez, ed. (Santa Barbara, Calif.: ABC-Clio, 2010).

83. Joseph M. Brewer, Sheril J. Hook, Janice Simmons-Welburn, and Karen Williams, "Libraries Dealing with the Future Now," *ARL Bimonthly Report* 234 (June 2004): 4.

84. DACS, *Describing Archives: a Content Standard;* LCC, Library of Congress Classification, DDC, Dewey Decimal Classification.

85. Grealy and Hall-Ellis, *From Research to Practice.*

86. Malcolm S. Knowles, *The Modern Practice of Adult Education* (Chicago: Follett Publishing Company, 1980), 41.

87. Malcolm S. Knowles, *Self-Directed Learning: A Guide for Learners and Teachers* (Englewood Cliffs, N.J.: Prentice Hall, 1975).

88. Barney G. Glaser, *Basics of Grounded Theory Analysis: Emergence vs. Forcing* (Mill Valley, CA: Sociology Press, 1993).

89. Antony Bryant and Kathy Charmaz, eds., *The SAGE Handbook of Grounded Theory* (Thousand Oaks, CA: SAGE Publications, 2007).

90. Etienne C. Wenger and William M. Snyder, "Communities of Practice: The Organizational Frontier," in *Organizational Learning* (Cambridge, MA: Harvard Business School Press, 2001), 1–20.

91. Patricia Benner, *From Novice to Expert: Excellence and Power in Clinical Nursing Practice* (Upper Saddle River, NJ: Prentice Hall: 2000).

92. Ibid.

18 CHRONOLOGICAL BIBLIOGRAPHY OF SELECTED WORKS RELATED TO CATALOGING AND LIBRARIES THROUGH 1800; AND, SELECTED BIBLIOGRAPHY OF LIBRARY AND CATALOGING HISTORY

Elaine R. Sanchez

"You have to know the past to understand the present."

Carl Sagan

"I like the dreams of the future better than the history of the past."

Thomas Jefferson

"With the past, I have nothing to do, nor with the future. I live now."

Ralph Waldo Emerson

"The past is not dead. In fact, it's not even past."

William Faulkner

So, toward which statement do you most gravitate? There are many more quotes and wise sayings about the past, the present, and the future, and how they are, or are not, related to each other and to each sentient being. Maybe some of these make sense to you, maybe not. They all reflect quite different attitudes toward past, present, and future. But, however you feel about these sayings and their meanings, we *do* have a long-ago cataloging past (well before the 1800s and our current cataloging era), and our present is based on those who came before us, just as future catalogers and metadata librarians will have their present stemming from our time. I wanted to include this short (and very incomplete) bibliographic essay on the history of ancient cataloging and libraries so that readers could learn about, or recall from their library school days, the great ancient past of our traditions, philosophies, and important personages of cataloging and classification.

Most catalogers are knowledgeable or aware of the great cataloging geniuses of the mid-to-late 1800s through our times: Panizzi, Jewett, Cutter, Dewey, Ranganathan, Lubetzky, Gorman, and others—they come to mind quite easily when thinking about those who we believe have established the foundations, ethics, and principles of our current cataloging times. It is true that they have done these things, but they were not the first of the noble group of cataloging geniuses and leaders, nor will they be the last. This chronological and selected bibliography of library and cataloging history goes far back into the dawn of civilized times, 4000 B.C.E., and briefly takes the reader through the era preceding our modern cataloging period which began in the 1800s.

CHRONOLOGICAL BIBLIOGRAPHY

The complete bibliography follows this chronological bibliography, and includes works not described in the chronology below. Rather than performing as a true bibliography, or a true chronology, contents of the works selected for this chronology are extracted and placed in broad time period categories, usually with detailed and/or interesting history and stories. There is some overlap in periods, however. I hope you will forgive the rather broad and sometimes disjointed scope of the histories presented, and find the content of interest. It's meant to give a flavor of our far past, rather an outline. The time periods are B.C.E., C.E. 0–1000, C.E. 1001–1500, and C.E.1501–1800.

B.C.E.

1. Norris, Dorothy May. *A History of Cataloguing and Cataloguing Methods 1100–1590: With an Introductory Survey of Ancient Times*, 1–5. London: Grafton & Co., 1939. Pages one through five describe the history of ancient libraries from the Babylonians, Sargon I in particular, founder of the Semitic Empire, who created the first library of clay tablets in 1700 B.C.E., which was cataloged by the librarian Ibnissaru; to the Royal Library at Nineveh, founded in 700 B.C.E., made public by Assur-bani-pal in 685 B.C.E., and arranged in a classified, numbered order; to the Alexandrian Library of ink on papyrus paper rolls, one part of which perhaps survived until perhaps 642 C.E., and which was cataloged in 240 B.C.E. by Callimachus, a poet and librarian, in a classified arrangement of one hundred twenty classes by the use of Pinakes, or clay tablets with systematic inscriptions which were used to arrange them in the library.
2. Tolzmann, Don Heinrich, Alfred Hessel, and Reuben Peiss. *The Memory of Mankind: the Story of Libraries since the Dawn of History*, 1–16. New Castle, DE: Oak Knoll Press, 2001. This work traces libraries back to the Tigris and Euphrates valleys and "Houses of Tablets" attached to temples and royal palaces, dating to the Sumerian city of Uruk, where the earliest inscribed tablets date before 3000 B.C.E. Other ancient libraries noted are in the Sumerian city of Ur, circa 2600 B.C.E., with cuneiform tablets, and the Syrian city of Ebla, around 2300 B.C.E, where a royal library existed and remained in its original classification system. The Royal Library of Nineveh is noted, including the fact that Scribes in the Nineveh library copied materials and added explanatory

notes, providing edition statements of sorts. Much of this library still exists today in the British Museum and Philadelphia's University Museum. The Library of Alexandria is also described.

3. Besson, Alain. *Medieval Classification and Cataloguing: Classification Practices and Cataloguing Methods in France from the 12th to 15th Centuries*, 3–5. Caldecote, Bigglewsade, Beds.: Clover Publications, 1980. The fifth century B.C.E. marks perhaps the beginning of classification systems used later in medieval times, specifically systems created by Plato and Aristotle. Plato employed a three-part division of knowledge, into Logic (rational science), Physical (natural philosophy), and Ethics (moral science). From this beginning, later systems evolved into educational categories of thinking, nature, and society, also known as liberal studies (as they didn't provide knowledge for employment). Plato subsequently seemed to add science as a specialized subcategory of "Nature" and included within it arithmetic, geometry, astronomy, and musical harmony. Aristotle changed "Logic" from a larger classification or philosophy, and recategorized it as a preparatory science, whose main divisions were Speculative and Practical sciences, with the broad subcategories as follows: Speculative: Physics, Mathematics, Theology (with further subcategories such as Meteorology, Biology, Music, Optics, etc.); and Practical: Ethics, Politics, Economics, and Rhetoric subcategories. Later philosophers and thinkers modified these original systems as they envisioned knowledge. Varro, a philosopher in the second half of the first century B.C.E. gathered all seven arts (Grammar, Dialectic, Rhetoric, Geometry, Arithmetic, Astronomy, Music), and included Medicine and Architecture as well. Other Romans in his time period seemed to have focused more on Grammar and Rhetoric, as philosophers such as Seneca (B.C.E.2–C.E.65) and Quintilian (C.E.35–95) had no idea of these seven liberal arts.

4. "Library of Alexandria." Wikipedia, the Free Encyclopedia, http://en.wikipedia.org/wiki/Library_of_Alexandria (accessed May 20, 2010). Describes the Royal Library of Alexandria, in Alexandria, Egypt, which was perhaps the largest, and one of the most ancient libraries, flourishing under the Ptolemaic dynasty, from the beginning of the third century B.C.E. through perhaps 391 C.E. (dates vary, as another section of the library may have existed until the mid-600s). The article discusses the history of the library, its collections, its users in ancient times, and its destruction at various times during the long history of its existence.

5. "Pinakes (Tables)." Wikipedia, the Free Encyclopedia, http://en.wikipedia.org/wiki/Pinakes_(tables) (accessed May 14, 2010). "The first library catalog was a set of indexes used at the Library of Alexandria in Alexandria, Egypt, starting in the third century B.C.E. . . . Callimachus . . . organized the library by authors and subjects . . . Eratosthenes of Cyrene succeeded him [another librarian after Callimachus] and compiled his . . . 'scheme of the great bookshelves' . . . the library collection at the Library of Alexandria contained more than 120,000 scrolls, which were grouped together by subject matter and stored in bins. Each bin carried a label with painted tablets hung above the stored parchments. Pinakes was [the name of] . . . these tablets and are a set of books or scrolls of index lists. The bins gave bibliographical information for every scroll. A typical entry started with a title. It also provided the author's name, birthplace, his father's name, any teachers trained under, and his educational background. It contained a brief biography of the author and a list of the author's publications. The entry had the first line of the work, a summary of its contents, the name of the author, and information about where the scroll came from."

C.E.: 0–1000

1. Besson, Alain. *Medieval Classification and Cataloguing: Classification Practices and Cataloguing Methods in France from the 12th to 15th Centuries*, 5–7. Caldecote, Bigglewsade, Beds.: Clover Publications, 1980.The seven liberal arts, even though not observed by many Roman philosophers, continued to have influence. Martianus Capella's *Liber de nuptiis Mercurii et Philologiae et de septem artibus liberalibus libri novem* (written between 410 and 429 C.E.) had the seven arts of Grammar, Dialectic, Rhetoric, Geometry, Arithmetic, Astronomy, and Music, which became the "cornerstone" of medieval age subject classification. Christianity shifted thinking during this period, as it had not earlier been included as a classification of knowledge, and was treated as a secular philosophy. At the end of 300 C.E., theology became a field of study, actually evolving into a main field of study to which all the other fields were made to relate. Boethius (480–525 C.E.) had his seven fields of liberal arts, to which he added a set called, "Quadrivium," or Mathematics: Arithmetic, Geometry, Music, and Astronomy. Discussion regarding Physics, Mathematics, and definitions of "Dialectica" and "Logica" during this time seemed to be muddied, and interchangeable.

2. Guthrie, Lawrence Simpson. "Monastic Cataloging and Classification and the Beginnings of 'Class B' at the Library of Congress." *Cataloging & Classification Quarterly.* 35, no. 3/4 (2003): 447. "This article explores the influence of medieval monastic libraries on the modern university, the break of monastic libraries from antiquity, and the cataloging and classification methods of medieval times, their influence on today, and their template for later historical eras." The earliest church collection that has been documented is the collection in the basilica of St. Lawrence, known as *chartarium ecclesiae Romanae* under the reign of Pope Damascus (C.E. 366–384). The author describes the many church and later college collections, such as the medical school at Salerno, Italy in the ninth century, Bologna in the late eleventh century, and so on. Monastic cataloging and classification was strongly linked to the regulations of religious orders, rather than the procedures of the ancient libraries. There were no rules on how to catalog books, so what is known has been inferred from surviving inventory lists, which often show no logic or consistency. As described in other essays, books were bound with each other, and inventories did not reflect all the titles in the volume, only the first one; this was performed in order to save binding costs. Manuscripts were often bound into catalogs or a Bible to protect them from thieves. Description of individual works within other works was not done, thus many works were never inventoried, and never appeared as being in the collection. The author notes the change in classification focus in the early Middle Ages, as Christendom caused a break from antiquity, such that by the end of the fourth century, scholars' main concern became the study of theology, and all other fields were related to this. Thus, monastic cataloging and classification was deeply influenced by theology and its place among all human knowledge. Various classification schemes were created, based on the books of the Bible, important authors, and classification of philosophy into subcategories of mathematics, ethics, and logic, such as the classification system of Isidore, Bishop of Seville. Boethius, C.E. 480, who classified knowledge into theoretical and practical categories, with various subcategories, exerted great influence on those who followed him.

3. Norris, Dorothy May. *A History of Cataloguing and Cataloguing Methods 1100–1590: With an Introductory Survey of Ancient Times*, 7–13. London: Grafton & Co., 1939. The author notes two interesting and unusual catalogs during this period. One is for

the collection of books given by Gregory the Great to the Church of St. Clement at Rome, dating from the eighth century. The catalog is engraved in the vestibule of the church on a marble slab, and is a brief introduction to the books of the Bible he offers, and a prayer. The second catalog Norris describes is that of Alcuin of York, England, and his collection of books from Gaul and Rome. He composed a metrical library catalog, consisting of a poem in Latin, which has no reference to the books in the collection, and only notes authors. Nothing much in terms of growth and change in libraries happened until after the Norman Conquest, when the growth of monastic libraries began during this period of relative peace. By the eleventh century, the Benedictines required monasteries to have two collections, one that would circulate to monks and others, and one that was secured for reference in the library. Traveling friars also set up their own libraries; however, their catalogs were generally in their memories! They had to know each book individually, and its exact position on the shelf.

4. "House of Wisdom." Wikipedia, the Free Encyclopedia, http://www.en.wikipedia.org/wiki/House_of_Wisdom (accessed May 20, 2010). The House of Wisdom was a library and translation institute in Baghdad, Iraq, founded by Abbasid caliphs Harun al-Rashid and his son. It was based in Baghdad from the ninth through the thirteenth centuries, for Muslim scholars. Foreign works were translated into Arabic from Persian, and studies of humanities, mathematics, astronomy, medicine, chemistry, and other areas caused great collections to be built. Even the idea for a library catalog was introduced in the House of Wisdom and other medieval Islamic libraries, as books were organized into genres and categories.

5. Strout, Ruth French. "The Development of the Catalog and Cataloging Codes." *Library Quarterly*, 26, no. 4 (October 1956): 259, 274. In JSTOR (accessed May 22, 2010). The author notes that she believes modern cataloging owes little to prior cataloging. Greeks taught the world to refer to books by their authors, and the catalog of the Middle Ages was mainly an unorganized inventory list, an early example being the ninth century catalog from the Benedictine House of St. Riquier. This was compiled in 831, using author entries (in no order) but listing contents of volumes and recording the number of volumes in a title. Starting in the tenth century, libraries became larger, such as the library of Bobbio in Italy with seven hundred volumes, although catalogs themselves had not changed.

C.E.: 1001–1500

1. Besson, Alain. *Medieval Classification and Cataloguing: Classification Practices and Cataloguing Methods in France from the 12th to 15th Centuries*, 8–79. Presents classification history, from Hugh of St. Victor and his classification system *Didascalicon: de studio legendi* (1120) with four branches of knowledge (Theoretical, Practical, Mechanical, and Logical) and twenty-one arts, differing from Plato's view, and changing scholars' views in his own and subsequent eras, as his cataloging system was translated into six languages; to Raoul Ardent, whose *Summa de vitiis et virtutibus* (1192–93) fourteen-volume work, with four broad categories, Theoretical (Physics, Mathematics, Theology), Ethics (Solitary/Personal, Political, Internal and External), Logic (Grammar, Dialectic, Rhetoric), and Mechanical (Food science, Fabric making, Architecture, Suffragetoriam, Medicine, Commerce, Military) was similar to Aristotle and Hugh of St. Victor, but with further categorization and relationships, and which also used

tables, showing that a concept could be viewed from multiple points of view; to Vincent of Beauvais, author of *Speculum majus* (before 1259), with a volume, *Speculum doctrinale*, devoted to science, contained in seventeen volumes, and with additional glossaries of 2,300 terms and facets in alphabetical order, thus having subjects categorized and displayed in lists as well as in hierarchical table formats; and finally, to classification systems from librarians of various collections who devised their own local classification schemes for their libraries (instead of overarching classifications of knowledge) such as Richard de Fournival, church chancellor of the Amiens church, and his work *Biblionomia* (1250), written for the citizens and using the liberal studies divisions of Plato and Aristotle and their successors, while shifting emphasis on Theology as an important category. Fournival applied subject category notation to all categories, using Roman letters, upper and lower case, and different colors to differentiate classification numbers from the various tables of classification, although conforming to a content-based classification with regular and predictable use of codification was not attempted, or achieved. Besson continues his history describing various cataloging methods and collections of the medieval period, and it is noted that intellectual pursuits in the early Middle Ages were only in religious institutions, but from the twelfth century forward, intellectualism, cataloging, and classification also spread to universities. As education had been monopolized by the church, knowledge was given religious overtones, leaving only clerics and church officers literate until the twelfth and thirteenth centuries; however, when education was broadened to universities (as noted) and other entities, knowledge, and the need to catalog and classify it, grew. During much of this closed, church-controlled period (as well as into the end of the 1400s), most catalogs were not meant to represent knowledge, but merely served as inventories, generally in list form with varying descriptions. Not all works were inventoried, either; some collections were ignored, additions to collections were not integrated into lists but were just tacked on in no particular order, and bound-together works were not individually listed. Three example catalogs, College of the Sorbonne, the Abbey of Saint-Pons de Tomieres and the library of the archbishop Guy de Roye, are detailed. Discussion on location devices on books, on bookcases, inscriptions on walls, murals, and stained glass, and arrangement of the books in some kind of subject class, at first meant for physical inventory control and later used to put works with similar content together, after the 1300s, is included, with examples of various libraries. One particular library, the library of St. Denis in the 1400s, had over 1,350 volumes arranged in more than thirty-nine classes, each with its own classification number of two elements: the first element was a subject division, and the second identified the individual volumes. For example, "XXXI.mxx" signified that the volume was in class thirty-one, and was the 1,020th book on the shelves. As education was extended beyond the church, universities and professors began to realize the need for more than an inventory, to find materials for teaching and quicker information. They saw that the inventory lists and the brief descriptions of the works were not useful for retrieval, and efforts at starting to create classified and more analytical catalogs began. The first semblance of a union catalog of various abbey collections also appears to have been created after 1350, although it remains only in a seventeenth-century description of its existence.

2. Guthrie, Lawrence Simpson. "Monastic Cataloging and Classification and the Beginnings of 'Class B' at The Library of Congress." *Cataloging & Classification Quarterly*. 35, no. 3/4 (2003). Many religious orders started their own systems during the time of the monastic library in the Middle Ages. The Augustinian order, founded in 1256,

had a library classification system supplied by a Dominican, Hugh of St. Victor. The Dominicans, founded by St. Domenica in Bologna in 1216, used the classification system of Vincent of Beauvais. Jesuits, founded in 1540 by Ignatius Loyola, had no set Jesuit classification scheme, and each library created its own. In 1209, the Franciscan order began, but its members were not able to own anything, or write anything, at the order of St. Francis of Assisi, as they were forbidden to own property. However, after his death, the parent house of this order had a large library with a catalog, beginning in 1381. The Cistercian order had a 740-volume collection, cataloged by Abbot John de Cirey, but the books were scattered throughout the house, in any place where there was a free space! The article then describes specific cataloging and classification systems in use at several important medieval libraries, including the Abbey of Saint-Pons-de-Thomieres (founded in 936), the Vatican Library (1481), and various cathedral and university libraries such as Richard de Fournival's chancellor library at the Amiens Cathedral (1246) and King's Hall (later Trinity College at Cambridge University) in 1394. However, it was not to last. Between 1536 and 1539, the monastic system was basically destroyed because of government breaks in France and England with the church in Rome, and thus its libraries. The remaining part of the essay describes the influence of medieval classification schemes. Library of Congress classification uses "B" for theology, which is near the top of the alphabet, and the classification schedule, thus reflecting the rank that monastic classification placed on holy writings. Other influences that the author mentions are that monastic classification not only used geographic classification, but also subject classifications, similar to the current subject classification system philosophy.

3. Norris, Dorothy May. *A History of Cataloguing and Cataloguing Methods 1100–1590: With an Introductory Survey of Ancient Times*, 15–125. London: Grafton & Co., 1939. Norris covers libraries and catalogs in detail from 1100 through 1500.

4. Kuang Neng-fu. "Chinese Library Science in the Twelfth Century." *Libraries & Culture*, 26, no. 2 (spring 1991): 357–71. In JSTOR (accessed May 20, 2010). This work covers the period of the Song dynasty, 960–1279, especially focusing on the work that established library policy and creation of libraries in the dynasty during this period, *A Tale of the National Library* (acquisitions, cataloging and classification, collation, arrangement, the writing of national history, and utilization of collections), contributed by two great librarians of this period, Cheng Ju and Zheng Qiao. Works were classified and stored according to Jing, Shi, Zi, and Ji, which are books on Confucian ideas, history, various schools, and literature. Cataloging was called "Jiao Chou" and catalogers were "men of Jiao Chou" (p. 367). Zheng Qiao proposed that it was absolutely necessary to appoint officials concentrating on Jiao Chou. Furthermore, he added, "if you want complete collections and a prosperous culture, why not give long-term posts to the Jiao Chou officials, who would take care of classifying, checking, revising, and cataloging books . . . if all the books are classified, then all school of thought and all knowledge are well organized and clearly systematized" (p. 367). He explained that "it was an undisciplined army that made soldiers scattered and lost. It was incorrect classification that made library books missed and lost. If you would like to use books, you should understand book classification and its subdivisions" (p. 367). Zheng Qiao also noted that scholars should search for books by classification and then perform research using the book record. His ideas on classification and cataloging demonstrated that standards were necessary for both. Books should be classified according to their contents, not by authors, as done in previous times. Books with similar content should be in one place. Other scholars after Zheng Qiao, such as Lu You (1125–1210),

Hong Mai (1123–1202), Zhou Mi (1232–1298), and many others expressed their views on library collections, but Zheng Qiao is attributed to having set Chinese library science as a science.

5. Strout, Ruth French. "The Development of the Catalog and Cataloging Codes." *Library Quarterly*, 26, no. 4 (Oct. 1956): 259–62, 274. In JSTOR (accessed May 22, 2010). In the eleventh and twelfth centuries, it seems that library lists made little progress. The thirteenth century produced a sort of union list of holdings for English libraries, the *Registrum librorum Anglaie*, of English monastery libraries, each with its own numeric code. The fourteenth century brought the idea of shelf-lists (for example, in Christ Church, Canterbury), location symbols, and more identification of editions and entries for all works in bound with titles, and analytical entries. The year 1372 saw a more truly classified arrangement, with the Augustinian friars in York, whose catalog separated an author's writings when the subject of his works required this, quite different than a straight author listing classification. In the fifteenth century, cross-references came on the scene, and a bibliography was compiled, along with an index to it. Toward the end of this century, German bibliographer and librarian Johann Tritheim developed a bibliography in chronological order, with an alphabetical author index.

C.E.: 1501–1800

1. Norris, Dorothy May. *A History of Cataloguing and Cataloguing Methods 1100–1590: With an Introductory Survey of Ancient Times*, 126–215. London: Grafton & Co., 1939. Norris covers libraries and catalogs in great detail through 1590.

2. Lubetzky, Seymour. *Writings on the Classical Art of Cataloging*, 345–47. Englewood, CO: Libraries Unlimited, 2001. Lubetzky recounts the story of Sir Thomas Bodley, of the Oxford University Library, who in 1598 went to buy books for the collection. So that he wouldn't purchase duplicates, he requested the librarian, Thomas James, to give him a copy of the catalog, which consisted of inventory lists. Books were divided into four classes: theology, medicine, law, and the arts, and further subdivided by size, such as folios, quartos, and so on. Each group was arranged in alphabetical order by author surnames on the bookshelves, and listed in the same order on sheets attached to the shelves (to show contents of each bookcase). Their purpose was as an inventory, and entries were informal and brief. Bound-with books were listed under the first book in the binding, with no other listing of the titles contained in the work. So, of course, Sir Thomas told the librarian that the inventory lists were not adequate to inform him as to the holdings of the collection. Because of this problem for Sir Thomas, the purpose of the catalog was broadened: to help determine if a library had a certain book, by moving from inventory list to finding list or finding catalog. By 1620, the next Oxford catalog was a finding catalog, in one alphabetical listing, of all books, regardless of their location in the shelves.

3. Hopkins, Judith. "The 1791 French Cataloging Code and the Origins of the Card Catalog." *Libraries & Culture*, 27, no. 4 (Fall 1992): 378–404. In JSTOR (accessed May 22, 2010). On May 15, 1791, the first national cataloging code and national card catalog were created by the revolutionary government of France, with playing cards as the medium. They needed to perform an inventory of church book and manuscript collections, which had been confiscated by the revolutionary government of the National Constituent Assembly, in order to see whether these should be sold, or kept to form libraries open to all. Revolution took its course, and the committee assigned to oversee

the library project changed along with the times. Two members of the Commission of the Four Nations (so-called because the college where they initially met was Mazarin, also called the College of the Four Nations) were assigned to write the code of catalog instructions, Gaspard-Michel LeBlond, librarian of the Mazarin Library, and Barthelemy Mercier, Abbe de Saint Leger. It was a cataloging course designed for new librarians. The idea of playing cards came from older catalogs, such as that of Conrad Besner, in his work *Pandects* (1548), where he proposed using paper slips for bibliographic records. Slips like these were used in the Vatican Library in the late 1600s. Entries were written on sheets, which were cut into strips, one strip per entry, alphabetized, and then pasted into the leaves of large books. This carried over into using playing cards for bibliographical records in 1775 as a general index to the publications of the Academie des Sciences of Paris, which was perhaps known to the Commission of the Four Nations. Work on creation of the catalog began, instructions were reissued in 1794, and work continued. By 1794, 1.2 million cards, or 3 million volumes, had been received, less than a third of the estimated 10 million volumes. Staff continued to be added to the Bureau of Bibliography, the agency now responsible for this project, increasing it to well over 40 staff members. The code itself is remembered more for its use of cards for bibliographic information, rather than by its excellence as a cataloging code.

4. Strout, Ruth French. "The Development of the Catalog and Cataloging Codes." *Library Quarterly*, 26, no. 4 (Oct. 1956): 262–67, 274. In JSTOR (accessed May 22, 2010). The sixteenth century saw catalogs with mention of editors and translators (librarian of the Priory of Bretton in Yorkshire, 1558), and for the first time, the entry word became important; this was along with the first use of entry under surname, and the uniform title entry for anonymous classics. A couple of remarkable publications by the Swiss bibliographer Konrad Gesner of Zurich were his author bibliography in 1545, and the subject index in 1548, which included cross-references. He created instructions for book arrangement, using his system of classification. Florian Trefer, a Benedictine monk, published his scheme of classification twelve years later, in 1560, which included a binding color notation. In 1595, Andrew Maunsell, an English bookseller, compiled his *Catalogue of English Printed Books*, also using entry under surnames, not personal names. Documentation on the creation of catalogs came with the seventeenth century. Sir Thomas Bodley founded the Oxford University Library, starting in 1600, and his cataloging code included a classified arrangement with an alphabetical author index arranged by surname, and including analytical entries. At the end of the seventeenth century, in 1697, new questions were asked to the Bodleian library curators by a staff member of the library, Humphrey Wanley: Should the catalog be classified or alphabetical? Should titles and dates of books be recorded in the language of the book? Should the size of a book be recorded? Should author/title analytics be included? Should the name of the publisher be in the imprint? Should it be noted if there is no date or place of publication? Should editions be noted, as well as a work's rarity, cost, or conditions? Amazing parallels to today's descriptive cataloging. Another key work was Frederic Rostgaard's work in Paris, in 1697, on the establishment of a library catalog with subject arrangement, subdivided chronologically, and by volume size, which was published in a printed catalog. The works were secondarily arranged, after chronology, by whether the books were totally about a subject, or only partially treated that subject. As with Sir Thomas Bodley, Rostgaard directed entry under surname, with analytics for bound with titles. The eighteenth century continued without much change except for the use of card catalogs (using playing cards) by the

revolutionary government of France at the end of this century, and a new French cataloging code of 1791. However, it is certain that catalogs were no longer viewed as inventories, and were now considered finding aids. In the nineteenth century, there was a marked interest in catalogs and in the meeting of user demands. Many modern catalogs appeared in the 1800s in Germany, France, England, and the United States. Reverend Thomas Hartwell Horne, of England, published a classification scheme and code of cataloging rules in English, which is listed in this essay's bibliography. Discussion over classified and dictionary catalogs was common. Monumental works and systems were created by cataloging giants such as Anthony Panizzi of Italy, in regards to the British Museum and his 91 rules; Charles C. Jewett's plan for a cataloging code in the early 1850s for the Smithsonian Institution; Charles Cutter, with his *Rules for a Printed Dictionary Catalogue* in 1876; Melvil Dewey's Dewey Decimal classification; and many others in Germany, Austria, Switzerland, Spain, the Netherlands, and so on, which all paved the way for our current cataloging concepts.

Selected Bibliography of Library and Cataloging History

All works cited below contain their own bibliographies, footnotes, source material, cited literature, illustrations, and so on, representing hundreds of additional sources on library and cataloging history. Many of the works in this selected bibliography have been used in the above chronological bibliography, and are so noted.

Besson, Alain. *Medieval Classification and Cataloguing: Classification Practices and Cataloguing Methods in France from the 12th to 15th Centuries.* Caldecote, Bigglewsade, Beds.: Clover Publications, 1980. Included in chronological bibliography by period.

Blum, Rudolf. *Kallimachos: The Alexandrian Library and the Origins of Bibliography.* Translated by Hans. H. Wellisch. Madison: University of Wisconsin Press, 1991. As the title indicates, this is a detailed study on the beginnings of bibliography with Kallimachos, an ancient librarian of the Alexandrian Library, and his Pinakes and other works and contemporaries, as well as how his work affected libraries and catalogs throughout early history.

Clark, John Willis. *The Care of Books: An Essay on the Development of Libraries and Their Fittings, from the Earliest Times to the End of the Fifteenth Century.* London: Variorum Reprints, 1975. Originally published, Cambridge: Cambridge University Press, 1901. 1901 ed., http://books.google.com/books?id=jKcFAAAAMAAJ&printsec=frontcover &dq=john+willis+clark+care+of+books&source=bl&ots=APy3m_cfm-&sig=lC3 Gg6B7JyGaOhdZloaKfPg8A_c&hl=en&ei=olT5S46LCYOB8gb21NHdCg&sa=X &oi=book_result&ct=result&resnum=1&ved=0CBoQ6AEwAA#v=onepage&q&f =falsehttp://books.google.com/books?id=jKcFAAAAMAAJ&printsec=frontcover&dq =john+willis+clark+care+of+books&source=bl&ots=APy3m_cfm-&sig=lC3Gg6 B7JyGaOhdZloaKfPg8A_c&hl=en&ei=olT5S46LCYOB8gb21NHdCg&sa=X&oi =book_result&ct=result&resnum=1&ved=0CBoQ6AEwAA#v=onepage&q&f=false (accessed May 22, 2010). This work encompasses libraries and their spatial and organizational layouts, catalogs, collections, reading rooms and library furniture, reading methods of the times, shelving, and organization as well as preservation of materials, from the span of time from Assur-bani-pal through the end of the eighteenth century, addressing royal, temple, abbey and monastic, collegiate, public, and private libraries. Many illustrations from the works of the period are included, as are architectural plans of buildings of the same times. Libraries covered include Assyrian Record-Rooms; libraries in Greece, Alexandria, Pergamon, and Rome; the Vatican Library of Sixtus V (ancient Roman library); libraries of many, many monastic communities and later, those attached to cathedrals such as Salisbury, Rouen, and more; university libraries of the Library at Queens' College, Cambridge, Zutphen, Oxford, etc; libraries in Italy such as Cesena, the Convent of Saint Mark, Florence, Medicean Library, Florence; later libraries, in the 1600s, such as the Library of the Escorial, Ambrosian Library, Milan, French libraries; and the private library of Abbat Simon, Charles V of France, Duke of Urbino, Library of Montaigne, and more.

Denton, William. "FRBR and the History of Cataloging." In *Understanding FRBR: What It Is and How It Will Affect Our Retrieval*. Edited by Arlene G. Taylor. Westport, CT: Libraries Unlimited, 2007. Available on the Internet, http://pi.library.yorku.ca/ dspace/bitstream/handle/10315/1250/denton-frbr-and-the-history-of-cataloging.;df? sequence=1 (accessed June 15, 2010) as well as having a URI: http://hdl.handle.net/ 10315/1250 (accessed June 15, 2010). The intent of this essay is to describe some of the ancient history of cataloging, the history of modern-age cataloging dating from the mid-1800s, the historical figures of our "modern age" (Panizzi, Cutter, Ranganathan, and Lubetzky), and the development of the precepts of FRBR in the twentieth century, stemming from past cataloging principles and philosophies. The short section on the ancient history of cataloging from 4000 B.C.E. to the late 1600s, and Thomas Hyde, a librarian at the Bodleian Library at Oxford University in the seventeenth century, is interesting. The main focus of the article, though is on modern cataloging from the 1850s forward and FRBR, and is a good summary with an excellent bibliography.

Edwards, Edward. *Memoirs of Libraries, Including a Handbook of Library Economy*. New York: Burt Franklin, 1859. This two-volume set was for many years the major aid to the study of library history, and it spans the beginning of libraries in the B.C.E. era, to 1850. This work of history covers all the ancient libraries, from the fourteenth century, "Library of Osymandyas" located in the palace-temple near Thebes (called "The Dispensary of the Mind"), to libraries in Europe and the United States through the early 1850s. The second half of the work is entitled, "Economy of Libraries," and covers working methods for book collecting, the handling of gifts, public printing, international exchange, acquisitions, building, library furnishings, internal administration and public service, and, importantly, sections on cataloging: Book III. Classification and Catalogues: Chapter I. Catalogues in General; Chapter II. Classificatory Systems (dating from 1498 through schemes available in 1856); Chapter III. Difficulties, Rules, and Details, for such cataloging topics as identification of authorship, name authority, pseudonyms, cataloging rules, full and short titles, and book sizes; Chapter IV. To Print, or Not to Print; Chapter V. Examples and Estimates (cataloging and catalog examples); Chapter VI. Local Arrangement, and its Appliances, addressing shelf catalogs, classification versus collocation, special collections and their arrangement, classification of prints, maps, charts and plans, and several example libraries.

Frost, Carolyn O. "The Bodleian Catalogs of 1674 and 1738: an Examination in the Light of Modern Cataloging." *Library Quarterly* 46, no. 3 (July 1976): 248–70. Not reviewed. ERIC abstract notes that these two catalogs were examined and compared, and analyzed against modern cataloging theory. Both catalogs presaged modern theories, and met the needs of their times.

Green, Arnold. "The History of Libraries in the Arab World: A Diffusionist Model." *Libraries & Culture* 23, no. 4 (Fall 1988): 454–73. This article only contains very limited information on cataloging, and none on classification. However, it is a broad history of libraries in the Arab world from 700 B.C.E. to present times, and has brief histories of the House of Wisdom begun by Abbasid Caliph al ma'mun, in Baghdad (after 833 C.E.), the library in Cordova begun by the Umayyad Caliph al-Hakam II (around 976), and the House of Science, established in Cairo by the Shi'i Fatimid Calpih al_Hakim, around 1021. There is much more history on the changes in the culture and education, related to mosques, universities, and seminary colleges, and the resulting libraries and collections, with great detail from the ancient through the modern period. In JSTOR (accessed May 22, 2010).

Guthrie, Lawrence Simpson. "Monastic Cataloging and Classification and the Beginnings of 'Class B' at the Library of Congress." *Cataloging & Classification Quarterly.* 35, no. 3/4 (2003): 447–65. Included in chronological bibliography by period.

Halporn, Barbara. "The Carthusian Library at Basel." *Library Quarterly,* 54, no. 3 (July 1984): 223–44. Not reviewed. ERIC abstract says this article describes problems faced by late medieval libraries during the transition from manuscript to printed book. Translation of a Swiss monastery 1520 library manual shows how librarian duties, arrangement of the library, circulation and public service procedures, and procedures for inventorying and cataloging were written.

Hanson, Eugene R. and Jay E. Daily. "Catalogs and Cataloging." In *Encyclopedia of Library and Information Science.* 2nd ed., 431–68. New York: Marcel Dekker, 2003. Complete, concise essay on libraries, their catalogs, and cataloging, from ancient times through the twentieth century. Of interest is an appendix with a list of codes of cataloging rules, starting with the 1791 French national cataloging code, and containing forty-seven total cataloging codes from many countries.

Hopkins, Judith. "The 1791 French Cataloging Code and the Origins of the Card Catalog." *Libraries & Culture,* 27, no. 4 (Fall 1992): 378–404. In JSTOR (accessed May 22, 2010). Included in chronological bibliography by period.

Horne, Thomas Hartwell. *An Introduction to the Study of Bibliography, to Which is Prefixed a Memoir on the Public Libraries of the Antients.* 2 vols. London: G. Woodfall for T. Cadell and W. Davies, 1814. In addition to much material on libraries from the ancient world through the early 1800s, this work also has the history and methods of recording the human record on stone, bricks, tree bark, vellum, leather, etc., and many different kinds of paper; the origin of writing, from hieroglyphics of early times to Mayans, North American Indians, Chinese, illuminations, and more; the origin, progress and mechanics of printing in England and other countries; a section on books regarding sizes, bindings, preservation, value and rarity; literary history and authorship; and, most importantly for this bibliography on catalogs, catalogers, and classification: classification is addressed on pages 358–72, with an example of a possible classification system for a classified catalog on pages 373–400, created by Mr. Horne; and a section of bibliographical systems and catalogs of various libraries of the world, both public and private (Denmark, France, Germany, Holland, Hungary and Poland, Italy and Sicily, Russia, Spain and Portugal, Sweden, Switzerland, Turkey, North America) and public and private libraries in Great Britain and Scotland, as well as booksellers of the period (pp. 551–742).

"House of Wisdom." Wikipedia, the Free Encyclopedia, http://en.wikipedia.org/wiki/House_of_Wisdom (accessed May 20, 2010). Included in chronological bibliography by period.

Jackson, Sydney L. "The Twelfth Century in the West, Its Libraries, and Hugh of St. Victor's Classification of Knowledge." *Journal of Library History* 2, no. 3 (July 1967):

185–200. In JSTOR (accessed May 22, 2010). Provides more detail and history, including future impact, of the classification system created by Hugh of St. Victor.

"Library of Alexandria." Wikipedia, the Free Encyclopedia, http://en.wikipedia.org/wiki/Library_of_Alexandria (accessed May 20, 2010). Included in chronological bibliography by period.

Lubetzky, Seymour. *Writings on the Classical Art of Cataloging.* Englewood, CO: Libraries Unlimited, 2001. Included in chronological bibliography by period.

Norris, Dorothy May. *A History of Cataloguing and Cataloguing Methods 1100–1590: With an Introductory Survey of Ancient Times.* London: Grafton & Co., 1939. Included in chronological bibliography by period.

Olle, James G. *Library History: An Examination Guidebook.* London: Clive Bingley, 1967. Covers general library history, as well as distinct periods, ancient libraries, institutional libraries, subscription and circulating libraries, national public libraries, local public libraries, private libraries, and other topics, including cataloging, page 53, which lists several works on the history of cataloging and classification, including some listed in this bibliography, as well as Sears Jayne's *Library Catalogues of the English Renaissance*, Berkeley: University of California Press, 1956, which compiles an inventory of 274 institutional and 574 private catalogs of the English libraries of the Renaissance (1500–1640); and W.C. Berwick Sayers, *A Manual of Classification*, 3rd ed., London: Grafton, 1955, which has a chapter on the history of classification in England.

"Pinakes (Tables)." Wikipedia, the Free Encyclopedia, http://en.wikipedia.org/wiki/Pinakes_(tables) (accessed May 14, 2010). Included in chronological bibliography by period.

Savage, Ernest A. *The Story of Libraries and Book-Collecting.* New York: E. P. Dutton & Co., 1909. There is little in this book regarding classification or cataloging, but in addition to the typical history of ancient and English and American libraries in general, it also has specific chapters on the principal libraries of Italy, France, Spain, Portugal, Germany, Austria-Hungary, Belgium, Holland, Russia, Scandinavia, Scotland, and Ireland, http://ia341207.us.archive.org/3/items/storyoflibraries00savaiala/storyoflibraries00savaiala.pdf (accessed May 20, 2010).

Smalley, Joseph. "The French Cataloging Code of 1791: A Translation." *Library Quarterly*, 61, no. 1 (January 1991): 1–14. Describes the importance of this very first national code of descriptive cataloging, as it became the first systematic mention and use of a card catalog, and provides detailed description on bibliographic transcription. Entries in the catalog contained the title and statement of responsibility; place of publication including publisher and date; and physical description, including extent, other details and dimensions. One access point was chosen, the author, and if that could not be determined, a title keyword was used. Cards were divided into three elements or fields: the first line was blank, the second line had the bibliographic information, and the third line had holdings. Some discussion on the use of playing cards is also included. The remainder of the article has actual examples of entries on cards.

Strout, Ruth French. "The Development of the Catalog and Cataloging Codes." *Library Quarterly*, 26, no. 4 (Oct. 1956): 254–75. In JSTOR (accessed May 22, 2010). Included in chronological bibliography by period. Strout explains that "catalog" is the Greek term *kata logos*, in which "kata" means "by" or "according to," but the "logos" term is not as easily pinned down. It can mean, "word," "order," or "reason," so, "is a catalog a work in which the contents are arranged in a reasonable way, according to a set plan, or merely word by word?" (p. 254). However it is defined, finally, it becomes "identical with the definition of its purpose" (p. 254). Cataloging and the organization and description of materials has changed, of course, through time, according to the needs of the collection and its owners and users, and the technologies available. From arranging books by binding color, to entering authors under the forenames, these may seem impractical now, but they were useful in their times. This essay describes the development of catalog codes, from prehistoric Nippur, 2000 B.C.E., through 1904. Each period is thoroughly described, and noted catalogers, classifiers, philosophers, libraries, cataloging and inventory codes, classification codes, and dates important to the tracing of the history of the catalog and cataloging codes are covered.

Thornton, John L. *The Chronology of Librarianship: An Introduction to the History of Libraries and Book-Collecting.* London: Grafton, 1941. This work covers ground already addressed in many of the other works in this bibliography, but it has an interesting chronology of librarianship, pages 145–220. It begins with the year 4000 B.C.E. as the beginning of civilization, and moves through time and across the world in relatively short intervals with important libraries and collections, librarians, kings, philosophers, great events in civilization and their effect on the human record, world history, great works, library catalogs and classification events and periods, cataloging philosophies and documentation, library associations, printing history, and laws affecting libraries and collections, finally ending the chronology in the year 1938. In the last section of his work, the author suggests that "entry word" is important as a basic concept in modern cataloging, and this idea only appeared in 1454 in the work of Konrad Gesner, but was not well developed until the 1800s when it was accepted, and the question regarding what component of the book constitutes entry arose. The oriental tradition was title, the Western tradition was author, and modern cataloging also brought up subject. Added entry, or the idea that there is more than one way to find a book in a catalog, appeared as indexes to catalogs, used initially by Johann Tritheim in 1494, and then used by later librarians. The dictionary form of catalog used cross references to perform the added entry function, rather than indexes. Analytical and "bound-with" entries began in the fifteenth century at St. Augustine's Abbey in Canterbury, and continue to be confusing to this day! Cataloging codes began with the rules of Trefler in 1560 and Thornton notes that cataloging codes are the very means through which cataloging progress has been achieved.

Tolzmann, Don Heinrich, Alfred Hessel, and Reuben Peiss. *The Memory of Mankind: The Story of Libraries Since the Dawn of History.* New Castle, DE: Oak Knoll Press, 2001. Included in chronological bibliography by period.

AFTERWORD

Sheila S. Intner and Susan S. Lazinger

If we were to sum up the dominant feeling running through *Conversations with Catalogers* in one metaphor, it would be fear of flying. And the metaphorical aircraft would be Resource Description and Access (RDA).

A striking number of the chapters in this varied collection by illustrious catalogers from all over the world reflects the apprehension engendered by the replacement for AACR2. RDA is more theoretical in content than any cataloging code in history, and so controversial that every time it has been due to be published, a cry demanding more testing has arisen from the global cataloging community. Finally scheduled for release in June 2010, the coming of RDA, even among a group of catalogers as knowledgeable and seasoned as the ones writing this book, is causing far more anxiety than anticipation. The plain fact is that most of the authors in *Conversations with Catalogers* think that the change from AACR2 to RDA is going to be a change for the worse. RDA will be published before *Conversations with Catalogers*, so time will tell how accurate or significant the issues raised in this current work will be once (or if) the code is adopted.

Why the anxiety? The fears are many and varied. Helen Buhler feels that RDA's writing is so lacking in clarity that even experienced catalogers have difficulty understanding newly released chapters. That RDA is based on the highly theoretical Functional Requirements for Bibliographic Records (FRBR) does not improve its clarity, nor does the "shortage of clearly stated principles," in a code that was billed as "principle-based." J. McRee Elrod notes that even though RDA is meant to be general enough for use outside the library community, it is so complex that this is unlikely. He isn't even sure that it will be used in small libraries. Some of the other problems Elrod sees are RDA's substitution of spelled-out phrases in the "language of the catalogue" for ISBD (International Standard Bibliographic Description) Latin abbreviations, which can cause difficulties, for example, in official bilingual provinces and countries; changes in AACR2 practice that will make brief displays less informative: omission of "[sic]" after a typographical error in the title will make it difficult to know if there is a mistake in transcription; and omission of a missing jurisdiction after city of publication will mean the patron won't know in which London (England? Ontario?) an item was published. Many patrons don't go beyond the brief display. If data doesn't appear there, it may not matter where else it can be found.

Martha Yee presents a long list of things that worry her about RDA in a chapter that revisits an article she wrote some time ago proposing the benefits of a single shared catalog. Ten years after she first declared that a single shared catalog that "we all cooperate in keeping under authority control" would be beneficial both to catalogers (who could then devote themselves to intellectual work rather than clerical work and to cataloging neglected works) and to users worldwide (who would have to learn only one piece of catalog-searching software), Yee sees two possible scenarios for creating this single shared catalog. The first paradigm uses OCLC WorldCat, and the second paradigm calls for putting cataloging data into the Semantic Web, connected by the new set of cataloging rules in RDA. After listing reasons why the WorldCat model would be problematic— e.g., OCLC WorldCat is not under authority control; noncatalogers can't access scope notes and cross references in authority records; users can't browse headings, but can only do keyword searches; users cannot search for a particular work using variants of the author's name and the title—Yee tests the other paradigm, the Semantic Web shared catalog, and finds it no less problematic, primarily because of the shortcomings of RDA: RDA, she notes, seems to take it on faith that the huge increase in granularity required to assemble records from bits of data scattered throughout the Internet is a good thing, without any experimentation demonstrating how these tiny bits of data will be reassembled into coherent displays and indexes. RDA takes a hierarchy-resistant approach, although hierarchy, Yee declares, is one of our main tools for allowing users to navigate vast quantities of information efficiently. RDA completely removes display from the rules; and thus, since from the catalog user's point of view, the catalog is display design, RDA "seems successfully to have removed cataloging from the cataloging rules." Finally, RDA has turned its back on the opportunity to call for identifying entities by the name commonly known in the community of the catalog. To illustrate the point, she cites a possible future scenario in which English-speaking users will have entities identified only in Chinese characters in their catalog's record for an item.

John Myers and Jay Weitz are less overtly pessimistic about Life After RDA, but the very titles of their chapters—"Cataloging Survival in a Sea of Change and a Surfeit of Acronyms" and "Judgment and Imagination: Carrying Cataloging through Times of Change," respectively—express the overwhelming uncertainty about the post-RDA world that pervades this collection. Myers laments that the days when one could get by with a knowledge of ISBD, AACR2, and MARC alone seem long gone amid the "current welter of acronyms and initialisms to befuddle and confound the work-a-day cataloger: MODS, METS, SGML, XML, DACS, DCRM, CCO, FAST, IME ICC, DC, FRBR, FRAD, FRSAD, RDF, RDA . . . and who knows what else." He also mentions, as a factor in the need for cataloger survival, that we have moved from the simple recording of the basic description of books to recording carrier type and extent, with extensive amplification in RDA. Weitz keeps his chin up in the face of all the change, remarking that catalogers have proven themselves to be "as resilient and adaptable as either AACR or MARC," while noting that those qualities will stand them in good stead as they move from the world of AACR to the world of RDA. Moving to that new world is not going to be easy. Hal Cain, noting that in RDA, catalogers not only face new rules but also a new mode of access (i.e., online), observes that as people who like stability, many catalogers feel threatened. In addition to new rules, the systems underpinning traditional cataloging are under fire: the value of controlled subject access and standard classification is being questioned, and there are signs that LC may decide that keyword access suffices for some resources. "My constant worry," he admits, "is that, in elaborating, consolidating, and applying new approaches, we'll find we've discarded elements that have real value for our users and ourselves, without setting in place sufficient replacement."

Not all is fear and trembling in this collection, however. There is also a minority view that the radical change catalogers and their catalogs are facing is a great opportunity to reinvent ourselves. Scott Piepenburg sees a new library automation model emerging that will allow a library, for a specified amount of money, to select only the functions it wants, eliminating the need to pay for functionality and features they don't need. Jennifer Eustis sees blogs as an opportunity to help catalogers learn about new directions and possible futures of the profession, and to communicate with others as part of a professional network. Jon Gorman dreams of building a new cataloging workflow, using technologies and scanning efforts and information retrieval to assist us. He wants links from bibliographic records to reviews, and terms from these linked reviews to be available for keyword searching. Ed Jones believes that, since going on the World Wide Web, library catalogs acquired the potential to interact with other Web-enabled databases, and widely recognized identifiers in records (e.g., ISBN, ISMN, or an OCLC control number, OCN) could link to related records in other databases. From the end user's perspective, the local library catalog in such a world would have ceased to exist. Jones's vision bears a functional similarity to Yee's concept of a shared catalog.

The final group of chapters explores transitioning catalogers into metadata librarians, teaching cataloging in a way that provides adequate preparation for this new incarnation, and attracting new catalogers to the field by encouraging awareness of what an exciting new profession it has become. Lynn Fields describes some interesting differences between "cataloger" and "metadata librarian": as a cataloger, she catalogs something that already exists, while as a metadata librarian, she often has to create the digital collection before addressing its metadata needs; as a cataloger, she knows exactly the tool she is going to use to store her bibliographic information in a computer record—MARC 21—while as a metadata librarian, she may choose among Dublin Core, MODS (Metadata Object Description Schema), METS (Metadata Encoding and Transmission Standard), VRA (Visual Resources Association Core Categories), and others. Christine Schwarz advises catalogers transformed into metadata librarians to shift away from standardization toward a multiplicity of options. She notes that while accepting this ambiguity might sound easy, it's actually one of the hardest parts of the transition process. She recommends steps to get into the new mind-set, such as getting away from the idea of cataloging one item at a time, since digital resources tend to be grouped into projects such as a full-run collection of journals published by the cataloger's institution or a complete archival collection going from microfilm to a digital version. In addition, she highly recommends learning to program. Besides gaining a new skill, she says, it is easier to do quality control on metadata using programming than editing by hand.

Sylvia Hall-Ellis worries that the decrease in required cataloging courses in LIS (Library and Information Science) education programs occurred precisely when the number of formats and employers' expectations have increased. Entry-level catalogers are expected to have a comprehensive background in descriptive cataloging, subject access, classifying, and programming language scripting, with skills in managing, training, and supervising thrown into the mix of demands as well. She suggests internships, practica, mentorships, and service learning to provide the experience LIS students are going to need to find jobs. Janet Swan Hill deals with attracting new catalogers to the field. She lists reasons why it is difficult to get people into cataloging—we are invisible and unknown; librarianship attracts from the wrong disciplines; career guidance is off target; women have more careers open to them than they once did; in LIS programs, the cataloging curriculum is limited and not required; classwork includes little exposure to actual cataloging; expert faculty are scarce; the jobs sound old-fashioned. She suggests solutions (some of them perhaps a touch tongue-in-cheek!)—get someone to "write a screenplay for a movie like *Major League*, and make Rene Russo a cataloger, or turn Noah Wyle as *The Librarian* into a cataloger"; "get to people in graduate school who are pondering whether they want to finish that PhD, or if there's anything else they might do with their background in taxonomy or Italian"; appear in webcasts, participate in discussions with online cataloging classes, act as online mentors; urge schools to be proactive in seeking and encouraging more teaching candidates interested in cataloging; and write recruiting materials that "describe jobs in ways that make cataloging sound important, satisfying, and intriguing." Like Hall-Ellis, Swan Hill is concerned that the cataloging curriculum has shrunk precisely when there is so much more to learn.

These conversations reveal much to concern catalogers, but also offer hope, advice for creative solutions, and a solid belief that cataloging and catalogers are here to stay. James Weinheimer sums these things up best in his chapter on the realities of standards in our time. He contends that blind adherence to standards, of which catalogers have often been accused, is not always such a bad thing. Standards, he continues, save both our libraries and our users time and money. He illustrates this by giving examples of how standardization of paging in cataloging records does just this. Standardized paging saves catalogers the trouble of having to check the stacks or confer with people at other libraries to confirm exactly what item they are holding. It enables library selectors to ascertain that the book they are considering buying is not the same book they already own. And it aids researchers to distinguish between textual variants of works in which they are interested. Finally, he asserts what for all catalogers might be viewed as the bottom line on why our profession, even now when keyword access seems to suffice for more and more users, is still relevant: as people begin to see problems with the vagaries of keyword access, they may start to appreciate the control our name and subject authority work provides. Library cataloging, he concludes, is capable of providing one thing and one thing only that automatic means cannot, at least not at this point in time, and that is quality.

INDEX

ABOUT THE EDITOR AND CONTRIBUTORS

ELAINE R. SANCHEZ is Head, Cataloging & Metadata Services, Alkek Library, Texas State University–San Marcos. She earned her BA and MLS from the University of Texas at Austin. She has worked as a cataloger and technical services librarian for over twenty-seven years at Texas State, Texas Legislative Reference Library, Travis County Law Library, and UT-Austin. She has several books, chapters, research surveys, and journal articles published by Primary Research, Greenwood Press, *Technical Services Quarterly*, the present work by Libraries Unlimited, and others; and she is an advocate for cataloging and catalogers (and metadata librarians).

* * *

HELEN BUHLER is Classification Coordinator at the University of Kent's Canterbury campus, with responsibility for policy and standards, and is also involved with catalogue maintenance. She was previously a descriptive cataloguer. Before that she worked on the interlending union catalogues at LASER and the Institute of Latin American Studies, University of London, and began her cataloguing experience at Queen Mary College, London. Her diploma in Library Studies is from the Queen's University of Belfast and her BA (French and Spanish) from the University of London.

HALVARD (HAL) CAIN, BA, AALIA, has worked in libraries in Victoria, Australia, since 1964, chiefly in cataloging, principally in academic, but also in school, public, and special libraries. Now Cataloguer at the Dalton McCaughey Library (formerly Joint Theological Library) in Melbourne, where he has worked since 1993, he is deeply interested in the relationship between cataloging theory and practice and what catalog users do with bibliographic information; work in smaller libraries has convinced him users matter most. Retirement beckons in 2010.

J. MCREE (MAC) ELROD, born in Gainesville, Georgia, was reared near Athens. After an AB (history magna cum laude) at the University of Georgia, he attended Emory, Peabody, Scarritt (two MAs and an MLS). Five years in Korea establishing a library school and organizing a university library, were followed by further study and teaching at Peabody. After college librarianship in Missouri and Ohio, Mr. Elrod became the Head of Cataloguing at the University of British Columbia in 1967. In 1979 he established Special Libraries Cataloguing, which catalogues for small libraries, does special projects for academic libraries, and prepares catalogue records for publishers and aggregators of electronic resources.

JENNIFER MARIE EUSTIS is the Catalog/Metadata librarian at Snell Library, part of Northeastern University Libraries, at Northeastern University. Jennifer graduated from the graduate program in library and information science at Simmons College in May 2008 where she was an ARL (Academy of Research Library) Fellow for the year 2006–2007. Jennifer came to librarianship after completing a PhD and work as an instructor in philosophy. Currently, she continues her work at Snell and writes for her blog, Celeripedean.

BERNHARD EVERSBERG is Head of Library Computing, Braunschweig Technical University, Germany, and is also subject specialist for physics, computer science, and music. He has a degree in mathematics and physics from Ruhr Universität Bochum, Germany. Since 1975, he has primarily been busy in developing software and writing much code himself. His main product is the *allegro* ILS, being used in several hundred special libraries of all sizes in Germany (see http://www.allegro-c.de). He has also made contributions in cataloging, including subject analysis.

LYNNETTE M. FIELDS is a Catalog and Metadata Librarian/Assistant Professor, Library and Information Services, at Southern Illinois University Edwardsville. She holds an MA in Library Science from the University of Missouri. She has worked in cataloging for various institutions, including the St. Louis Public Library and the Lewis and Clark Library System. She has been a cataloging trainer for The MARC of Quality, SCCTP, and an adjunct instructor for the University of Missouri, School of Information Science and Learning Technologies.

JON GORMAN acquired a BA in Computer Science from the University of Minnesota–Morris. A lifelong bibliophile, he went on to obtain an MSLIS from the University of Illinois. After graduation, he accepted a position at the University of Illinois University Library. He is a member of the Infrastructure and Software Development group. Some of his current interests include linked data, library mashups, cataloging interfaces, and open source library systems. He irregularly posts on his blog at http://codexmonkey.blogspot.com.

MICHAEL GORMAN worked, for fifty years, in public libraries in London, for the British National Bibliography, the British Library, the University of Illinois library and that of the California State University, Fresno. He was the first editor of AACR2 and AACR2R and the drafter of the first ISBD (the ISBD-M) and of the ISBD-G. He is the author and editor of a number of books and too many articles. He is the recipient of the Margaret Mann Citation and the Melvil Dewey Medal, an Honorary Fellow of the Chartered Institute of Library & Information Professionals, and a past president of the American Library Association.

SYLVIA D. HALL-ELLIS is an Associate Professor, Library and Information Science Program, at the Morgridge College of Education, University of Denver. She received her MLS, University of North Texas, and PhD, University of Pittsburgh. A library educator since 1993, Dr. Hall-Ellis has personal, in-depth experience teaching adults, and integrating technologies and assessments into classroom instruction. Her thirty years of experience working in diverse, rural communities and with librarians and paraprofessionals, project design and management, strategic planning, professional development, and continuing education make her uniquely qualified to consult on this project. A multilingual, bicultural librarian, Dr. Hall-Ellis is a long-standing member of state, regional, and national professional organizations. She has conducted fourteen field-based research studies, and has published numerous technical reports, articles, and four monographs. She currently serves as the Principal Investigator on the IMLS grant that has funded the Law Librarian Fellowship program at the University of Denver.

JANET SWAN HILL is Professor and Associate Director for Technical Services at the University of Colorado Libraries in Boulder, having also held positions at Northwestern University and the Library of Congress. She holds an MA in Librarianship from Denver University and a BA in Geology from Vassar College. She has published and spoken regarding cataloging, technical services, professional education, and tenure for librarians. She has served as President of ALCTS, ALA Councilor, and member of the ALA Executive Board. See http:// spot.colorado.edu/~hilljs/Vita4CU.pdf for her full vita.

SHEILA S. INTNER is Professor Emeritus at Simmons College GSLIS. In 2001, she was founding director of its MLIS program at Mount Holyoke College. Since retiring in 2006, she taught as an adjunct faculty member at Catholic University and the University of Maryland. She teaches currently at Rutgers University. Dr. Intner served as an ALA Councilor-at-large, President of the Association for Library Collections & Technical Services, and Chair of Online Audiovisual Catalogers. She was a Senior Fulbright Scholar to Israel, was awarded the Margaret Mann Citation, and won the annual awards of New England Technical Services Librarians and Online Audiovisual Catalogers. She is author or principal editor of many books, including *Metadata and Its Impact on Libraries* (2006), *Standard Cataloging for School and Public Libraries* (2007), and *Fundamentals of Technical Services Management* (2008).

ED JONES is Assistant Director of Assessment and Metadata Services at National University, San Diego. He has worked in cataloging for more than thirty years at various institutions, including Harvard University, where he was head of the CONSER Office for eight years. He has taught cataloging courses at Dominican University and the University of Illinois at Urbana-Champaign. He holds a PhD from the University of Illinois at Urbana-Champaign, an MLS from Kent State University, and an MA in Modern History from Youngstown State University. Ed has been published in various library journals, including *Library Resources & Technical Services, Serials Review, Cataloging & Classification Quarterly*, and the *Serial Librarian*. Current research involves libraries and Google Books.

SUSAN S. LAZINGER is Senior Lecturer (Emerita), School of Library, Archive and Information Studies, Hebrew University of Jerusalem, Israel, where she was Head of the Academic Program. In addition she was Adjunct Lecturer in digital preservation and metadata at the Department of Information Studies and Librarianship, Haifa University. She is the author of three books and numerous articles on cataloging and metadata, as well as a number of invited chapters in books edited by others. Currently, she is an Associate Editor for the Greenwood Publishing Group/Libraries Unlimited, as well as Co-Editor (with Professor Sheila Intner) of their Third Millennium Cataloging Series.

JOHN F. MYERS is Catalog Librarian at Union College. He has transitioned from public to technical services and from public to academic libraries. His MLIS is from the University of South Carolina. John has provided regional training in cataloging and serves on ALA/ALCTS's Cataloging Committee: Description and Access.

For eight years, including a brief period of consulting firm work and other work, SCOTT PIEPENBURG has been Library System Administrator/Intellectual Properties Supervisor, of the Dallas Independent School District (DISD)—the tenth-largest U.S. school district. With an MLIS and an MA in history, from the University of Wisconsin–Milwaukee, Scott has worked in school and academic libraries, for three different vendors, and has served as District Cataloger and System Administrator for DISD, 1994–2000. Scott was a cocreator of the original DALLINK library system, and has written books and journal articles on cataloging (popular Easy MARC), authority control, and technology and libraries. He has conducted workshops and spoken at library and user group conferences, and has worked with library automation vendors in product design to help users optimize their automation systems.

CHRISTINE SCHWARTZ has worked in cataloging and metadata in theological libraries for twenty years. She holds the position of Metadata Librarian at Princeton Theological Seminary. Christine writes the blog Cataloging Futures, which focuses on the future of cataloging and metadata in libraries. Among her accomplishments, she has served on a Task Force to Review the Draft of RDA for the American Theological Library Association (ATLA) and more recently was a member of the Editorial Committee of the *Code4Lib Journal*. Christine holds an MA and MDiv from New Brunswick Theological Seminary and an MLS from Rutgers University.

JAMES WEINHEIMER is currently Director of Library and Information Services at the American University of Rome. In previous positions, he was Slavic cataloger at Princeton University and an information specialist at the Food and Agriculture Organization of the United Nations. He is the creator of the online Slavic Cataloging Manual, now with ACRL, authored several articles, and most recently initiated the open project, The Cooperative Cataloging Rules Wiki.

JAY WEITZ is Senior Consulting Database Specialist at OCLC and was previously Assistant Catalog Librarian at Capital University, Columbus, Ohio. He is the author of *Cataloger's Judgment*, both editions of *Music Coding and Tagging*, and the cataloging Q&A columns of the *Music OCLC Users Group Newsletter* and the *Online Audiovisual Catalogers Newsletter*. Since 1992, he has presented dozens of cataloging workshops in the United States, Canada, and Japan. He has a BA in English from the University of Pennsylvania, an MLS from Rutgers University, and an MA in Education from Ohio State University.

MARTHA M. YEE has been Cataloging Supervisor, UCLA Film & Television Archive, since 1983. Her PhD in Library and Information Science and specialization in moving image material cataloging are from UCLA's Graduate School of Library and Information Science. Her extensive publication list is at http:// myee.bol.ucla.edu/workspub.htm. Active in the Cataloging and Classification Section, ALCTS (ALA), she has also served as a member of the Cataloging Committee: Description and Access, the Subject Analysis Committee (SAC), and as chair of the Machine Readable Bibliographic Information Committee (MARBI).